U··· Uni··· ··y···

Emergency
Relief Operations

INTERNATIONAL HUMANITARIAN AFFAIRS
Kevin M. Cahill, M.D., series editor

1. Kevin M. Cahill, M.D., ed., *Basics of International Humanitarian Missions.*

Emergency Relief Operations

Edited by
KEVIN M. CAHILL, M.D.

A Joint Publication of
FORDHAM UNIVERSITY PRESS
and
THE CENTER FOR INTERNATIONAL
HEALTH AND COOPERATION
New York • 2003

International Humanitarian Affairs, No. 2
ISSN: 1541–7409

Library of Congress Cataloging-in-Publication Data

Emergency relief operations / edited by Kevin M. Cahill.—1st ed.
     p. cm. – (International humanitarian affairs ; no. 2)
  Includes bibliographical references and index.
  ISBN 0-8232-2239-X (hardcover)—ISBN 0-8232-2240-3 (pbk.)
    1. Disaster relief. 2. Humanitarian assistance. 3. Emergency man-
  agement. I. Cahill, Kevin M. II. Series.

HV553.E495 2003
363.34'8–dc21

                                                           2003040792

Printed in the United States of America
03   04   05   06   07   5   4   3   2   1
First Edition

For Michel Veuthey

CONTENTS

Acknowledgments   ix

Abbreviations and Acronyms   xi

Introduction   xv
    Kevin M. Cahill, M.D.

PART 1   1

1. Early Warning Systems: From Surveillance to Risk
   Assessment to Action   3
       Ted R. Gurr and Barbara Harff

2. Initial Response to Complex Emergencies and Natural
   Disasters   32
       Ed Tsui

3. Evidence-Based Health Assessment Process in Complex
   Emergencies   55
       Frederick M. Burkle, Jr., M.D.

4. Concern Worldwide's Approach to Water and
   Sanitation and Shelter Needs in Emergencies   80
       Tom Arnold

PART 2   113

5. Internal Displacement: A Challenge of Peace, Security,
   and Nation Building   115
       Francis M. Deng

6. Protection Strategies in Humanitarian Interventions   135
       Gerald R. Martone

7. Issues of Power and Gender in Complex Emergencies 153
   Judy A. Benjamin

8. Clinical Aspects of Malnutrition 180
   Kevin M. Cahill, M.D.

PART 3 189

9. Military/NGO Interaction 191
   Major General Timothy Cross

10. An Introduction to NGO Field Security 225
    Randolph Martin

PART 4 265

11. Resolutions, Mandates, Aims, Missions, and Exit
    Strategies 267
    Larry Hollingworth

12. The Transition from Conflict to Peace 284
    Richard Ryscavage, S.J.

Selected Web Sites 295

Chapter Notes and References 299

Appendixes 335

The Center for International Health and Cooperation and
   the Institute of International Humanitarian Affairs 367

About the Authors 369

Index 373

ACKNOWLEDGMENTS

THIS BOOK is made possible by the generous contributions of many individuals and organizations. All the chapters were written by colleagues who accepted the challenge on short notice and for no honorarium because they shared my belief in the need to record their vast experience and knowledge for future humanitarian workers. All authors had participated in the International Diploma in Humanitarian Assistance offered by the Center for International Health and Cooperation (CIHC) in concert with Fordham University, the University of Geneva, and the Royal College of Surgeons in Ireland.

This book was supported, in part, by a generous grant from the William H. Donner Foundation. Special thanks are due to Ms. Phaedra Annan, Rev. Joseph A. O'Hare, S.J., Mr. Saverio Procario, and the staff of the Fordham University Press. The Executive Secretary of the CIHC, Renee Cahill, and Ms. Yvette Christofilis helped with editing and made a complex and difficult task a pleasure.

ABBREVIATIONS AND ACRONYMS

AI	Amnesty International
AIDS	Acquired Immune Deficiency Syndrome
ALNAP	Active Learning Network for Accountability and Performance in Humanitarian Action
CAP	Consolidated Appeals Process (UN)
CDC	Centers for Disease Control
CEDAW	Convention on the Elimination of All Discrimination against Women (also called Women's Convention)
CERF	Central Emergency Revolving Fund
CHAP	Common Humanitarian Action Plan
CIA	Central Intelligence Agency
CIHC	Center for International Health and Cooperation
CIMIC	Civilian-military cooperation
CMR	Crude mortality rate
CNN	Cable News Network
CPJ	Committee to Protect Journalists
CRED	Center for Research on the Epidemiology of Disasters
CRS	Catholic Relief Services
CWS	Church World Services
DAC	Development Assistance Committee
DFID	Department for Foreign International Development (U.K.)
ECHO	European Community Humanitarian Office
ECOSOC	Economic and Social Council (UN)
EM-DAT	A comprehensive disaster database
ERC	Emergency relief coordinator
EU	European Union
FAO	Food and Agriculture Organization
FAWE	Forum for African Women Educationalists
FGM	Female genital mutilation (also called female genital cutting)

FTS	Financial Tracking System
GBV	Gender-Based Violence
HDC	Humanitarian Dialogue Center
HEWS	Humanitarian Early-Warning System
HIC	Humanitarian Information Center
HIV	Human Immunodeficiency Virus
HRW	Human Rights Watch
IASC	Inter-Agency Standing Committee
ICC	International Criminal Court
ICJ	International Court of Justice
ICRC	International Committee of the Red Cross
ICTR	International Criminal Tribunal for Rwanda
ICTY	International Criminal Tribunal for the Former Yugoslavia
ICVA	International Council of Voluntary Agencies
IDHA	International Diploma in Humanitarian Assistance
IDP	Internally displaced person
IFJ	International Federation of Journalists
IFRC	International Federation of Red Cross and Red Crescent Societies
IHL	International Humanitarian Law
IIHA	Institute of International Humanitarian Affairs, Fordham University
ILO	International Labor Organization
IMF	International Monetary Fund
INSARAG	International Search and Rescue Advisory Group
IOM	International Organization for Migration
IRC	International Rescue Committee
JDC	Joint Distribution Committee
MCDU	Military and Civil Defense Unit
MSF	*Médecins sans frontières*—Doctors Without Borders
NATO	North Atlantic Treaty Organization
NGO	Nongovernmental organization
OAS	Organization of American States
OAU	Organization of African Unity
OCHA	Office for the Coordination of Humanitarian Affairs (UN)
OECD	Organization for Economic Cooperation and Development

OFDA	Office of Foreign Disaster Assistance (U.S.)
OSCE	Organization for Security and Cooperation in Europe
OSOCC	On-Site Operations Coordination Centers
POW	Prisoner of War
PVO	Private Voluntary Organization
RADARS	Reporting, Analysis, Decision-Making, and Response System
RCSI	Royal College of Surgeons in Ireland
RHC	Reproductive Health Consortium
SCHR	Steering Committee for Humanitarian Response
SGBV	Sexual and Gender-Based Violence
SITREP	Situation Report
SOS	Emergency call: Save Our Souls
TRC	Truth and Reconciliation Commission (South Africa)
UNAMIR	United Nations Assistance Mission in Rwanda
UNDAC	United Nations Disaster Assessment and Coordination
UNDP	United Nations Development Program
UNEP	United Nations Environment Program
UNESCO	United Nations Educational, Scientific, and Cultural Organization
UNFAO	United Nations Food and Agriculture Organization
UNFICYP	UN Peacekeeping Force in Cyprus
UNHCR	United Nations High Commissioner for Refugees
UNICEF	United Nations International Children's Emergency Fund
UNIENET	UN International Disaster Management Information Network
UNJLC	UN Joint Logistic Centers
UNPROFOR	United Nations Protection Force (in Yugoslavia)
UNRWA	United Nations Relief and Works Agency for Palestine Refugees
USAID	U.S. Agency for International Development
VOICE	Voluntary Organizations in Cooperation in Emergencies
WCC	World Council of Churches
WFP	World Food Program / UN World Food Program
WHO	World Health Organization
WV	World Vision

INTRODUCTION

Kevin M. Cahill, M.D.

EMERGENCY RELIEF operations are the starting point for most international humanitarian assistance programs. Wanton killing and brutality within supposedly sovereign borders, ethnic and religious strife, millions of near-starving refugees, other millions of migrants fleeing their homes out of fear for their lives, human rights trampled down, appalling poverty in the shadows of extraordinary wealth, inhumanity on an incredible scale in what was supposed to be a peaceful dawn following the Cold War—these are the awesome challenges that face the world community and are quite different from the nation state rivalries and alliances that preoccupied statesmen during most of the last century. More and more, these humanitarian crises are immediately known to us in an era of instant communications, demand a response, and, as is pointed out in the companion volume, *Basics of International Humanitarian Missions,* that response, to be effective, cannot be mere compassion or sympathy but must reflect an emerging science and the strengths of multiple partners.

The desire to respond to natural or man-made disasters is strong in every culture and on every continent. However, as the contributors to these books point out, the disasters of today are more complex and more dangerous than ever before, and an effective and well-coordinated response must be multidisciplinary. Some areas of the world, for historical, ethnic, and political reasons, are disaster prone. Complex humanitarian crises, sadly, have become a common interface between developed and developing nations, between rich and poor, the haves and the have nots. Those of us privileged to participate in great humanitarian dramas have the opportunity adversity offers to build a new framework, using, and sometimes rediscovering, the best of the old structures, but realizing that a new spirit and innovative methods are necessary for international discourse in a new millennium. Our success—or failure—will, to a large extent, define the chances for the very survival of the world.

Almost five hundred years ago, in a small book that remains a classic text on politics and diplomacy, Machiavelli shrewdly employed the semantics of health to explain a fundamental tenet of governing; he wrote: "When trouble is sensed well in advance, it can easily be remedied; if you wait for it to show, any medicine will be too late because the disease will have become incurable. As the doctors say of a wasting disease, to start with it is easy to cure but difficult to diagnose; after a time, unless it has been diagnosed and treated at the outset, it becomes easy to diagnose but difficult to cure. So it is in politics." And so it is in humanitarian assistance.

This is the second volume in Fordham University Press's "International Humanitarian Affairs" series. In this book we consider the challenges that one must deal with before, during, and immediately after a disaster—from trying to identify disaster-prone areas and predict crises, to developing early warning systems, devising rapid assessment measures for health, nutrition, and housing in the early days of a humanitarian crisis. Contributors consider the incredible problems faced by refugees and internally displaced persons and focus especially on the plight of women and children and the severely malnourished. But merely measuring medical abnormalities fails to provide a true picture of societies in crisis, and this book also offers reflections on those fundamental violations of human rights that underlie most disasters. The logistical needs for supplying potable water, adequate shelter, and basic sanitation systems are part of any emergency relief operation. We review the response of international organizations, such as the United Nations, and the interaction of the military and nongovernmental organizations during the emergency relief phase. Security for staff deserves the careful attention that a separate chapter provides. One of the important first steps in entering a complex humanitarian crisis is figuring out how and when one is going to depart, and to attempt as smooth an exit as possible. The book is divided into four sections.

Part 1

Emergency relief operations begin long before a disaster occurs. As the discipline of international humanitarian assistance has become ever more professional, there has been an emphasis on learning from past efforts, especially from earlier failures.

This section opens with a review of early warning systems for disasters. Sophisticated analyses permit scientists to map disaster-prone areas, much as the study of winds and tides allows weather experts to forecast hurricanes. Predicting where and what, and how as well as why, a disaster is likely to occur allows major relief agencies and organizations to plan, stockpile, and begin coordinated efforts that must flow from policy rooms to field operations.

At the very beginning of a disaster the United Nations initiates a process that rapidly involves many offices and agencies of the organization. Representatives from the United Nations High Commissioner for Refugees, the World Food Programme, the International Organizations of Migrants, the World Health Organization, and other branches of the world body participate in a coordinated UN response. But they cannot act alone, and local governments, donor nations, the International Red Cross, and nongovernmental organizations must be involved if chaos is not to complicate existing disasters. The long-term Chief of Policy in the UN Office of the Coordinator for Humanitarian Assistance (OCHA) describes the initial response to a reported disaster.

An appropriate reaction to a complex emergency requires estimates that must be extrapolated from rapid surveys. Assessments for health, shelter, food, water, and security needs must be available so proper supplies and personnel can be mobilized. One of the most experienced and scholarly experts in this critical field provides a thorough introduction. To offer an NGO perspective I asked the leader of one of the front-line NGOs, Concern Worldwide, to present their plans for supplying emergency shelter, water, and sanitation in a humanitarian disaster.

1
Early Warning Systems:[1]
From Surveillance to Risk Assessment to Action

Ted R. Gurr and Barbara Harff

THE IDEA of early warning is simple and widely accepted in the international community. Officials and practitioners who must deal with the consequences of local conflicts and humanitarian disasters need early warnings of impending crises to buy time—time to build political support for action, time to design and implement proactive strategies, time to plan for assistance and rescue.[2] Dr. Cahill has made the point elsewhere: the thrust of international policy should be on long-term foreign assistance, conflict resolution, and development programs that could prevent many disasters from happening in the first place.[3]

The challenge is translating the early warning idea into systems, like those used to monitor threats to public health, that provide and help interpret information on emerging conflict situations on a global scale. The key concept is *system,* as distinct from an unstructured flow of public and private reports from observers who happen to be on the ground in places that are ripe for conflict. Early warning systems may no longer be needed to call attention to ongoing and potential conflicts in the Caucasus, the Balkans, or the Greater Horn of Africa. These regions are the focus of close international scrutiny and preventive efforts. The challenge for early warning systems is to search beyond the time horizon to identify latent and low-level conflicts that have not yet attracted CNN crews or fact-finding missions.

Warfare within states and its handmaidens, including large-scale killings of civilians and refugee flows, are now the leading challenges to security in most of the world. Recent findings by researchers at the University of Maryland suggest the dimensions of the problem. At the beginning of 2001 there were ten serious armed conflicts within states (for example, in Afghanistan, Sierra Leone, and Colombia) and another eighteen low-level armed conflicts (for example, the Moro rebellion in the Philippines and the anti-Taylor insurgency in northwestern Liberia). There were also twenty-three suspended-armed conflicts, for example, in Azerbaijan and northern Iraq, in which fighting could resume at any time. Fighting did in fact escalate seriously in some societal conflicts in 2001, for instance, in Macedonia, Israel/Palestine, Afghanistan, Nepal, and Liberia. International bodies were committed to containing some of these fifty-one active or suspended conflicts, as in Kosovo and Iraq, but most attracted little international attention.[4]

At the beginning of the twenty-first century an estimated one hundred ethnic and religious minorities throughout the world were targeted by discriminatory public policies that substantially and selectively limited their political, economic, or cultural rights. In a handful of instances the victimized groups, like Hutus in Burundi and the Lhotshampas of Bhutan, have benefited from preventive international efforts. Most, however, are of serious concern only to human rights observers. Some of these groups support armed conflicts, enumerated above. Most others have mobilized to promote or protect their collective interests but have not yet rebelled openly or been victimized by state repression.[5]

International attention to societal conflicts and group discrimination is selective. Ethnopolitical conflicts in Western democracies are not usually of international concern because, it is assumed, conflicts about the status of, say, indigenous peoples in North America and Muslim minorities in Europe are likely to be worked out through the democratic process. Some armed conflicts are ignored because of triage decisions, based on a tacit consensus that little or no international leverage can be brought to bear on them, as in Chechnya and Kashmir. And there is the problem of attention deficit: the sheer number and diversity of societal conflicts, open and potential, overwhelms the capacity of international officials to monitor, assess, and respond.

Enter early warning systems. In which of the present and future societal conflicts will large-scale humanitarian assistance be needed, where will political pressures build for international responses? In which latent ethnic conflicts are the risk factors highest? Where and when are the openings for early, low-cost preventive measures? Which preventive strategies have been used in the past, and with what effects? A global system for conflict early warning is a means to efficiently monitor such situations. Analysis is the essential component to monitoring: analysis provides assessments of risks and openings. An early warning system cannot answer fundamental policy questions about optimal preventive measures, but it should be able to provide increasingly reliable information and assessments that will help decision-makers answer those questions.

This chapter addresses some specific issues raised in this preamble. It begins by identifying some organizations working to develop early warning systems and concludes with evidence from a study, designed and directed by the second author, that aims at identifying potentially genocidal conflicts for U.S. foreign policy-makers.

Who Is Working on Early Warning?

A potent impetus for research on early warning of conflicts with grave humanitarian consequences came from the UN Secretary-General's *Agenda for Peace* of June 17, 1992. Dr. Boutros-Ghali focused attention on threats to international security arising from "ethnic, religious, social, cultural or linguistic strife" (par. 11) and called for strengthening early warning systems that incorporate information about natural disasters and "political indicators to assess whether a threat to peace exists and to analyze what action might be taken by the United Nations to alleviate it" (par. 26).[6] Efforts to design and employ early warning systems for international policy planning were undertaken by several UN agencies.

In New York, the UN's Office for the Coordination of Humanitarian Affairs (OCHA) developed the Humanitarian Early Warning System (HEWS) in the early 1990s, a database of quantitative and qualitative information on countries vulnerable to humanitarian crises. HEWS was used to support interpretive analyses and reports for decision-makers in UN operational agencies but was shut down in the late 1990s for lack of funding. A second project is ReliefWeb, established and maintained by OCHA's Geneva office. ReliefWeb is an internet-based compendium of current information and assessments on complex emergencies. Its information is publicly accessible and thus has been widely used by humanitarian organizations and private activists.

A third UN-related early warning project focuses on food crises rather than the civil conflicts that cause most humanitarian crises. The Global Information and Early Warning System (GIEWS), run by the Food and Agricultural Organization in Rome, monitors demand and supply for all basic foods throughout the world and provides alerts of imminent food crises. It is an exemplar of what could be done for conflict early warning given sufficient resources and political support from the UN's member states.[7]

The European states also support early warning and preventive action programs. The Organisation for Security and Cooperation (OSCE) in Europe maintains the research-oriented Conflict Prevention Center in Vienna, while the OSCE's High Commissioner on National Minorities (Max van der Stoel, based in the Hague) has responsibility for reporting on and planning diplomatic responses to emerging ethnonational conflicts.[8] The European Union supports the work of the Conflict Prevention Network of academic institutions and NGOs, designed to provide analytic and operational input to the EU system. The Organisation of African Unity (OAU) also initiated an early warning system in the mid-1990s, based at OAU headquarters in Addis Ababa, the first such effort by a regional organization outside Europe.

A number of Western governments have developed risk assessment and early warning systems to support post–Cold War policies of developmental and humanitarian assistance. The long-run planning question for development administrators is how to design programs to forestall future crises; the short-run question is whether impending crises will destroy the gains of ongoing programs. The U.S. Agency for International Development makes such assessments, as does the Canadian Ministry of Foreign Affairs, the Swiss Foreign Ministry (under contract with the Swiss Peace Foundation), and the Foreign Ministry of the Netherlands (at its Clingendael center). Beginning in the early 1990s the U.S. Department of Defense and intelligence agencies began to shift their early warning efforts from the interstate conflicts with which they were preoccupied during the Cold War to intra-state conflicts and humanitarian crises that may call for U.S. rescue, assistance, and peace-keeping operations.[9] A vivid illustration of increased U.S. concerns about humanitarian issues was the Clinton administration's establishment, early in 1999, of an interagency center for early warning of genocides, based in the Department of State and headed by Ambassador for War Crimes David Schaeffer.

Parallel to these national and international efforts at early warning are the research and action programs of numerous nongovernmental organizations.[10] The Carnegie Commission on Preventing Deadly Conflict carried out a major program of action research between 1994 and 2000. Its numerous books and reports dealt with the general causes of ethnonational and religious conflicts and with means by which international entities could prevent mass violence and promote nonviolent problem-solving. The Center for Preventive Action, supported by the New York–based Council on Foreign Relations, has a more narrow focus. The Center has assembled expert teams for in-country assessments of conflict situations and has increasingly emphasized preventive strategies.[11]

The London-based Forum on Early Warning and Early Response (FEWER) is an umbrella organization that pursues similar objectives through a network of affiliated organizations. FEWER was founded in 1996 as a consortium of NGOs and academic research institutions and has built a global network for information exchange and action partnerships with governmental and private organizations. It has working links with regional early warning networks in Africa and the CIS, for example, the Moscow-based Network of Ethnological Monitoring on Early Warning of Ethnic Conflict, and distributes information from organizations doing early warning research. Examples of its work include early warning of the outbreak and escalation of conflicts in the Democratic Republic of Congo, and developing conflict and peace indicators for the Caucasus and Great Lakes regions (for current reports, see http://www.fewer.org).

The International Crisis Group (ICG) is the largest and best-funded private organization now working on conflict risk assessment and early warning. Founded in 1995 and currently (2002) directed by Gareth Evans, former Australian foreign minister, it aims to provide independent assessments of crises and emerging conflicts for officials, practitioners, and the media. It has a substantial Brussels-based staff plus eleven field offices—in the Balkans, Asia, and Africa—that prepare dozens of in-depth reports each year. A forty-two-page report, "Liberia: The Key to Ending Regional Instability," issued in April 2002, is representative. It describes the origins of the current anti-Taylor insurgency, assesses the internal political situation in Liberia, analyzes the conflict's international context, and sets forth recommendations for action by interested governments (Nigeria, the United States, the United Kingdom, and France), by the UN Security Council and Secretary General, and by international donors.[12]

The next link in the chain that begins with risk assessment and early warning is prevention. Whereas FEWER and ICG focus on assessment first and prevention second, other NGOs give priority to prevention. One very active umbrella organization is the Utrecht-based European Platform for Conflict Prevention and

Transformation, which exchanges information and advocates prevention activities by participating NGOs. Its publication projects include a handbook that inventories conflict prevention centers worldwide and a series of regional Conflict Prevention Surveys.[13]

A great many other entities doing research related to early warning and preventive action might be cited. Annual tracking of armed conflicts are reported by university-based researchers in Sweden, Germany, and the U.S. Periodic human rights assessments are prepared by Amnesty International, Human Rights Watch, the Human Rights Internet (Canada), and the U.S. Department of State. Political risk analyses are prepared for corporate clients by applied research groups in the U.S. and London. Refugees and the crises that generate them are assessed by university researchers and NGOs in North America, Europe, and Japan.

It is obvious from this overview that early warners have diverse objectives and methods and work in different kinds of environments. The specific "bads" they warn about include civil wars, massive human rights violations, and refugee flows. Some collect and report data, others do case studies, still others disseminate information. Some prepare rigorous risk assessments, others try to focus preventive efforts on impending crises. Some work in NGOs and university research programs, others provide staff support to national and international policy-makers. But some issues cut across this diversity and are dealt with in the sections that follow.

THE CONNECTION BETWEEN EARLY WARNING AND EARLY ACTION

Advocates of early warning assume that credible warnings of impending conflict, however derived, will make it possible to initiate preventive action and plan for humanitarian assistance. Skeptics point to the collapse of the Yugoslav federation at the beginning of the 1990s and the onset of the new Balkan wars, which were anticipated by many local observers and the U.S. Central Intelligence Agency, among others, as instances of early warning that failed. What failed in this instance was not "early warning" but the governments and international organizations that should have responded more quickly and coherently to the emerging crisis. The warning signals were present in prospect as well as in retrospect. Either they were ignored, or the preventive actions were inadequate to the crisis.

Effective early responses are by their nature less visible, and less often analyzed, than failures. An antidote to skepticism about early warning is to cite briefly some post–Cold War cases in which early warnings led to international responses that checked the escalation of crises into humanitarian disasters.[14]

(a) Early warning of drought in southern Africa in the spring of 1992 prompted a concerted international program of relief and rehabilitation that forestalled significant loss of life.[15] Information networks that provide early warning of ecological disasters are better developed than the conflict early warning programs discussed in this chapter. The international community also is predisposed to respond to them. The example calls attention to what in principle should be possible in the political realm. It also illustrates the role political factors play in preventive responses: the international response depended on cooperation of governments in southern Africa with relief agencies. The successful outcome contrasts sharply with the Horn of Africa, where similar conditions in the 1980s and early 1990s caused enormous suffering, population displacement, and loss of life. Most contenders in civil wars in the region, both governments and their opponents, refused to cooperate fully with international relief agencies, and as a consequence humanitarian efforts were crippled.[16]

(b) After Macedonia seceded from the Yugoslav federation in 1992, early warnings of a Bosnian-type civil war in Macedonia were widely echoed, and heeded, by the international community. The major threats at the time included ethnic rivalries between the Macedonian majority and Albanian and Serbian minorities; diplomatic and economic sanctions by a hostile Greek government; and serious economic deterioration. Among the responses were intensive diplomatic efforts by international, regional, and U.S. diplomats directed at the Macedonian government and its neighbors; the stationing of Scandinavian and U.S. troops as "trip-wire" peacekeepers; and initiation of grass-roots conflict resolution efforts by a U.S.-based NGO, Common Ground. The conflict was contained, and in one significant respect lessened: in autumn 1995, in response to U.S., European, and UN pressure, the Greek and Macedonian governments reached an accord that led Greece to suspend its embargo and to open their common border.[17] Spillover of refugees and armed fighters from Kosovo in 1999–2000 severely tested the delicate ethnic balance in Macedonia and led to a rebellion by ethnic Albanians, but intensified international engagement has secured an uneasy truce that makes it possible to pursue a political settlement.

(c) The Congo Republic in late 1993 was in a state of incipient civil war between rival political groupings following disputed elections. The Organisation of African Unity and the government of Zaire provided mediation that led to a peace accord in early 1994. The peace accord checked the escalation of conflict, though it did not end it.[18]

(d) In Burundi the assassination of the newly elected Hutu president in October 1993 by elements of the Tutsi military precipitated a series of massacres and contributed indirectly to the Rwandan genocide in spring 1994. Since late 1993 Burundi has been the focus of intensive efforts by the United Nations, the OAU, the U.S. and West European governments, and NGOs to check further communal and political violence. Serious massacres have occurred, and the situation is very tense, but orchestrated violence on the scale of Rwanda has been prevented as of this writing (April 2002).

(e) The nationalist leaders of a number of post-Communist states in the early- to mid-1990s proposed and imposed restrictions on the rights of national minorities, seeking in some instances to encourage them to emigrate. The targets have included Magyars (Hungarians) in Slovakia and Romania, Russians in the Baltic states, Gagauz and Russians in Moldova, and the Roma throughout East-Central Europe. Most of these situations were the focus of diplomatic and political initiatives by the UN, the OSCE, the Council of Europe, and West European governments (and the Russian government, in the case of Russian minorities in the near abroad). The governments in question were encouraged to abide by international standards for the protection of national minorities. These efforts included reminders about the political and economic costs of rights violations as well as inducements (especially assistance programs). In all the instances cited, the nationalist governments in question have modified their policies and threats of ethnic warfare have subsided.[19]

Most of these successes of preventive diplomacy occurred in regions that have been the subject of intensive international scrutiny and concern. Regional organizations as well as the UN and European powers have been actively engaged. Detailed information about emerging crises usually was available to all interested parties, and except in the case of Congo-Brazzaville, major international actors had stakes in checking the escalation of conflict.

Two critical questions are raised by these examples. One is whether the collection, dissemination, and assessment of information on prospective societal violence and humanitarian disasters can be done systematically and in a timely fashion. From the perspective of the research community there is little doubt that the answer is yes, given some modest but sustained investment of resources in information technology, data analysis and display, and the further testing of forecasting models of internal conflict. The second question is whether the results of such assessments are credible enough that they help guide policy-makers and activists about where to invest efforts in prevention. On this question the jury is out. Most diplomats, desk officers, and activists are accustomed to relying on their own fly-by-wire understanding of a situation and often are skeptical of outsiders using new information technologies and lists of risk factors. The value of the systematic approach may be most appreciated by high-level decision-makers who are responsible for planning regional and global strategies of prevention. They are most acutely aware of the value of long-range risk assessments and systematic monitoring.

DESIGN CRITERIA FOR EARLY WARNING SYSTEMS

The capacity to collect and disseminate information on emerging crises has vastly increased since the mid-1980s, due especially to electronic networking, the widespread availability of personal computers, and advances in technology for data management and analysis. It is fair to say, however, that the capacity for assessing this information's policy implications has developed much more slowly. Discussions of early warning systems too often ignore the implications of the growing gap between the capacity of observers to generate information and the capacity of analysts and policy-makers to interpret it. The point can be highlighted by contrasting three different approaches to early warning.

Early Warning as Field Monitoring

This is the long-established practice by which diplomats and local representatives of international organizations report any event or intelligence they receive that suggests an imminent escalation of conflict. The Human Rights Watch organizations and other NGOs have carried out this kind of monitoring and reporting for a number of years. UN agencies concerned with humanitarian issues have done so for decades. In early 1993, after years of planning, the UN's Office of Humanitarian Affairs held its first "consultation" to synthesize such information as it related to potential flows of refugees. On the basis of these assessments ten countries, such as Zaire and Cambodia, were identified as being at risk of escalating conflicts and refugee flows.

Field monitoring is of great potential value because the information it generates on emerging crises is generally of high quality and immediacy. Four further steps are needed if field monitoring is to make an optimal contribution to a systematic early warning system. First, standard protocols are needed to increase the consistency in the kinds of information reported by field representatives. Second, those who assess field information need explicit models to guide its interpretation. Third, those who plan and carry out preventive diplomacy, humanitarian assistance, and peace-keeping operations must be committed to the early warning process and give close attention to its signals and assessments—even if in specific instances they choose to discount them. Finally, it is necessary to overcome the political constraints facing the UN Secretariat and other international organizations when reporting on high-risk situations. Their member states are highly sensitive to adverse evaluations and will seek to suppress them. Organizations like FEWER and IGC are much better able to offer full and frank assessments.

Early Warning as Monitoring of Indicators

Much discussion and planning for the establishment of early warning systems in the early 1990s focused on using indicators to assess risks and monitor trends. Planners envisaged systems based on available statistical indicators and construction of new indicators that would be easily accessible to desk officers and policymakers. The concept is that when decision-makers confront or anticipate crises, they will turn to the system for background data and for indicators that enable them to track the situation over time. The UNOCHA's Humanitarian Early Warning System (HEWS), referred to above, was designed beginning in the summer of 1993 with this in mind. It consisted of an electronic database of statistical indicators on more than one hundred countries plus headlines on recent political, humanitarian, and other developments in a smaller number of countries. Until HEWS was shut down, the system was regularly used to prepare assessments of emerging crises in response to requests from senior UN offi-cials, but its extensive information was never subject to systematic analysis, because of a combination of political and bureaucratic constraints. In short, HEWS was a system for managing informa-tion on potential humanitarian crises, not for its analysis.

Systems that rely mainly on indicators have great potential value for systematizing information and making it readily avail-able, but such systems also have two general limitations. First, conflicts evolve through phases. The transitions among phases, for example, from disputes to armed violence, usually are abrupt and not predictable from analyzing trends.[20] Indicators are more suitable for tracking country situations than for anticipating rapid changes in them. Analyses based on indicators are more likely to lead to "late warning" or to quantified description that lags behind events than to "early warning."

Second, reliance on indicators may help regulate the flow of information to planners, analysts, and policy-makers but does not give them tools to interpret it. Conversations with UN and U.S. officials suggest they often are skeptical about indicator-based early warning systems for two reasons. First, they are already flooded by more information than they can cope with. Second, what they need most are filters to guide them in screening and interpreting that information. Their own "filters" tend to be the presuppositions and policy orientations of the bureaucratic and political contexts in which they work.

Systematic, Model-Based Early Warning

The essential complement to field monitoring and indicator con-struction is the development of explicit frameworks, or models, that analysts and policy-makers use to interpret the flow of infor-mation. Models for systematic early warning should meet three general design criteria:

- Specify what disease is to be warned about. Ethnic warfare, re-gime failure, massive human rights violations, and refugee flows

are the result of different combinations of factors, hence require
somewhat different models

- Specify the combinations of risk factors and sequences of events
  that are likely to lead to crises. Lists of variables or indicators are
  only a starting point; models should identify which measurable
  conditions, in what combination and relative importance, establish a potential for which kinds of crisis
- Distinguish between remote and proximate conditions of crises.
  This may be done in either of two ways. One is to specify the
  conditions associated with each phase in the development of
  crises (see note 20). The second is to distinguish between background conditions, intervening processes, and the accelerators
  or triggers that lead to rapid escalation. Such distinctions are
  essential for analytic clarity and help in planning long-term versus short-term responses

It should be evident that early warning models that meet these
design criteria not only structure analysis, they help determine
the kinds of information sought; that is, they stipulate what kind
of information is especially needed as well as how to interpret it.
They are thus information-management tools as well as analytic
tools.

The Challenge of Developing and Testing Models for Early Warning

To design and test valid models of the etiology and epidemiology
of crises is a demanding task. Substantive knowledge about a
number of cases of humanitarian crises is a necessary condition.
Once outlined, models need to be validated; that is, they require
testing against the empirical reality of a large number of conflict
situations to ensure that they identify the potential for escalation
with acceptable levels of accuracy.[21] Also, significant resources
need to be invested to collect and test such models. These activities are interdependent. To test models adequately requires extensive data and sustained research effort. If early warnings are
to be credible to those who might act on them, they should be

based on good data that is analyzed by tested models. But if organizations that want early warnings fail to give adequate support to this research, "early warnings" are likely to include too many "false negatives" (unanticipated crises) and too many "false positives" (predicted crises that did not happen).[22] If early warnings are too often inaccurate, early warning research may be discredited in the eyes of skeptical policy-makers.

A number of social science models have been developed with early warning of civil conflict and humanitarian crises in mind. For example, forecasting refugee flows is the objective of early warning models developed by Akira Onishi at Soka University (Tokyo) and by Susanne Schmeidl and Craig Jenkins at Ohio State University.[23] The first author of this chapter has developed and statistically tested models that can be used to forecast magnitudes of ethnic rebellion.[24] Since 1994 the U.S. government has supported the work of the State Failure Task Force, which uses empirical techniques to identify the conditions linked to the onset of episodes of state failure worldwide. The purpose is to identify, two years in advance, the risk factors that predict ethnic and revolutionary war, regime collapse, and genocides and politicides (political mass murders). The Task Force has achieved 75 percent to 80 percent accuracy in identifying the preconditions of past episodes of these kinds of failures and has helped establish the credibility of empirical early warning research for U.S. intelligence analysts and foreign policy-makers. Its results have become a significant input into foreign policy planning.[25]

The use of statistical analysis of indicators on large numbers of cases is one approach to developing and testing early warning models. This "large n" approach should be complemented by comparative case studies in which sequences of events can be examined in much greater detail. Case studies can focus on less tangible factors as cultural context, the significance of ideology, the role of leaders, and the impact of preventive actions—factors that rarely can be measured precisely in broad statistical studies. Especially recommended is what Alexander George calls "structured, focused comparison." Such studies ask a specific theoretical question and seek answers through comparative examination of cases that resemble one another in a number of respects, but differ on one or a few theoretically significant factors. A hypothetical example of a "structured, focused comparison" of communal conflict is a comparison of Sri Lanka and Malaysia; the theoretical question is why Tamil-Sinhalese conflict has escalated since the early 1980s, contrasted with the largely successful management of Chinese-Malay conflict. A not-so-hypothetical example is a comparative study of Rwanda and Burundi that asks what conjunction of internal conditions and international events led to genocide in the first country and more limited political massacres in the second.[26]

Design Criteria for a Global Early Warning System

Embedded in the foregoing discussion are suggestions about the steps needed to institute a global early warning system in support of international efforts at preventing ethnic warfare and humanitarian disasters. The criteria are similar to those used by in monitoring potential epidemics. These are seven guidelines:

- Highest priority should go to identifying and monitoring latent and emerging crisis situations, well before the onset of armed conflict and massive human suffering
- Information should be gathered and reported using standard protocols, designed to ensure that assessments are comprehensive and precise. Prototypes exist: they use various combinations of text and quantitative indicators, not only statistical data
- Information should be interpreted by reference to risk factors known or thought to be associated with the occurrence of specific kinds of conflict and crises. This implies using simple etiological models for related phenomena such as ethnic warfare, regime instability, and massive human rights violations. Distinctions need to be made among remote, intermediate, and proximate conditions
- Risk assessment and early warning are distinct but complementary activities. Risk assessments are based on the systematic analy-

sis of remote and intermediate conditions. Early warning requires near-real-time assessment of events that, in a high-risk environment, are likely to accelerate or trigger the rapid escalation of conflict

- The monitoring and analysis of conflict situations should be done independently of political control and considerations so that its results are, and are seen to be, as objective as possible
- Risk assessments and early warnings should get close attention from officials with operating responsibilities for preventive diplomacy and humanitarian assistance. There is little point in establishing early warning systems if their results are not communicated in a timely way to officials who give them some degree of credibility
- Risk assessments should be widely circulated to international, regional, and nongovernmental organizations as well as practitioners, activists, journalists, and scholars. No effort should be made to shield potential contenders from knowing that they are under international observation. On the other hand it may be necessary to limit the publicity given to close-to-real-time early warnings because, if they become known to contenders, preventive efforts may be compromised

Assessing Risks of Genocide and Political Mass Murder for U.S. Foreign Policy Planning

In late 1998, the Clinton administration started a policy initiative on early warning and prevention of genocide. The State Failure Task Force, which was established in 1994 to do empirical studies of the preconditions of internal wars and regime failures (see note 25) was asked whether its methods could be used to assess risks of one particularly deadly kind of state failure, namely, genocide and politicides (political mass murders). The second author, a senior consultant to the Task Force, drew on her data and expertise on these deadly events to design two such studies. The first, which is described here, identifies countries and situations at risk of future episodes. The second monitors political events in high-risk countries, looking for patterns that signal that the onset of mass killings is imminent.[27]

The first step in any systematic study of conflict is to identify the universe of cases for analysis. Genocides and politicides are defined as *the promotion, execution, and/or implied consent of sustained policies by governing elites or their agents, or in the case of civil war, either of the contending authorities that are intended to destroy, in whole or part, a communal, political, or politicized ethnic group.* In genocides, the victimized groups are defined by their perpetrators primarily in terms of their communal characteristics. In politicides, by contrast, groups are defined primarily in terms of their political opposition to the regime and dominant groups. The general definition (and operational guidelines not discussed here) guided the compilation of a list of genocides and politicides since World War II. New information and the critical advice of other genocide and conflict researchers led to successive refinements of the list, which has been widely accepted and used by other researchers, including the State Failure Task Force. The thirty-five cases used in the risk assessment study described below include all those that began after 1955, from Sudan's first genocide (1956–72) to Serbia's attempted politicide against Kosovar Albanians in 1998–99.[28]

A Model of Risk Factors for Genocide and Politicide

The beginning point for analysis of genocides and politicides is *political upheaval,* a concept that captures the essence of the structural crises and societal pressures that are preconditions for authorities' efforts to eliminate entire groups. All geno/politicides since 1955 occurred in response to or immediately after some combination of revolution, anticolonial rebellion, ethnic war, coups, or adverse regime changes that brought extremist political elites to power. Not all such conflicts lead to mass killings, however. The State Failure Task Force has identified 126 failures between 1955 and 2001, of which only thirty-five included genocides or politicides. The empirical research question, therefore, is what risk factors distinguish state failures that lead to geno/politicide from those that do not.

The first of the six variables in the risk assessment model is the *magnitude of political upheaval,* measured by the total extent of all internal wars and adverse regime changes in a country during the fifteen years prior to the onset of the current failure. The argument is that the greater the extent of violent conflict and adverse regime change, the greater the likelihood that geno/politicide will occur.[29] The second variable is a binary (yes/no) indicator of whether a country headed into state failure has a history of *previous geno/politicide.* This parallels Helen Fein's observation that regimes committing genocide may become habituated to using this kind of response to challenges, as was the case historically in the USSR and in contemporary China, Rwanda, Burundi, and Indonesia.[30]

Political upheaval is a necessary but not sufficient condition for geno/politicide. Two characteristics of governance have vital intervening effects—the ideological commitments of elites and the extent of democratic constraints on their actions. Governing elites usually have many strategic and tactical options for defeating or neutralizing contending groups. Episodes of genocide and politicide become more likely when the leaders of regimes and revolutionary movements articulate an *exclusionary ideology,* a belief system that identifies some kind of overriding purpose or principle that justifies efforts to restrict, persecute, or eliminate categories of people who are defined as antithetical to that purpose or principle—because they belong to the wrong ethnic group or religion or class. The second author developed a binary indicator, applied to all country-years from 1955 to 2001, of the presence or absence of exclusionary ideologies among the political elite—defined as including doctrines of ethnonational superiority or exclusivity, strict variants of Marxist-Leninism, rigid anti-Communist doctrines, Islamic rule justified on the basis of strict observance of Shari'a law, and doctrines of strict secular nationalism that exclude political participation of Islamic religious movements.

Democratic and quasi-democratic regimes have institutional checks on executive power that constrain elites from carrying out deadly attacks on citizens. Moreover the democratic norms of most contemporary societies favor protection of minority rights and the inclusion of political opponents, while competitive elections minimize chances for adherents of exclusionary ideologies to be elected to high office. The proposition is that states that maintain *democratic governance* in the face of state failure are much less likely to commit geno/politicide than autocratic regimes. A binary indicator is used that distinguishes full and partial democracies, on the one hand, from autocracies, constructed from the Polity global dataset's coded information on political institutions.[31]

Ethnic and religious divisions are often identified as preconditions of geno/politicide. We tested the effects of the extent of ethnic and religious diversity, the presence of small minorities in otherwise-homogenous societies, and indicators of discrimination against religious or ethnic minorities. *Elite ethnicity* was the only factor that remained significant when nonethnic factors—upheaval, ideology, democracy, economic interdependence—were taken into account. If the political elite disproportionately represents a minority in a heterogeneous society, like Afrikaaners in Apartheid South Africa and Tutsis in Burundi, under-represented groups are likely to challenge the elite's unrepresentativeness, and elites fearing such challenges are likely to define their interests and security in communal terms—for example, by designing policies of national or racial exclusion. The more narrow the ethnic base of a regime, the greater the risks of conflict that escalates to genocidal levels. The second author supervised the coding of a binary indicator of minority elite ethnicity to test this argument.

Finally, international context matters for geno/politicides. There was very little international concern with genocides in Uganda, Rwanda, and Burundi in the 1970s and 1980s; they happened in countries of low economic status and did not threaten the security interests of the major powers. At the other end of the scale many international actors have been concerned about crises in Tibet and Kashmir but lack means of pressuring China and India. The general proposition is that the greater a country's interdependency with others, the less likely it is to attempt geno/politicides—and the more likely to face international repercussions if it does so. Interdependency has two dimensions, economic and political. The State Failure studies have consistently showed that countries with a high degree of *trade openness*—exports plus imports as a percentage of GDP—are less likely to experience state failures, leading to the conclusion that trade openness serves as a highly sensitive indicator of state and elite willingness to maintain the rules of law and fair practices in the economic sphere. In the political sphere a high degree of trade openness implies that a country has more resources for averting and managing political crises. An indicator of political interdependence is a country's memberships in regional and intercontinental organizations. Countries with greater-than-average memberships in such organizations should be subject to greater influence, and get more political support, when facing internal challenge, and their regimes should be less likely to resort to geno/politicide.

The Impact of the Six Factors on the Risks of Geno/Politicide

The study employs a case-control research design widely used in epidemiological research. The basic procedure is to match problem cases—people (or countries) affected by a disorder—to a set of controls that do not have the disorder. In this analysis the problem cases are countries in which state failures led to geno/politicide, the controls are state failures without such deadly outcomes. Logistic regression is used to analyze data on conditions in problem countries one year before the onset of state failure in comparison to conditions in the controls. The results are expressed in odds ratios that tell us the relative risks associated with each such factor. Table 1.1 shows the odds ratios for the six factors in the final model and reports statistics on how accurately the model classifies the cases.

The risks of geno/politicide, given the occurrence of a state failure, are 3.5 times greater in autocracies than democracies and 3.4 times greater in countries with a prior genocide. Next in importance is trade openness (an alternative indicator of regional political interdependence was significant by itself but had no effect independent of trade openness). Characteristics of the political elite also make a major difference in risks. Minority elites, and elites motivated by an exclusionary ideology, are both 2.5 times more likely to commit geno/politicides than are more representative and nonideological elites. Less important, but still significant, countries with high historical levels of political upheaval have substantially greater risks of future geno/politicide.

Taken together the six risk factors correctly classify all but nine of the thirty-five historical cases of genocide, and most of the nine "false negatives" are in fact consistent with the model. Sudan 1956 is misclassified because the genocide is dated from the beginning of the first southern rebellion, whereas mass killings began an indeterminate number of years later. If the onset of genocidal policies were dated from the mid-1960s, when the Sudanese regime was no longer democratic and the magnitude of upheaval was high, it would be correctly classified. Afghanistan 1978 (the onset of Soviet-supported Marxist rule) and El Salvador 1980 (elite instability and the ascendancy of the right) probably are misclassified for the same reason as Sudan: policies aimed at destruction of the opposition—Mujahdeen in Afghanistan, leftists in El Salvador—came into play later, after other counterinsurgency strategies failed.

Chile 1973 (targeting the left) and the Philippines 1972 (targeting rebellious Moros) are misclassified because of lags in the data used to estimate the model. Both regimes are classified as democracies because all model variables are measured one year

Table 1.1   Risk Factors for Genocide and Politicide, 1955–2000

Variable	Countries at Greater Risk	Countries at Lesser Risk	Odds Ratio
Political upheaval	Above average	Below average	1.70
Prior genocide	Prior post-1955 genocide	No prior genocide	3.39
Ideological orientation of ruling elite	Exclusionary ideology	No exclusionary ideology	2.55
Regime type	Autocracies	Partial or full democracies	3.50
Ethnic character of ruling elite	Represents an ethnic minority	Represents most or all groups	2.56
Trade openness	Lower	Higher	2.58
Model summary statistics			
c	0.83	A measure of the model's accuracy	
Number of problems	35		
Number of controls	91		
Percentage of genocides correctly classified	74% (26 cases)	Misclassified genocides: Afghanistan, 1978; El Salvador, 1980; Chile, 1973; Uganda, 1972; Iraq, 1963; Yugoslavia, 1992; Sudan, 1956; Philippines, 1972; Sri Lanka, 1989	
Percentage of nongenocides correctly classified	73% (66 cases)	Highest-risk nongenocides (model scores >0.50): Pakistan, 1983; Brazil, 1961; Algeria, 1991; China, 1988; Mozambique, 1976; Bangladesh, 1974	

Note: Effects of political upheaval and trade openness are calculated using interval data on the full range of scores; other variables are binary. The odds ratio for upheaval is based on the odds associated with the seventy-fifth percentile of upheaval scores relative to the twenty-fifth percentile. The odds ratio for trade openness is based on the odds associated with the twenty-fifth percentile of openness scores relative to the seventy-fifth percentile. All odds ratios are statistically significant at the 0.05 level except for prior genocide and ethnic character of the ruling elite, which are significant at the 0.10 level.

prior to the onset of state failure. In fact, both geno/politicides were carried out by authoritarian leaders after they suspended democratic rule: General Pinochet overthrew the democratically elected Allende government; Marcos effectively ended Philippine democracy by declaring martial law.

Uganda 1972 and Yugoslavia 1992 have two traits in common that help account for their misclassification. Both cases were instigated by authoritarian leaders with a single-minded commitment to eliminating opponents (in Milosevic's case, to cleansing non-Serb areas of Bosnia), and were carried out in a permissive international environment. There was very little international concern about Uganda, and although NATO members tried to check the Yugoslav civil wars by diplomatic means, they also were afflicted by collective political paralysis that Serbian (and Croat) leaders interpreted as a license to pursue genocidal policies.

In sum, at least five and more likely seven of the nine misclassified "false negative" cases are in fact accounted for by variables within the model. If they are added to the twenty-six correctly classified geno/politicides, we conclude that the model provides accurate after-the-fact predictions of over 90 percent of the genocides and politicides of the last half-century. It also flags a number of other state failures in which the model gives "false positive" predictions. It suggests, for example, that Algeria at the onset of the Islamist insurgency in 1991 had a high risk of geno/politicide, and so did China at the onset of the Uygur separatist rebellion in Xinjiang province in 1988.

Using the Genocide Risk Model to Generate a Watch List

Assuming that the risk factors for genocide and politicide during the past half-century have changed little in the first decade of the twenty-first century, the model provides a framework for assessing and comparing the vulnerability of countries to future genocide and politicide in a systematic and consistent manner. When the model is applied to current information it provides the basis for a global "watch list" that identifies countries in which the conditions for a future episode are present, as we show below.

Table 1.2 lists fourteen countries with recent armed conflicts—the political upheavals that are necessary preconditions for genocide and politicide—that have three or more of the six risk factors. Specific risk factors are listed for each, and possible victim groups are identified based on country-specific information from our case files on past genocides, minority groups, and political opposition movements. A more formal analysis would apply the coefficients from the final model to numeric data and calculate model scores; here we rank countries according to their numbers of positive risk factors.

Eleven countries currently are high on four or more of the risk factors for genocide and politicide. Iraq is the only one in which all six risk factors are present; Afghanistan also had all six factors prior to the overthrow of the Taliban regime, but still faces considerable risks depending on the outcome of current efforts to reconstruct a nonideological coalition government. The three countries with five factors are Burma, Burundi, and Rwanda. Another five African countries have four factors, as does Algeria. The Peoples Republic of China, responsible for three previous episodes, has three risk factors, as do Liberia and Pakistan.

For this approach to be useful for policy analysis, listings of risk factors must be complemented by assessment of the political circumstances in which they might be activated, as is suggested in the following sketches of Burma, Burundi, and China.

Burma: The SLORC, the military council that controls Burma, has relied mainly on repression to control its domestic opponents, including communal separatists such as the Karen and Shan and the urban-based democratic opposition. They also targeted the Muslims of the northwest Arakan region for destruction or expulsion in 1978 and again in the early 1990s. The potential that any of these conflicts might lead to future geno/politicide is moderated by several factors. First, the SLORC has sought negotiated settlements with most regional separatists, indicative of a shift away from exclusive reliance on repression. Second, it is seeking an accommodation with the democratic opposition, partly in response to international pressures. Finally, the country is being opened up to foreign investment in ways that will continue to reduce its rulers' future options about how it deals with opponents.

Burundi: Burundi has been wracked by recurring Tutsi massacres of Hutus, and observers have repeatedly warned of risks of

Table 1.2 Countries with Armed Conflicts and Three or More Risk Factors for Geno/Politicide in 2001

Countries (Number of Risk Factors)	Prior Geno/ Politicides	Upheaval since 1986[2]	Risk Factors				Possible Target Groups
			Minority Elite	Exclusionary Ideology	Type of Regime	Trade Openness[3]	
Iraq (6 of 6)	Yes: 1961–75, 1988–91	High	Yes: Sunni Arabs dominate	Yes: Secular nationalist	Autocracy	Very low	Kurds, Shi'a, political opponents of Hussein
Afghanistan 2000 (6 of 6)	Yes: 1978–89	Very high	Yes: Pushtuns dominate	Yes: Islamist	Autocracy	Very low	Hazaris, Tajiks, Uzbeks
Afghanistan 2002 (4 of 6)	Yes: 1978–89	Very high	No: Coalition in formation	No	No effective regime	Very low	Supporters of Northern Alliance
Burma (5 of 6)	Yes: 1978	High	No: Burman majority dominates	Yes: Nationalist	Autocracy	Very low	Democratic opposition; Karen, Shan, Mon; Arakenese Muslims
Burundi (5 of 6)	Yes: 1965–73, 1993, 1998	Very high	Yes: Tutsis dominate	No	Autocracy	Low	Hutus
Rwanda (5 of 6)	Yes: 1963–64, 1994	High	Yes: Tutsis dominate	No	Autocracy	Low	Supporters of exiled Hutu militants
Congo-Kinshasa (4 of 6)	Yes: 1964–65, 1977	Very high	Yes: Narrow coalition of Kabila supporters	No	No effective regime	Medium	Hutus, Tutsis, political and ethnic opponents of Kabila regime

Somalia (4 of 6)	*Yes: 1988–91*	*Very high*	No: Clan rivalries	No	*No effective regime*	*Very low*	Isaaq in Somaliland; clan rivals in south
Sierra Leone (4 of 6)	No	*Very high*	*Yes: Mende dominated*	No	*No effective regime*	*Low*	Supporters, targets of Revolutionary United Front (RUF)
Ethiopia (4 of 6)	*Yes: 1976–97*	*High*	*Yes: Tigreans dominate*	No	*Autocracy*	Medium	Supporters of Oromo, Somali secessionists
Uganda (4 of 6)	*Yes: 1972–79, 1980–86*	*High*	No	No	*Autocracy*	*Low*	Supporters of Lords Resistance Army
Algeria (4 of 6)	*Yes: 1962*	*Very high*	No	*Yes: Secular nationalist*	*Autocracy*	Medium	Islamists, government supporters
Liberia (3 of 6)	No	*High*	No	No	*Autocracy*	*Low*	Krahn, Mandingo; political opponents of Taylor regime
Pakistan (3 of 6)	*Yes: 1971, 1973–77*	Medium	No: Punjabi majority dominates	No	*Autocracy*	*Low*	Sindhis, Hindus, Shi'a, Christians
China (3 of 6)	*Yes: 1950–51, 1959, 1956–75*	Medium	No	*Yes: Marxist*	*Autocracy*	Medium	Uighers, Tibetans, Christians

Note: Countries are listed according to their number of risk factors, as identified in table 1.1. Data are from the State Failure dataset posted at http://www.bsos.umd.edu/cidcm.inscr. All indicators use 2000 information except that Trade Openness is for 1999. Bold italic entries are high-risk conditions.

future genocide. Those risks may be overstated. The crucial change in Burundi in the last few years has been the emergence of moderate leaders, both Tutsi and Hutu, who want to contain communal violence. So long as they control the regime, genocide initiated or condoned by the government is highly unlikely. The risks are of a different sort: militant Hutus in eastern Congo repeatedly attack Tutsi villagers and officials in Burundi, sometimes in collusion with Hutus living in Burundi. These incursions sustain the cycle of Hutu-Tutsi communal violence. If militants of either group came to power, genocidal violence almost certainly would follow. International attention and support has reinforced the government's commitment to moderate policies. However, it is essential that regional powers stop supporting competing rebel groups. Long-term reduction of the risks of geno/politicide is possible only when and if international engagement brings an end to anarchy in eastern Congo.

China: Three geno/politicides have been carried out during Communist rule in China, one after the Communists took power in 1950–51, the second in Tibet in 1959, the last during the Cultural Revolution from 1966 to 1975. Some risk factors remain high, but in our judgment they are declining. Beijing's rulers in the 1990s are more pragmatic in doctrine and practice than their predecessors. China is more engaged economically with the rest of the world, with the likely long-term result of constraining domestic policies that offend trading partners and investors. Nonetheless the regime has responded harshly to resistance by Tibetans and Muslim separatists in Xinjiang province, and to imagined security threats from Christians and the Falun Gong movement. Unless and until the Chinese government becomes more willing to accommodate national minorities and unauthorized religious sects, the risk remains that repression may escalate into policies aimed at eliminating the offending groups.

Concluding Comments

The risk analysis helps highlight situations that should have the highest priority for remedial and preventive action. By whom and how? The answers depend on which actors have the will, the political leverage, and the resources to act. International and regional organizations are most likely to pursue effective preventive strategies in areas where the Western powers have vital interests, which means Europe, Latin America, the Middle East, and Central Asia. Conflicts and potential humanitarian disasters in Africa and elsewhere in Asia are more remote and resistant to external influence. When preventive strategies fail, or are not attempted in the first place, the international challenges are different: how to provide humanitarian aid and how to contain the regional dispersion of conflict.

2

Initial Response to Complex Emergencies and Natural Disasters

Ed Tsui

ON JANUARY 17, 2002, one of Africa's most active volcanoes unexpectedly erupted in the Democratic Republic of Congo (DRC). As lava rapidly advanced toward the lakeside city below, fuel depots erupted into slow burning fires, tremors and shocks crumbled buildings and collapsed houses, heat and lava flows destroyed water and electrical systems, ash covered the landscape, and lava-turned-to-rock covered parts of the lake.

As a result, about 400,000 of Goma town's 500,000 habitants were forced to flee to unstable areas of the DRC and Rwanda, where rebel elements remained active. Nine died and one hundred were wounded. About 40 percent of the town's infrastructure was destroyed, leaving thousands without electricity or potable water.

If ever there were a typical natural disaster, the eruption of Mount Nyirangongo was not it. Its location on a contentious border in an area plagued by armed conflict placed it squarely in the middle of a long-standing, regional, complex emergency, where state and nonstate actors compete for control, misinformation is rampant, and humanitarian access limited.

A number of other factors added to the complexity of the response, including the many actors involved; the threat of further eruptions or factures from associated volcanic *and* seismic activity, whose interplay was classified by both vulcanologists and seismologists alike as a new phenomena; and the potential for contamination of Lake Kivu, a primary source of both food and drinking water in an already impoverished area and, ironically, of noxious gases that threatened to ignite.

Yet the international humanitarian response was as quick as it was comprehensive, and, in spite of the complexity of the situation, largely succeeded in alleviating the immediate needs of those most affected.

The Office for the Coordination of Humanitarian Affairs (OCHA) was but one of many players who made this response a success. OCHA and its partners over the past ten years have learned a great deal about the types of tools, mechanisms, and processes needed for an effective emergency response. New technologies, increases in the scope and magnitude of both complex emergencies and natural hazards, as well as the need for common tools to address them, and a growing appreciation by member states of the importance of humanitarian assistance and the protection of civilians to the achievement of peace, security, and development are only a few of the trends that have shaped the nature of emergency response as we know it today. But despite the growing need for humanitarian interventions in ever more complex operating environments, the key lessons learned by the international humanitarian community regarding emergency response in the past decade are straightforward. In short, over time we have come to understand that an effective response depends on the following:

1. Solid needs assessments that allow relief agencies to jointly determine who does what where, under the umbrella of a comprehensive humanitarian action plan
2. The proper staff and emergency response tools available at the right time in the right place
3. Common tools for natural disasters and complex emergencies, which build on the comparative advantage of the other without losing their ability to be applied in unique situations
4. Emergency funding mechanisms that ensure money is readily available and easily dispersed
5. Well-developed information management networks through which accurate-as-possible data are immediately available to key decision-makers

6. Reviews that draw the lessons learned from each response and help apply them to the next

Each of these lessons was manifested in the Goma response, which included, among other actions, early reinforcements of experienced humanitarian staff, including a senior emergency manager; the provision, through daily updates, of credible and timely information about the crisis at both the field and international levels; the on-site establishment of extraordinary information exchanges and a specialized center to process, analyze, and share humanitarian data; the issuance of an inter-agency emergency appeal for funds; the rapid dispatch of vulcanologists to the field; and the procurement of emergency nonfood items for the affected population.

As such, this particular response to a sudden onset emergency highlights not only the need for, but also the increasing efforts by, aid actors, in particular OCHA, to ensure that the above elements are consistently at the disposal of the international system, so that each response is timely yet flexible, specialized when needed, and above all, well coordinated.

As an example of how aid can effectively reach its victims, it also provides a benchmark of comparison to other international emergency responses, where, for whatever reasons, action was neither as swift nor as decisive. Thus, it further highlights the need for greater consistency in the application of the emergency response tools and mechanisms at the disposal of the international humanitarian community.

Before I elaborate on these lessons and themes, it is useful to understand the increasingly challenging and multifaceted backdrop against which aid workers struggle to deliver assistance in the field and that has shaped the formulation of emergency response.

Natural Disaster and Complex Emergencies

In the last two decades alone, more than three million people have died in natural disasters caused by extreme weather resulting from global warming and other related atmospheric changes, as well as by deforestation and soil erosion caused by unsustainable development practices. Combined with poverty and population pressure, growing numbers of people are being forced to live in harm's way—on flood plains, unstable hillsides, and earthquake-prone zones.

Similarly, the end of the Cold War has resulted in profound changes not only in the number but also in the nature of armed, internal conflicts. In the last decade of the twentieth century, regions once thought to be beyond war, such as Western Europe, became entrenched in it; simmering socio-economic tensions in many African countries resurfaced; and the war on terrorism gave way to far-reaching humanitarian implications in Central Asia and the Middle East. In this period, conflicts have claimed more than five million lives and driven many times that number of people from their homes. At present, it is estimated that more than 40 million people have been displaced by conflict worldwide.

Increasingly, as we saw in Goma, the traditional distinctions between the two types of crises—natural disasters and complex emergencies—are not always so clear. Interplay between the two has become common. This is particularly true in the case of drought, which differs from most natural disasters in that it is slow in onset and may continue for a prolonged period of time, which can lead to a conflict over scarce resources. In ongoing emergencies, drought can also exacerbate existing tensions.

Whatever the cause, the resulting effects of these emergencies are similar. They include extensive violence and loss of life, increasingly among innocent noncombatants and civilians, massive displacements of people, and widespread damage to societies and economies. But despite the similarities, key differences in the immediacy, duration, scope, and political complexity of a crisis have increasingly called for specialized capacities or services in the initial response.

Immediacy

In the event of a natural disaster, such as an earthquake or volcano, thousands of lives are put at immediate risk. Many can be lost within hours or days of the incident if search and rescue and other life-saving efforts are delayed. In these cases, a rapid initial response is critical, and often more easily applicable, to the goal of saving lives.

Complex emergencies, on the other hand, are characterized by a total or considerable breakdown of authority. They usually involve more deliberate violence—and therefore violations of human rights and international humanitarian law—targeted at civilians, as well as political and military constraints that hinder response and pose more significant and sinister security risks to aid workers. Aid actors are not always able to reach populations, and the type of assistance required is often varied. For instance, immediate, on-the-spot assistance can consist of medical treatment for war-related injuries. But this is often combined with sustained and cumulative needs, arising from weeks and months of deprivation due to lack of access to basic social services and food, over long periods of time. Thus, the provision of timely assistance may be as critical, but the operating environments are usually more complex and require a more tailored response.

Duration

As a result of these differences in immediacy, the life-saving stage that follows a natural disaster response may be over within a matter of days or weeks, notwithstanding the reconstruction efforts that may follow.

The chronic humanitarian needs arising from war, however, often continue for months and even years. Additionally, as the nature of an emergency changes—for example, from the immediate aftermath of military action, to a long-simmering standoff between government and militant groups, to a negotiated peace—humanitarian assistance programs may evolve and become more varied, encompassing simultaneous relief programs as well as rehabilitation and reintegration activities. These situations necessitate longer-term initiatives designed to minimize human suffering over time.

Scope

Natural disasters increasingly span several countries. For instance, when successive cyclones hit southeastern Africa in February 2001, rivers and dams overflowed throughout the region, resulting in widespread flooding in Mozambique, Swaziland, Botswana, Malawi, Zimbabwe, and South Africa, affecting more than two million people. But although several neighboring countries can be affected by the same natural disaster, especially in case of drought, their relationships are not always strained, and cooperation is more common.

In complex emergency situations, however, the international and cross-border dimensions are almost always characterized by political differences between those concerned. One need not look further than the former Federal Republic of Yugoslavia, the Great Lakes region of Africa, or the West African subregion for examples of how conflict spreads, displacing thousands in a tangled web of cross-border movements. Responding to such crises requires a higher level of regional coordination and interaction with a greater multiplicity of actors, who are often at odds with each other.

KEY ELEMENTS OF A SUCCESSFUL RESPONSE

Against this backdrop, the international community has seen an increasing trend toward more integrated, as well as a more standardized, yet flexible, application of initial response procedures, tools, and mechanisms in crises. This versatility entails being able to deal with the full range and potential interplay of crises, from purely complex emergency and natural disaster situations to every possible combination in between, based on a common platform of response practices, tools, and mechanisms that consist of the following:

1. Solid needs assessments that allow relief agencies to determine jointly who does what where, under the umbrella of a comprehensive humanitarian action plan.

When a crisis erupts, the international community—including government, nongovernmental organizations (NGOs), donors, member states, the Red Cross Movement, and the United Nations—is usually alerted by an array of monitoring systems, including individual as well as shared sources of information, ranging from field reports to earthquake bulletins, weather notices, and press reports. Once alerted to a crisis, the international humanitarian community must gauge the willingness of the affected state to accept assistance. Although the primary responsibility for taking care of the victims of crisis always rests with the affected state, governments whose national capacities are not sufficient to meet the needs may either directly request assistance or pose no objections to humanitarian intervention.

Once the acceptance or nonobjection to aid is established, the humanitarian community focuses its attention on ensuring the impartial and timely inter-agency assessment of the humanitarian situation on the ground. These assessments, often led by OCHA in its role as a nonoperational and therefore unbiased facilitator of humanitarian response, are vital to ensuring that a wide spectrum of policy and decision makers are well informed from the outset of a crisis, when time-sensitive decisions regarding funding, deployments of staff and assets, and staff security must be made under enormous pressure. OCHA's experience has shown the importance of striking a balance between the depth and speed of reporting and the accuracy of the initial assessment. In crisis situations, initial assessments often must be updated hourly to reflect new, incoming information resulting from fast-moving events. Emphasis must therefore be placed on conveying what is known at the moment.

They also form the basis for the coordination of assistance in a rapidly evolving situation involving a multiplicity of actors, with sometimes overlapping mandates. Especially critical is the prioritization of needs—whether they be in the food, shelter, health, water, sanitation, or protection sectors—and the subsequent assignment of tasks and responsibilities based on the individual mandates, strengths, and comparative advantages of each organization. Thus, in response to a sudden onset crisis, initial actions may focus on determining who does what where. OCHA's role is to ensure that, drawing on systemwide capacities, all needs are met without duplication and that often scarce resources are efficiently used.

Ongoing assessments throughout the crisis will then form the basis of longer-term inter-agency planning efforts designed to ensure that there is (1) a common understanding of the problems and constraints besetting affected populations, (2) a joint and complementary action plan for addressing them, and finally (3) an effective use of limited resources for those activities that are of mutual concern to all—such as communication, logistics, security, and information management. These are often realized through the development of a Common Humanitarian Action Plan (CHAP), which forms the basis of an inter-agency appeal process, of which OCHA is the custodian. Through this process—known as the Inter-Agency Consolidated Appeals Process (CAP)—national, regional, and international relief organizations jointly develop a common humanitarian programming, strategic planning, and resource mobilization document, which is regularly reviewed and revised. In the event of a sudden deterioration of an existing emergency for which a CAP has already been developed, the plans to respond to the evolving crisis may already have been incorporated in the CAP as possible planning scenarios. If not, the CAP may be rapidly reviewed and revised to reflect the new needs. Similarly, in cases where a natural disaster occurs in a country with a CAP, a revised CAP is usually issued, reflecting the new needs presented by the natural disaster.

In natural disaster settings, needs are determined jointly by the resident agencies on the basis of rapid assessments, which are conveyed along with funding needs in situation reports that are issued within the first twenty-four hours of a crisis and then updated daily.

2. The proper staff and emergency response tools available at the right time in the right place.

No matter how experienced the first, in-country responders to an emergency are, the sudden onset of a crisis is inevitably marked by alarm and confusion as national authorities and their UN and NGO counterparts struggle to assess the situation, often in conditions of extreme danger and limited access. Depending on the type of crisis, the leading humanitarian official on the ground, usually the UN Resident Coordinator (RC), may be forced to deal with many competing concerns, ranging from assessing the situation to evacuating nonessential staff to dealing with the media. Coordination at this stage is especially critical to ensuring that humanitarian assistance is delivered in a targeted, effective, and complementary manner.

OCHA facilitates this process by either rapidly establishing a field presence and coordination structures in country or by providing extra support to actors already in the country in the form of temporary rapid response teams, otherwise known as "surge" capacity.

Usually, existing resident agencies—headed by the RC—will support the government's efforts to respond to a disaster or complex emergency. If new structures are needed, OCHA's head, the Under-Secretary-General for Humanitarian Affairs and the Emergency Relief Coordinator (USG/ERC), in consultation with a range of humanitarian actors, determines—based on an analysis of the humanitarian, political, military, and security situation—whether the crisis warrants a country or regional response, and decides which coordination mechanisms best fit, including whether there is a need to appoint a Humanitarian Coordinator (HC) to oversee the coordination of international aid efforts. Often the Resident Coordinator will also serve as the Humanitarian Coordinator (R/HC). These permanent structures help ensure not only the success of the initial response, but the development of common strategic planning and monitoring of humanitarian assistance throughout a crisis.

Either way, quick and decisive leadership from OCHA, in specific the USG/ERC, in the initial phase of an emergency is critical. In consultation with UN agency and Secretariat department heads in New York, the USG/ERC may decide to visit the striken country himself in order to assess the damage first hand, and then report back to the Secretary-General, the Security Council, donors, agencies, and NGOs on a appropriate course of action. Or he may deploy one of OCHA's senior managers or an OCHA Regional Disaster Response Advisor (RDRA) already in the region to the emergency site, in order to support resident UN agencies, the R/HC, and the local government in the initial assessment.

It has become clear from numerous evalutions of OCHA's initial response that such senior leadership is a prequisite to success. The presence of these additional senior staff can lend the necessary authority and legitimacy to build consensus for effective coordination; deal with other senior officials, especially in situations requiring access negotiations or interface with the peace-keeping and political authorities; and draw worldwide attention and resources to the aid efforts. In East Timor, for instance, despite the lack of a meaningful contingency plan to respond to the outbreak of mass destruction and violence on September 4, 1999, the Assistant Emergency Relief Coordinator managed to fly into Dili by September 6, 1999, where he remained as one of only two international humanitarian representatives in East Timor until the re-entry of the humanitarian community on the twentieth. Under his leadership, coordination fora were immediately established and a preliminary assessement document begun.

The ERC may also decide to deploy interdisciplinary rapid response teams or "surge capacity" to support the government and/or the R/HC in assessing the situation and coordinating the relief response.

These working-level emergency reinforcements, by providing specialized capacities or boosting existing ones in times of extreme demand, can help take strain off governments, resident UN agencies and other organizations; focus attention on the need for extraordinary levels of coordination and contingency planning; and if necessary reorient resident agencies from their normal development focus to the different demands of disaster response.

Their timely arrival can also be critical to the success of an initial response. In the past decade, OCHA has been increasingly called upon to provide such surge capacity on very short notice to R/HCs at the ouset of a new crisis, when an existing emergency intensifies or to relieve temporarily or replace a critical staff member of an existing unit. In Goma, for instance, within thirty-six hours OCHA had within fielded a UN Disaster Assessment and Coordination (UNDAC) team and staff with specialized skills from nearby offices in Eritrea and Kenya, as well as from Geneva. The Assistant Emergency Relief Coordinator (AERC) was on the ground within forty-eight hours. Within seventy-two hours, OCHA had a total of fourteen staff members on the ground, backed up wth support from desk officers in New York and Geneva.

While OCHA in the past has drawn staff on an ad hoc basis to respond to a sudden onset or deterioriation in a complex emergency, the need for more systematic internal procedures has been recognized. As a result, OCHA, borrowing from the expertise of its more automated initial response to natural disasters, is in the process of building its own in-house capacity to deploy within twenty-four hours OCHA-trained staff, who are fully conversant with OCHA's mandate and the operational specifics of the organization, in order to establish immediate and effective coordiantion mechanisms in a sudden-onset emergency. Depending on the crisis, these may include information management and technology, operations, logistics, administration, and communications capacities.

Increasingly one of their first tasks is to establish what has become known as a Humanitarian Information Center (HIC). By providing a venue for humanitarian exchange, HICs promote communication and cooperation, especially in crises involving a multitude of actors. Typically staffed by information managers and data specialists borrowed from humanitarian agencies and international NGOs, HICs offer a range of products and services that make coordination and response possible. These include, but are not limited to, Internet-based data repositories containing baseline information on at-risk countries; *Who? What? Where?* (3W) databases containing vital statistics on population, internal displacement, refugee movement, and needs; country encyclopedias and digital libraries of UN reports and documents; road maps to assist relief convoys and missions; and thematic maps illustrating key sectoral data including housing damage, schools and clinics, and the location of mines. HICs also often provide humanitarian aid workers with accessible, central meeting rooms, common office equipment and announcement boards, as well as Internet and fax access.

3. Common tools for natural disasters and complex emergencies, which build on the comparative advantage of the others without losing their ability to be applied in unique situations.

The international humanitarian community has increasingly recognized the need to have at its disposal a range of flexible and integrated emergency response tools that can be used in either complex emergency or natural disaster situations. OCHA itself has long maintained relatively separate response tools for both types of crisis. But based on its experience over the past ten years and the increasing demands of its partners, it is increasingly attempting to provide the international humanitarian community with an integrated menu of emergency response tools, which include the following subjects.

United Nations Disaster Assessment and Coordination (UNDAC)

Originally designed to provide assessment capacity and support for the coordination of incoming relief at the site of a sudden-onset natural disaster, UNDAC teams are drawn from a roster of 164 volunteer national emergency managers, who are nominated and funded by more than forty participating countries, together with staff from OCHA, UN agencies, and other international organizations. They can be deployed within twelve to twenty-four hours anywhere in the world and are capable of performing a variey of tasks, including assessment, coordination, and information management, as well as providing experts in specialized fields of disaster management, such as search and rescue, chemical spill management, and infrastuctural engineering.

Until very recently UNDAC was used primarily as a natural disaster response mechanism, having been deployed since 1993 in only ten complex emergencies, but efforts are now underway to strengthen UNDAC's capacity to respond to complex emergencies.

International Search and Rescue Advisory Group (INSARAG)

At the same time, OCHA recognizes the benefit of retaining the unique nature and purpose of some specialized response mechanisms. To that end, OCHA continues to help mobilize international urban search and rescue (SAR) teams, who specialize in rescuing victims trapped by rubble. They are drawn from a network of government-provided experts known as INSARAG. Additionally, in cooperation with the United Nations Environmental Program (UNEP), OCHA facilitates the deployment of rapid response teams with environmental expertise to coordinate the UN emergency response to environmental emergencies, such as chemical or oil spills and forest fires.

If OCHA determines a need for specialized capacities not already on stand-by, it can make special arrangements to provide them on behalf of the international community. In response to the Goma crisis, for instance, OCHA rapidly identified and funded the dispatch of expert vulcanologists to the site of Mount Nyiragongo within days of the eruption. Ultimately, while nothing could be done to stop the flow of lava, the vulcanologists were able to provide invaluable information and assessment, allowing humanitarians to work with as much a degree of certainty as was possible given the fluidity of the situation.

On-Site Operations Coordination Centers (OSOCC)

The rapid establishment—usually by UNDAC or the first international search and rescue team on the ground—of a temporary

OSOCC at the site of a disaster can help provide a locus for information management and sharing as well as the coordination of various aid actors, particularly when infrastructure or communication facilities are lacking. But although initially conceived of to assist local authorities of the affected country in managing the disaster, in particular to coordinate international search and rescue teams, OSOCCs have proved valuable in their flexibility and adaptability to various situations and needs. At the most basic level, an OSOCC can be established with reduced needs, such as to act solely as a humanitarian information clearinghouse, or as a coordination center for UNDAC teams and other humanitarian actors. As opposed to HICs, OSOCCs are usually more temporary in nature.

Internet-based virtual OSOCCs can also be used in both complex emergency and natural disasters to exchange information, identify needs, and plan ongoing responses in real time from anywhere in the world. Virtual OSOCCs proved vital in the initial response to the earthquakes in El Salvador, India, and Peru, as well as in Afghanistan.

Civil-Military Cooperation (CIMIC)

In crises in which there is a peacekeeping mission already in place or in which militaries are heavily involved in the humanitarian response, OCHA staff, sometimes based in HICs, will often liaise with CIMIC staff attached to various militaries or peacekeeping operations in order to ensure the complementarity of peacekeeping and humanitarian programming and to share vital security information. They also help facilitate the most effective use of military and civil defense assets in humanitarian operations by promoting interaction between the humanitarian and military cells of a relief operation. In most cases, individual UN agencies and the larger NGOs establish their own links with military cells. However, in some instances OCHA will serve as the hub for the mobilization and deployment of these assets and act as a direct liaison between the humanitarian and military cells during a humanitarian relief operation. In this case, OCHA identifies personnel experienced in civil-military coordination to work closely with the R/HC.

UN Joint Logistic Centers (UNJLC)

OCHA may also assist in the establishment of UNJLCs where logistical information, data about the estimated global need for food and nonfood items, and information about distribution of relief to beneficiaries is exchanged and shared with the humanitarian community. For example, during the response to the floods in Mozambique in early 2001, OCHA's Military and Civil Defense Unit (MCDU) participated in establishing a joint logistics center to coordinate the use of military planes, boats, and communications equipment for rescue, water purification, food distribution, and shelter activities.

Physical Assets

It goes without saying that the rapid deployment of emergency aid items is critical to meeting the needs of the affected population. But when contingency plans are lacking or the emergency is entirely unpredicted, it can take days for relief organizations to reposition stocks. Recognizing the need for instant access to relief supplies, the UN, with support from key donors, has established a permanent renewable stock of donated disaster relief items at the UN Humanitarian Response Depot in Brindisi, Italy, which includes tents, blankets, kitchen sets, generators, water purification/distribution equipment, and tools. Together with the World Food Program (WFP), which administers the depot, OCHA organizes the immediate transport free of charge of these basic nonfood survival items to disaster-affected areas, subject to the donor agreement and availability. In response to the Goma crisis, for instance, a twenty-five-ton shipment of nonfood items donated by the governments of Italy and Norway within seventy-two hours were transported to the DRC and distributed to those affected by the crisis.

OCHA also maintains a database of relief sources for use by the broader humanitarian community. Designed to function as a humanitarian yellow pages, the Central Register includes a list of stockpiles for noncommercial equipment and supplies, directories for search and rescue teams, national emergency response offices, a register of available military and civil defense assets, and a roster of disaster management experts. This enables emergency response staff to identify and approach quickly the potential providers of the required international assistance.

4. Emergency funding mechanisms that ensure money is readily available and easily dispersed.

It goes without saying that an effective response to sudden-onset emergencies and disasters depends heavily on the availability of funds to support immediate needs. The willingness of donors to fund such response is often high, largely because when compared to protracted emergencies, the immediate needs of an initial response are more easily defined, direct life-saving results are more visible, and public pressure to act is at its greatest. But, in its efforts to capitalize on this fact, the international humanitarian community faces two main challenges.

The first is to provide donors accurately and quickly with interagency funding and needs assessments. In natural disaster situations, this is typically accomplished by including funding needs, determined jointly by the resident agencies on the basis of rapid assessments, in its situation reports, which begin being issued within the first twenty-four hours of a crisis.

In a new complex emergency situation, the mechanisms for immediately communicating needs to donors are less clear. Typically, ad hoc "flash appeals" or "donor alerts" covering needs for one month may be issued within the first few weeks of a new crisis. As the crisis evolves, the initial requirements presented in flash appeals or donor alerts are subsequently incorporated into the more formal CAP.

While valuable for longer-term planning and coordination, this appeal process has not yet developed the flexibility needed to address sudden-onset emergencies. At the same time, although the situation reports issued in the first days of natural disaster rapidly communicate funding needs to donors, neither they nor the "flash" appeals issued in an emergency follow the standard guidelines for appeals endorsed by both UN and non-UN humanitarian actors.

Recognizing the need to capitalize on the strengths of both of these mechanisms by establishing a common fundraising tool for both natural disasters and complex emergencies, OCHA and its partners are exploring the development of a Common Appeal Framework, which would include clear, simple guidelines for preparing a coordinated inter-agency appeal from the first twenty-four hours of an emergency onward and would be flexible enough to cover either a natural disaster or a complex emergency.

The second challenge to accessing emergency funds is more easily solved. Although donors may be willing to fund a sudden-onset emergency, they are often unable—and less frequently unwilling—to release funds quickly enough to have an impact in the initial phase of crisis. This can hamper relief efforts.

To ensure the immediate availability of funding in a sudden-onset emergency, ten years ago OCHA created the Central Emergency Revolving Fund (CERF), a cash-flow mechanism under the authority of the USG/ERC and administered by OCHA New York, to bridge the gaps between needs and available funding. Since then many UN agencies and larger NGOs have created their own emergency funding mechanisms, and use of the CERF has declined. To that end, OCHA is reviewing ways to keep the CERF viable.

In support of broader humanitarian objectives, OCHA also provides emergency cash grants of up to U.S.$50,000 from its own reserves to meet immediate, specific relief needs, such as the purchase and transport of blankets, tents, and tools; manages a Trust Fund for Disaster Relief for life-saving activites; and often acts as a channel for bilateral donor contributions in sudden-onset natural disasters.

5. Well-developed information management networks through which accurate-as-possible data are immediately available to key decision-makers.

Although vital to coordination throughout an emergency, the role of information technology and management in initial response is increasingly being recognized by a wide spectrum of policy and decision-makers as being the most vital at the outset of a crisis, when accurate, timely data are needed to make time-sensitive decisions. Technological advances, as well as the increased expectations they generate, among ourselves and the public at large, are in part responsible for this dilemma. As television and satellite transmissions increasingly focus public attention on poverty and suffering through real-time images of the victims of disaster and conflict across the globe, we face greater pressure to respond not within weeks, but within days or hours. Indeed, it is not uncommon for journalists to reach the scene of a disaster and start broadcasting before we do. In short, humanitarian actors must ensure that accurate information rises quickly to top decision-makers.

Although the first task of the R/HC, with support from rapid deployment or assessment teams, is to survey the situation quickly and define the needs and type of assistance required, doing so in a both timely and accurate manner can be challenging, especially in the deep field. Information flow in an emergency is often limited by the lack of national information management capacity, limited access, damaged communication systems, insecurity, and poor communication among actors, all of which can lead to isolated decision making on the basis of disparate analysis.

All too often, when a crisis erupts, valuable time is wasted gathering baseline information about an affected area, which is often already available on the Internet. Even more troubling are the instances in which our greatest challenge is not the *lack* of information but rather too much of it from too many, sometimes conflicting, sources—making it difficult to discern the most critical and relevant data from the not so useful. Just as the uncoordinated arrival of relief supplies can clog a country's logistics and distribution system, the onslaught of unwanted, inappropriate, and unpackaged information can impede decision-making and rapid response to an emergency.

These challenges highlight the need for more systematic ways to process and standardize information, as well as to begin information gathering and sharing on vulnerable countries well in advance of crises.

At the most basic level, OCHA does this by issuing situation reports on the overall humanitarian situation in country. These situation reports chronicle information on changes in the military/humanitarian situation, loss of life, material damage, national response, agency response, relief needs by sector and region, and the resultant funding appeals. Before on-site actors are able to develop or adjust their Common Humanitarian Action Plan and present comprehensive funding needs, these situation reports serve as a vital conduit for communicating to donors the scope of the needs. They are ideally informed by the individual or joint assessments by actors on the ground. On the basis of these assessments, the R/HC typically issues these reports at least daily, and often twice a day, during the first few days of a crisis and then weekly or biweekly as the crisis becomes less acute. The reports are shared with the host government of the affected country, the UN system on the ground, donor embassies, and with the NGO community.

Just five years ago, time-critical documents such as these were still distributed by fax, telex, and cable. Today they are available to these partners and the public through two OCHA information-sharing platforms, the Integrated Regional Information Network (IRIN) (www.irinnews.org) and ReliefWeb (www.relief web.int). The former is a humanitarian news service that provides unbiased reporting on humanitarian crises through updates, analysis, and alerts on a range of political, economic, and social issues on forty-six countries in Africa and eight in Central

Asia. The latter provides, via the Web, twenty-four-hour coverage of relief, preparedness, and prevention activities for complex emergencies and natural disasters worldwide and acts as a gateway to documents and other sources of information related to humanitarian assistance and relief.

As part of its efforts to provide a more integrated response through all phases of a crisis, OCHA can also deploy information specialists to the field as part of its surge capacity or rapid response teams. Similarly, information management, as opposed to technology, is increasingly being recognized as a core function of UNDAC.

The immediate deployment of experienced information managers, in both the DRC and Afghanistan, demonstrate the potential for rapid, effective, and coordinated inter-agency information management during an initial onset of a crisis, as well as the flexibility needed to respond to different types of crisis.

For example, in the extremely complex operating environment of Afghanistan, OCHA information managers helped enhance existing information systems maintained by UNDP, FAO, and various NGOs to create one common information framework dealing with emergency as well as transitional issues—demonstrating not only the potential effectiveness but the high level of inter-agency involvement in information sharing. At the opposite extreme is the response to the volcanic eruption in Goma—a comparatively small, localized, and short-lived disaster. In this case, OCHA, with the full support of its partners, was able to deploy—at very little cost and relatively quickly—existing information management capacities to provide up-to-date information services to the agencies and organizations on the ground through a rudimentary, but effective, humanitarian information center.

At the more sophisticated level, OCHA information managers also support initial response by working closely with their humanitarian partners to develop information products and tools, such as geographical and thematic maps, databases and digital reference libraries, and virtual coordination centers that improve the coordination of humanitarian assistance. In particular, much work remains to be done in the critical area of identifying cost-effective and simple technologies that work in the deep field, from which information is often most scarce.

For example, during flooding in Mozambique in February 2001, OCHA's Field Information Support (FIS) unit sent GIS specialists to develop a geo-referenced database of humanitarian needs so that helicopter pilots could pinpoint overlooked villages. In Kosovo, information specialists created a needs database that highlighted duplication and gaps in assistance and developed a series of common road maps to help humanitarian convoys find their way to remote locations.

6. Reviews that draw the lessons learned from each response and help apply them to the next.

When all is said and done, continued improvements in the initial response to crises depends largely on the extent to which the lessons learned in one situation are both recorded and then applied in similar contexts. To this end, lesson-learning reviews can help to identify strengths and weaknesses in international response coordination mechanisms and ensure that lessons identified are integrated into future contingency planning and coordination structures. Given the need for actors to focus on the work at hand, so-called "real-time" exercises may be less appropriate in the context of an initial response but should be undertaken almost routinely at the end of each emergency activity. These need not be full-fledged and lengthy exercises—key to their success is a relatively light design, one that fully involves the key actors and that uses a method that facilitates joint learning and provides instant feedback.

OCHA is fully committed to such systematic reviews of lessons learned for all its emergency activities and is currently experimenting with different modalities for such reviews—one of the first being a lessons review of the 2002 Goma earthquake. Clearly the usefulness of these reviews depends very much on the interest and will of participants—staff and key partners alike—to gen-

uinely reflect on what worked and what did not and to iden..,
workable recommendations for future activities. Over time
OCHA hopes to distill lessons from these country-specific exercises and review their broad validity for similar activities and complex emergency situations.

Another way to identify lessons are external evaluations undertaken by independent consultants. In 2001, for example, OCHA
asked independent evaluators to analyze its performance in response to the 2000 Gujarat earthquake, address some broader
issues about the efficacy of the UN system's disaster-response capacity, and identify lessons for future activities. Similarly, OCHA
also commissioned an independent evaluation of its response to
the East Timor crisis in 2000. Both exercises produced sound
recommendations and lessons, apart from providing an objective
and transparent basis for reviewing OCHA's performance.

However, unless such individual activity or country-specific exercises are systematically reviewed for their potential application
in similar activities, fully incorporated into institutional memory
and applied in policy-making and decision-making, their usefulness is limited. Recognizing this challenge, OCHA recently created an Evaluation Studies Unit within its Policy and Studies
Development Branch and is in the process of putting in place an
evaluative framework and strategy, in consultation with its key
partners.

The strategy recognizes that evaluation activities provide little
added value, if their recommendations and lessons are not applied in current and future programming, as well as policy and
decision-making. To that end, OCHA's strategy aims also to create and/or improve systems for sharing the results of evaluations
and reviews in a meaningful way, and to establish follow-up
mechanisms.

CONCLUSION

Through this combination of shared experience, the international humanitarian community has in the last decade made

great strides in its efforts to create a common platform of response practices and tools. Overall, it is reacting more quickly and in a more coordinated manner to bring relief to the victims of disasters and emergencies. But as the war on terrorism and other sources of conflict continue, we are certain to face ever increasing and perhaps unanticipated challenges in the delivery of humanitarian assistance. To that end, we must look beyond improvements in how we respond to crisis. We must learn to be quicker to detect and prepare for crises before they occur. The earlier we intervene, the more likely we are able to have a meaningful impact on the ground. Similarly, we must more consistently enter all crisis situations with a clearly defined and viable exit strategy that guides all of our actions, even in the initial response, toward the ultimate stability and recovery of the affected country. Greater advocacy efforts before, during, and after an acute crisis can also help us to better harness public and political attention, especially in the early days of a crisis when international attention is highest. The very fluidity of the situations in which we work has forced us to remain flexible, and that has led to many improvements in our response. In the coming years, we must continue to demonstrate the same level of versatility and ability to learn from our past interventions so that we may ultimately save more lives.

3

Evidence-Based Health Assessment Process in Complex Emergencies

Frederick M. Burkle, Jr., M.D.

Introduction

DISASTER ASSESSMENT is defined as the "survey of a real or potential disaster to estimate the actual or expected damages and to make recommendations for preparedness, mitigation, and relief action."[1] In natural disasters, such as rapid onset earthquakes and cyclones, the health consequences are usually the direct results of injury or death. Often, however, the greatest toll on humans comes from the unappreciated long-term secondary effects, as seen with slow-moving droughts and massive flooding.

Zwi has defined complex emergencies as "situations in which the capacity to sustain livelihood and life are threatened primarily by political factors and, in particular, by high levels of violence."[2] The most common complex emergencies of the past two decades have involved famine and forced migration. Since the 1980s, few famines have occurred that were not human induced, and many famines catalyzed the onset of complex emergencies.

The most severe consequences of population displacement have occurred during the acute phase, when relief efforts have not yet begun or are in the early stages.[3] Refugees (populations that cross borders) and internally displaced populations have experienced high mortality rates during the period immediately following their migration. Internally displaced populations, in contrast to refugees, do not enjoy the immediate protections under international law that are afforded to refugees by the United Nations High Commissioner for Refugees (UNHCR). They must fend for themselves without benefit of basic health-care services, food, water, or sanitation that make up the protective infrastructure of refugee camps. Therefore in complex emergencies the health consequences are both directly and indirectly related to the conflict itself (table 3.1).[4]

Historically, response activities in both natural and human-generated disasters have often been ineffective, because of both the poor quality of the information available as well as the manner in which an assessment was conducted. Disaster assessment and assistance activities are often hampered by organizational problems that ultimately diminish the effect of these efforts on the population they intended to help.[5] Unfortunately, lack of personnel, medical records, and financial resources often hinders the assessment of the health situation in a complex emergency by conventional epidemiological methods practiced in traditional development programs. Epidemiological methods established for situations of restricted resources employ a simpler method of statistical analysis to be performed. The technique offered by these epidemiological methods became known as a "rapid assessment."[6] The outcome of an appropriately organized

Table 3.1   Direct and Indirect Effects of Complex Emergencies[4]

Direct Effects	Indirect Effects
Injuries/Illnesses	Population displacement: internally displaced and/or refugees
Deaths	Disruption of food
Human rights abuses	Destroyed health facilities
International Humanitarian Law violations and abuses	Destroyed public health infrastructure
Psychological stresses	
Disabilities	

and directed assessment is an efficient and effective response. During the 1990s, both health and nutritional assessments in complex emergencies gained a reputation for quality. With critical advances in indicator identification, epidemiological analysis, data retrieval technologies, and education and training of relief personnel, health and nutritional assessments have continued to improve as an art and science.

The immediate priorities of assistance in complex emergencies are the protection of the affected populations and the reduction of mortality and morbidity.[7] The effective response to complex emergencies requires timely, accurate public health information and data.[8] The rationale for an assessment is to provide objective information for planning, prioritizing needs, implementing health programs, evaluating the relief process, and identifying health issues needing further investigation.[9,10]

The humanitarian community (international organizations, nongovernmental organizations, private governmental organizations, and peace-keeping militaries) has a professional obligation to base the assistance on the best evidence available.[11] This assumption is the cornerstone of the concept of evidence-based health care. The need and demand for health care in complex emergencies are increasing at a rate determined, in part, by the rate at which public health infrastructure is destroyed and the moral integrity of governance disappears. Initially healthcare needs may be greater than the rate at which resources are being made available.[12] Use of an evidence-based approach makes it possible for decision makers (policy, operational, and field levels) to differentiate the needs of the population, the resources available, and the costs of any decision. An evidence-based approach helps to differentiate between what is supported by evidence and that made on unsubstantiated assertion. Health assessments today are expected to be reliable and valid and, as such, are inextricably linked to the analysis of specific performance and outcome indicators, region- and disaster-specific epidemiological studies, and measures of effectiveness.[13]

The assessment tool used can vary depending on the phase of

the disaster event: prevention, preparedness, response, recovery, rehabilitation, and reconstruction. Much has been written concerning the assessment process in each phase of natural and human-generated disasters. This chapter concentrates on the rapid health assessment of a complex emergency where disaster managers and decision-makers require immediate and accurate data necessary to allocate available resources rationally according to the emergency needs of the humanitarian organization. In addition, there is a brief discussion of the role rapid assessment has in stimulating the development of more organized and focused surveys and the longer-lasting surveillance system. The actual methodology for data collection and recording are beyond the scope of this chapter. However, suffice it to say, during the early 1990s response initiatives suffered because of poor and inconsistent humanitarian response and lack of assessment standardization. By the late 1990s, WHO rapid assessment protocols[14] and the Sphere Project's *Minimum Standards* provided the needed standardization guidelines to assess and assist in water supply and sanitation, nutrition, food aid, shelter and site planning, and health services.[15] The Project's Humanitarian Charter describes the core principles that govern humanitarian action and defines the legal responsibilities of states and parties in conflict to guarantee the right to assistance and protection.[16] When states are unable to respond, they are obliged to allow the intervention of humanitarian organizations—*which begins with an assessment.*

RAPID ASSESSMENT PROCESS

All health and nonhealth interventions in support of the public health in complex emergencies are determined by rapid assessments, focused surveys, and surveillance. Poor surveillance design, at all three levels, will lead to a predictable resurgence of disease and public health disruption (see fig. 3.1). If survey indicators and surveillance methodologies are incomplete or inaccurate, the ability to monitor the sensitive relationships between health, nutrition and environmental indicators, endemic disease, injury prevention (for example, landmine injuries), and gender- and age-specific vulnerabilities will be lacking. Evaluation and monitoring programs based on these three levels are the essential management tool for all health- and nutrition-related programs in complex emergencies. The important role of epidemiological surveillance in infectious disease control in a long-term refugee camp is illustrated in the applications of simple epidemiological methods in camps on the Thai-Burmese border. Here, agency collaboration organized a Health Information Office to facilitate the collection of demographic and vital statistics data, administration of a disease surveillance system, regular monitoring of hospital and outpatient discharge diagnoses, and investigation of disease outbreaks.[17] This was the forefront of Health Information Systems (HIS), which are now an essential component of all refugee camp protocols. How rapidly and how accurate an assessment and an HIS can be implemented is often used as a measure of efficiency and effectiveness of camp management.

The objectives of a rapid assessment in the emergency phase of a complex emergency are to:[18,19]

- Determine the magnitude of the emergency
- Identify existing and potential public health problems
- Measure present and potential impact, especially health and nutritional needs
- Assess resources needed, including availability and capacity of a local response
- Determine and plan an appropriate external response
- Set up the basis for a health system

The initial or rapid assessment comprises both situation assessment (a definition of the problem and an assessment or measurement of its extent) and needs assessment (a systematic procedure for determining the nature and extent of problems experienced by a specified population that affect health either directly or indirectly). This is performed in the early, critical stage of a disaster

Figure 3.1

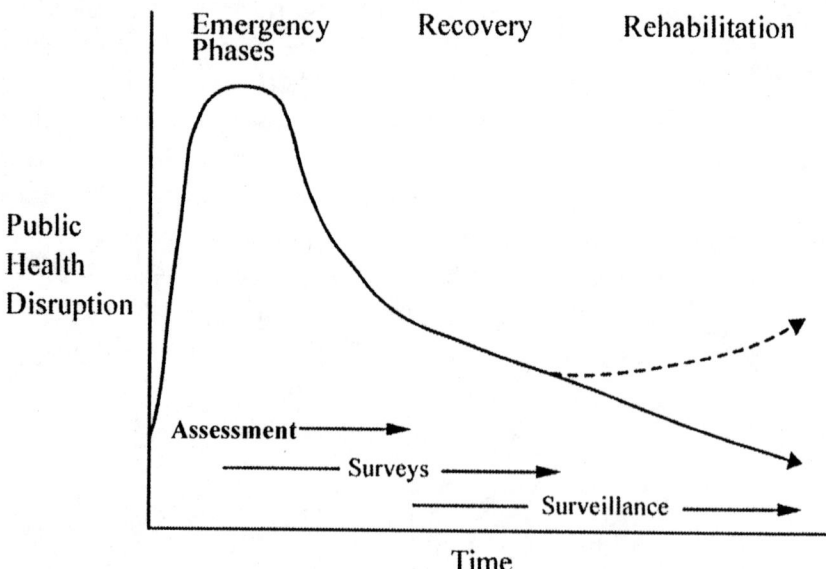

Rapid assessment is only the first phase in the overall and ongoing assessment process. If the survey and surveillance process fails to monitor potential post-disaster health problems appropriately, resurgence may occur, especially if the preventive public health infrastructure has not yet been rehabilitated.

to determine the type of relief needed for immediate response. It must identify the impact on a society, its infrastructure, the most vulnerable population groups, and the ability to cope. A rapid assessment requires data and interpretation of data. Therefore, data critical to interpretation of the needs of a population affected by a complex emergency begin with background data on the political, social, and economic status of the country (and also the region where refugees might migrate), the size and demographics of the population, and vital health information.

Facts and figures are "indispensable tools" for health personnel.[20] A simple graph of daily mortality rates can work miracles by catalyzing the mobilization of human and material resources, focusing the attention of decision-makers, and guiding and refining the assistance program that is being put into place. The five areas that are most useful are (1) mortality, (2) incidence of the most important diseases, (3) nutritional status, (4) "activities data," such as immunizations performed, and (5) the "vital sectors," namely, food, water, sanitation, shelter, and fuel. All assessment tools have been minor variations on this original theme. An effective way of presenting information is graphically, so that everyone can see the trends over time.[21]

Data collection commences before the field assessment and originates from existing country profiles, maps, census data, previous demographic and health surveys, early warning system tools, and previous or ongoing in-country assessments.[22] These are routinely performed by international organizations (United Nations Agencies, International Committee of the Red Cross), nongovernmental organizations both operational and advocacy, governmental institutions such as donor organizations—examples being the Office of Foreign Disaster Assistance (OFDA) and Department for Foreign International Development (DFID)—and academia and research centers. Additional data may come from over-flights and satellite imagery, especially useful in tracking refugee migration. Background health information is gleaned from previous reports inherent to organizations such as the World Health Organization, the Disaster Epidemiology Research Center in Belgium, Epicentre, or the Centers for Disease Control and Prevention *Mortality and Morbidity Weekly Report (MMWR)* publications. Such information may include, but is not restricted to, baseline data on:[23,24,25,26]

- Endemic diseases
- Mortality rates
- Morbidity-incidence rates
- Nutritional status
- Sources of health care
- Impact of disruption of health services

Documents are available that provide detailed checklists, information on the principles of an assessment, planning techniques, methods, and forms. The initial assessment must be carried out as soon as it is clear that an emergency exists. An experienced interdisciplinary team is required for a rapid health assessment. Time must not be lost if the desired team expertise is not readily available; however, they must be totally independent of any political or other influence. Ideally, an assessment team will include three to five members skilled in public health, epidemiology, nutrition, water and sanitation, and logistics. Assessment teams should strive to include members from the country at conflict, if possible, as well as trained interpreters. More detailed assessments, in the form of surveys and surveillance, will follow as the emergency develops and needs evolve. Assessment never stops.[27,28]

Initial assessments serve to provide a structural cornerstone for a more robust survey and surveillance system. There is often an overlap of the rapid assessment and the process implemented by the more organized survey teams (fig. 3.1). Field surveys are intermittent focused assessments that collect population-based health, nutritional, and environmental data found to be of concern or potential concern during the rapid assessment phase. To increase the power of a survey, it is combined with statistical analysis. To increase the validity of a survey and affirm or deny the suspicions drawn from the initial assessment, surveys are repeated after a certain time has elapsed or after some intervention (for example, vitamin A) has been completed. In addition, surveys are performed to gather baseline data on endemic diseases, locally and regionally, and serve as the foundation for an ongoing surveillance system. The quality of the survey instruments used and the population studied increases as one moves from the rapid assessment to the more sophisticated surveillance system. In the survey and surveillance phases, the evaluation process screens and monitors all children within the camp and at the time of entry and registration.

DATA AND INFORMATION SOUGHT

Assessments must be sensitive and specific enough to identify the most vulnerable groups and to target them with assistance appropriately. In complex emergencies, indicators are used as assessment, monitoring, and evaluation tools to inform for practical decision-making in the field. Indicators are defined as quantitative or qualitative criteria used to correlate or predict the value or measure of a program, system, or organization.[29] In the acute emergency phase, based on best practice, only the most essential indicators should be selected.

Rapid Assessment Indicators

POPULATION SIZE AND DEMOGRAPHICS

These data are necessary for determining the denominator for indicator rates (e.g., infant mortality rates) to determine who and how many people are entitled to material assistance, and to facilitate legal identity and protection of those at risk. The age and gender structure (age- and sex-specific rates) of the population is also necessary to identify the vulnerable groups and to target necessary assistance programs (e.g., immunizations). In a refugee camp setting these data are obtained early on from the camp registration system, convenience and cluster sampling of the camp population, aerial photographs, and global positioning system (GPS)–assisted population estimates.[30,31] Humanitarian assistance is slowly moving to an urban setting where the majority of the world's poor now reside[32] In an urban setting household surveys, records of beneficiary of aid, and city and country records (if recent) can be used.[33]

VITAL HEALTH INFORMATION

The goal is to confirm or deny the above background data against actual field data. The indicator data required from the field are summarized in table 3.2.[34,35]

These rates are essential for the recording of disease, trend analysis, a comparison of populations at risk, and for developing a baseline for future surveillance. A public health emergency may be defined as a situation where the daily crude mortality rate

Table 3.2   Vital Health Data

Crude mortality rate (CMR): This is the most specific indicator of a population's health. It is recorded as total deaths/10,000 population/ day. In the post-emergency phase, this reverts to total deaths/1,000 population/month
Under age 5 mortality rate (U5MR): Measured as total deaths < 5 years/10,000/day
Cause-specific mortality rates: Specifies proportion of deaths according to cause, e.g., trauma
Case fatality rates (CFR): Proportion of individuals with a specific disease that die within a specified time, e.g., CFR for children with malnutrition that die from measles
Age- and sex-specific mortality rates: Incidence rates collected during survey phase
Sphere Project Minimum Standards in Health Services add:
Sex- and age-specific breakdown (at least < 5 years and > 5 years)
Average family and household size
Age- and sex-specific incidence rates of major problems and diseases

(CMR) is significantly higher than the baseline level in the affected population. A threshold of one death per 10,000 population per day is commonly used to define an emergency in a developing country.[36] In Africa, the CMR has been as high as sixty to eighty times the baseline rates.[37] Unaccompanied orphans, not easily recognized in densely populated refugee groups, lack care and protection usually afforded by adult supervision. As such, it is not unusual for them to experience CMRs over two hundred times the baseline. CMR benchmarks are illustrated in table 3.3.[38]

A concerted effort must be made during the assessment process to identify these vulnerable populations. The most common causes of death among refugees and the internally displaced are diarrheal diseases, measles, acute respiratory infections, and malaria.[39] Most people become refugees only after their health and security have been severely compromised, and during their flight their health status deteriorates even more. Except in retrospective

Table 3.3   Crude Mortality Rate Benchmarks

Normal rate in developing countries	< 0.5/10,000/day
Serious condition	> 1.0/10,000/day
Emergency condition	> 2.0/10,000/day
Severe famine or disaster	> 5.0/10,000/day
Effective relief effort	< 1.0/10,000/day

assessments, those who died prior to reaching the camps are usually never recorded. In addition, mortality rates, particularly of those under age five (U5MR) and infants, increase when the rate of newly arriving refugees is higher.[40]

Obviously, these data are not always easy to obtain in a conflict setting. Sources of information are traditionally obtained from hospital and burial records, but many who die never had access to a health facility or formal record keeping. Improved data acquisition may require a twenty-four-hour grave site surveillance, the counting of burial shrouds used (NGOs provide the shrouds to the population), or the hiring of, for data retrieval, truck drivers used by the families to transport the dead to the grave sites.[41,42] Verbal autopsy (VA) is a procedure for gathering systematic information to be made of the cause of death in situations where the deceased has not been medically attended.[43] VA is widely used in the absence of medical certification of deaths and in situations where the proportion of people who die while under medical care is low. It is based on the assumption that the most common and important causes of death have distinct symptom complexes that can be recognized, remembered, and reported by lay respondents (for example, surviving family members). VA has been used extensively to assess causes of childhood deaths, but studies have shown this to be equally applicable to adult deaths, especially those dying during childbirth.[44,45] VA is a useful way to enhance the quality of mortality statistics. VA methodological approaches have varied widely in field settings and among aid agencies. However, results have improved with efforts to improve questionnaire design, mortality classifications, training of interviewers, and in reserving the final diagnosis to reviews by panels of physicians.[46]

Protein energy malnutrition (PEM) has three components: malnutrition, micronutrient deficiency diseases (especially vitamins A, C, and B_1), and secondary infections. PEM is often used instead of kwashiorkor or marasmus to define the state of illness. Indeed, many cases are mixed (marasmus-kwashiorkor) in their presentation and difficult to distinguish clinically. Nutritional assessments are performed by population convenience samples, screening new arrivals at the refugee camps, and through cluster sample surveys (see table 3.4). The malnutrition rate of children under age five years is next to crude mortality rates as the most specific indicator of a population's health.[47,48,49,50] It also determines the urgency for food ration delivery and requirements for supplementary feedings and therapeutic feeding centers. Some interventions are now so routine that they no longer require an assessment before implementation in the acute phase of complex emergencies. Most demonstrable is the use of vitamin A and measles vaccines in refugee populations in developing countries. Studies from the early 1990s in complex emergencies have shown that vitamin A will reduce mortality and morbidity in malnourished children, especially those with measles (active, susceptible, and exposed) and other respiratory illnesses. Indeed, vitamin A supplementation reduces all-cause mortality in children.[51] By the time measles becomes identified in a population-dense camp environment the mortality and morbidity already may be out of control. Based on this evidence it has become protocol to provide all children between one and six years of age, at the time of registration into the camp, both a measles vaccine and vitamin A. This being the case, the initial assessment will focus on identifying the population in need of services and in ensuring continuing monitoring through program outcome surveys and surveillance. Relief programs emphasize a primary health care (PHC) approach, focusing on oral rehydration, feeding centers, immunization, promoting involvement by the refugee community in the provision of health services, and stressing effective coordination of programs and information sharing among the NGOs that deal directly with the recipients of care.[52]

As the nutritional assessment moves from the rapid assessment phase through to the surveillance phase the evaluation methodologies used become more sophisticated. For example, in the rapid assessment phase, the mid-upper arm circumference (MUAC) studies performed through convenience or cluster sampling provides the decision makers information to determine whether a serious malnutrition problem exists, but not necessarily the full extent (i.e., micronutrient status, age, and gender specifics, etc.). By moving to more exact weight-for-height and Z-score monitoring in the survey and surveillance phases the evaluation process screens and monitors all children within the camp and at the time of entry and registration.

Environmental health assessments: disruptions in basic water, sanitation, shelter, and fuel indicators are indicative of public health infrastructure loss and most commonly contribute to rising acute respiratory illnesses (e.g., pneumonia, tuberculosis) and gastrointestinal diseases (e.g., dysentery, cholera, common pathogen diarrhea). In large refugee camps the mortality may increase as the population of the camps exceeds the environmental resources available.[53] In the last decade, environmental health assessments have become increasingly a critical means of defining the causes

Table 3.4   Nutritional Assessment

Goal: Prevalence of acute protein energy malnutrition (PEM) Prevalence of micronutrient deficiencies (especially vitamins A, C, B_1)
Data retrieval: Rapid Screening: Mid-upper arm circumference (MUAC) Survey and Surveillance phase data: Weight-for-height, Z-scores Clinical evidence of micronutrient deficiencies
Levels of acute malnutrition: Minor, moderate, serious (presence of edema/kwashiorkor)
Prevalence of malnutrition: > 10% of < age 5 population = SERIOUS STATUS > 20% of < age 5 population (with edema/kwashiorkor) = CRITICAL STATUS

of the mortality and morbidity seen in complex emergencies (see table 3.5).[54,55,56,57,58]

A recent critical environmental assessment was performed in war-affected areas of the Eastern Democratic Republic of Congo (largely inaccessible to aid organizations and assessments because of insecurity).[59] The ongoing fighting drove hundreds of thousands of internally displaced people into forests, jungles, and other remote areas where they had no food, medicine, or shelter. Health systems and basic environmental public health infrastructure were destroyed. At considerable risk, an epidemiologist conducted a series of eleven mortality surveys in five provinces throughout eastern Congo. He was able to determine that over a thirty-two-month period, approximately 2.5 million excess deaths (deaths greater than expected during the period studied) had occurred because of the conflict in that country. Previous reports had documented that approximately 100,000 people had died as a result of war.[60] The assessment surveys revealed that the war casualties were not limited to victims of violence, but rather that 90 percent of the deaths were attributed to infectious diseases (malaria, diarrheal diseases) and other nonviolent causes (malnutrition) directly or indirectly related to the environmental disruptions. The destruction of the region's health infrastructure

Table 3.5   Environmental Health Assessment Indicators

Water	Sanitation Services	Shelter	Fuel
• Quantity: 15–20 liters/person/ day • Quality of supply • Sources of water and accessibility	• Types of facilities: e.g., latrines, defecation fields, etc. • Recommended pit latrines/family: *Minimum*: 1 pit latrine/20 people *Serious*: < 1 pit latrine/50 people	• Types of structures: e.g., tents, plastic sheeting, etc. • Percentage of households without water-resistant shelter • Percentage of households without any form of shelter • Recommended area: 3.5m2/ person	• Types of fuel, access, and security • Recommended: 5kg of wood/ family/day

and lack of regional security meant that the vast majority of the population had minimal access to medical and public health services, making them more prone to these and other diseases. In addition, this assessment provided the only evidence that a humanitarian crisis of "staggering proportions" existed.[61] The assessment demonstrated the critical importance of how an epidemiological approach to an assessment can be used to document the denial of human rights associated with a lack of access to medical care, and basic public health and environmental services. While the study lacked the empirical scrutiny guaranteed with exact numbers, the assessment did reveal that a massive international response was indicated.

EPIDEMIOLOGICAL-BASED DEFINITION OF COMPLEX EMERGENCIES

The core evidence (knowledge) base for war and public health management comes from these assessments, surveys, and surveillance studies that, with other more advanced epidemiological research, provide a working definition and description of the phases of complex emergencies. Burkholder and Toole first described complex emergencies in developing countries as having acute, late, and postemergency phases, each of which is characterized by predictable patterns of health indicators and expected public health responses.[62] If these patterns are addressed with appropriate management responses, a decline in mortality and morbidity and a shortening of the duration of each epidemiological phase will occur. In this developing country model, the acute phase is characterized by high mortality rates for infants and those under the age of five years from severe malnutrition and outbreaks of communicable disease. Epidemiological indicator studies in the acute phase in developed countries (e.g., Yugoslavia, Chechnya) appears to be characterized more by violent trauma from advanced weaponry and untreated chronic disease (e.g., diabetes, high blood pressure, and stroke), increased incidence of communicable diseases and malnutrition in the elderly, and in neonatal health problems.[63,64]

MEASURES OF EFFECTIVENESS

With an increased understanding of the knowledge base and consequences of these internal conflicts resulting in complex emergencies, the humanitarian community has moved to attempt to define whether the interventions to provide relief and assistance have actually been beneficial or not. A theme of many recent humanitarian evaluations has been that the effectiveness of the relief process has been lacking.[65] In part, this has been attributed to a lack of clearly stated program objectives and monitoring information used in both the overall program and the sector and project components. To answer this problem, the humanitarian community is mandated to use clear and explicit statements of objectives starting with the initial assessment phase. This mandate has encouraged that assessments be redefined over three levels of management and response: strategic (or policy), operational and field levels all using goals based on indicators most relevant to the individual level. For example, "strategic frameworks" should be established to set system- (country and region) wide objectives by the international community. Second, "country (operational response) strategies" should be clearly articulated by the donor organizations, and "logical framework analyses" (LogFrame) are valuable as a way of articulating the goal, purpose, outputs, and indicators for humanitarian projects in the field. Some donor organizations have made LogFrame use mandatory.[66]

Outcome or performance measures of effectiveness (MOEs), developed primarily from analysis research, use quantitative or qualitative criteria (indicators) to correlate or predict the value or measure of a system or organization, and to make decisions or judgments on performance. Table 3.6 lists desired goals for MOEs.[67]

Table 3.6 Measures of Effectiveness

Appropriate	Mission-Related	Consistently Measureable	Cost-Effective	Sensitive	Timely
MOEs should be appropriate to the objective of the stated mission	*MOEs should be related to the mission*	*Those measuring MOEs should be able to assign a value*	*MOEs should be reasonable*	*Must be sensitive to the goals and objectives of the mission*	*MOEs should be responsive to changes*
1) To help the decision makers understand the status of the situation in different geographic areas	1) The mission is clearly understood by all participants	1) Quantitative values (i.e., indicators)	1) So as not to levy too high a burden on limited resources	1) Must change as progress toward meeting the mission objectives changes	1) Must be sensitive in time to what the participants are trying to measure
2) To present information to higher authorities	2) Focus on assessing the effectiveness of the mission and not on the accomplishment of the supporting tasks	2) Qualitative descriptors (i.e., criteria)		2) Not be greatly influenced by other (external) factors	2) Must be timely enough for participants to act
3) To support authorities in making better decisions	3) Cover all aspects of the mission and expand as the mission expands			3) Be measured in sufficient detail that changes will be apparent	

MOEs have been used in complex emergencies to correlate a variety of diverse but interrelated humanitarian, security, economic, and infrastructure indicators, and in determining whether effectiveness or success of assistance goals exists within the overall relief program. MOEs can be used with medical and public health indicators to determine trend analyses in various sectors, compare geographic sectors and programs, and identify areas in which additional program scrutiny or security is needed. Medical and public health MOEs rely on data that are already collected in the initial assessments and surveys. For example, crude mortality rates are an MOE that is an indicator of improving or deteriorating health status and is used to show impact of the overall mission. As a security MOE the measured number (fraction) of the security assumed by the security guards at the distribution centers by the host nation indicates the ability of the host nation to conduct the security mission themselves, and functions as a transition indicator (measures capability of host nation to assume responsibility).[68] In a complex emergency, there are always MOEs (at a minimum) that address security, infrastructure, medical/public health, and agricultural and economic factors.[69] Additional MOEs may address more directly the human rights issues (improvements) as a measure of success in aid relief.

ORGANIZATION-SPECIFIC HEALTH ASSESSMENTS

Humanitarian organizations provide assessments based on their particular and often diverse roles and responsibilities in the relief response. The examples provided here paint a picture of how the initial assessment process is interpreted across the humanitarian community. There is often an overlap in the interpretation of data sets among organizations, and sharing of these data should be performed as soon as possible to ensure the most efficient and effective coordination of available resources and response.

UNHCR

The objective of the initial assessment and problem analysis is to "provide UNHCR with a clear and concise picture of the emergency situation, in both quantitative and qualitative terms." The initial assessment should answer the following questions:[70]

1. How many refugees are there?
2. Where have they come from and why?
3. What is the rate of arrival?
4. What is the gender ratio, age specific?
5. What are the vulnerable groups?
6. Who are the sick and injured?
7. Is there excess mortality?

Initial assessments should:

1. Involve the affected population from the outset
2. Use agreed and appropriate standards
3. Involve appropriate technical support
4. Record sources of information
5. Cross-check information
6. Have a quick turnaround

World Health Organization (WHO)

WHO rapid assessments function to ensure an effective Ministry of Health and WHO country representative response by collecting and circulating information and assisting to coordinate health relief. WHO headquarters in Geneva and regional offices (e.g., Pan American Health Organization) function to support WHO representatives in the field with technical and personnel assistance. Assessment teams use WHO's "Rapid Health Assessment Protocols."[71] The initial assessment should:[72]

1. Assess the situation and trends: Look at the causes, magnitudes, affected areas, likely evolution of the emergency and its impact, and identify the groups and areas most at risk
2. Assess the needs: Look at the vital needs of the population—

security, water, food, shelter and sanitation, blankets, and health care
3. Assess resources: Look at what remains of local systems, what can be quickly mobilized from other partners (UN, NGOs, religious institutions), and what are the gaps in response capacity
4. Determine the area of priorities for WHO action, draft projects for immediate priorities, and contact local donors

Nongovernmental Organizations (NGOs): The example of Médecins sans frontières (MSF)

Assessments preformed by the NGO community vary greatly depending on the type, size, and work mission the individual NGO traditionally performs. MSF, like many other major NGOs, sees a first-phase priority as a rapid decision on whether or not to intervene and the type and size of the intervention. This will also lead to a decision whether a second and more comprehensive assessment is required and when it should take place. This will define the priorities of the intervention, plan the implementation of the priorities and deciding strategies, and determine the resources and time frame needed. MSF's rapid assessment phase can be completed in less than three days, although action in the field and assessment may go on at the same time, especially when there is a critical infectious disease outbreak that requires immediate attention.[73] Critical to an MSF assessment is the requirement to pass on information, as well as observations of the refugee conditions and the human rights situation, to the international humanitarian community and donors. The data collected and analyzed are classified into six categories:[74]

1. Geo-political background to include cause(s), duration, and conditions under which the displacement took place, the political situation, and the security situation
2. A description of the population, including demographics, ethnicity, sociocultural characteristics, and vulnerable groups
3. Characteristics of the environment where the refugees have settled
4. The major health problems

5. The requirements in terms of human and material resources
6. Local and international operating partners

Military

A complex emergency will include a military element for purposes of civil safety, relief security, or logistical expertise. The initial health assessments performed by the military will focus first on the military force health protection. This information may or may not be shared with the humanitarian community. Civil-Military Information Centers (CMICs), mandated by UN peace-keeping forces, are designed to be a coordination tool for relief convoys and security issues but informally function as a forum to share assessment information.

In principle, under a UN Charter peace enforcement mandate, the military may be the only asset in the field available to protect the civilian population, immediately bring about a decline in the mortality, and cease human rights abuses.[75] To date, no formal military assessment tools exist that approach the evaluation process of the civilian population during the heat of a conflict.

CHARACTERISTICS OF COMPLEX EMERGENCIES THAT RESULT IN ASSESSMENT BIAS

Decision-makers require data rapidly in order to clarify rumors and make reasonable judgments on response management. Early on, there is much pressure to act. Complex emergencies result in a rapidly changing situation in the field, in and out migration of the population at risk, and a higher vulnerability to disease and injury. The rapid assessment is time dependent, suffers from limited data resources and data quality, and occurs within an unstable or disrupted infrastructure that is insecure and intolerant of scrutiny. There may be pressure to interpret data to reflect a certain political or media agenda (e.g., intervention versus non-intervention).[76,77]

Several examples are illustrative of the need for well-designed and measured assessments. In the early stages of the Somalia debacle, many countries were eager to obtain data that would justify a larger intervention. Media reports described a rural area where there were few if any children under the age of four left alive. The report suggested that the children had died from the violent conflict that raged throughout the country. The report immediately became a rally point for intervention and began to drive the logistical efforts for relief. Several months later an assessment team visited the area. They confirmed that, yes, there were few children under age four alive, but that the reasons for this were more likely due to prolonged infertility from secondary amenorrhea of malnourished women of childbearing age, and lack of adult males who were either killed or long absent and fighting in another area of the country. Childhood deaths from violence or trauma were not above the expected norm.

Similarly the peace-keeping forces were eager to show success in the humanitarian mission, transfer duties to other organizations, and redeploy their troops. The singular indicator they were following was the infant mortality rate that had skyrocketed with the onset of fighting throughout the country. They used as an objective the baseline infant mortality rate present before the conflict escalated. When this objective was reached, mission success was unilaterally declared, and plans were put in place to begin redeployment. Concurrently, the UN Secretariat spoke to the humanitarian community on the status of the relief effort and communicated that there was a tenuous and alarming situation with infants, in that half were still considered ill and half remained malnourished. In both examples, the data were interpreted as a particular self-interest and decision.

Many early studies were "often hastily planned rapid assessments, executed under less than ideal circumstances, and too often did not culminate in a formal report."[78] Of twenty-three assessments studied in Somalia between 1991 and 1993 all revealed extensive methodological differences. Target populations and sampling strategies varied widely. Of sixteen that assessed mortality, only eight assessed cause of death. None of the studies provided confidence intervals around the point estimates of the rates. Use of units of measurement and inclusion of denominators in rate calculations were inconsistent. Concerns were that some studies may have influenced policy and program management decisions, but even here, these effects "may have been limited by failure to adequately document results and by differences in objectives, design, parameters measured, methods of measurement, definitions, and analysis methods."[79]

Because there is no clear population denominator, it has been said that complex emergency assessments consist of numerators searching for an accurate denominator. With denominator estimation, data accuracy may be uncertain ("dirty").[80] Unfortunately, incomplete assessments or unscrupulous interpretation of assessment data has led to misuse of scarce resources and incorrect analysis of the etiology of observed mortality and morbidity. Given the context of shifting populations and unstable political conditions, population size is especially difficult to assess.[81] Hansch stresses that current methods are inadequate for dealing with large-area emergencies, especially where populations are unregistered, uncounted, migratory, and likely to be mobile in response to aid.[82] In these situations relief agencies must employ improved sampling strategies, and population tracking and unique demographic retrieval techniques, such as advanced satellite and GPS/GIS methods.[83] In conflict areas where little or no data are available, collected, or analyzed, proxy or surrogate data collections have been employed. Cross-border assessments of North Korean migrants seeking assistance in China have provided the most accurate view of the nutritional status within the country. These data are limited to one province and may not reflect conditions elsewhere.[84] Although there will never be complete accuracy in the rapid assessment phase, the assessment must emphasize uniformity in analysis and appropriate restraint on descriptive judgments to act.[85]

SUMMARY AND FUTURE DIRECTIONS

Rapid assessment is the first step in designing and developing a surveillance system in complex emergencies. The data interpretations of the rapid health assessment will launch the initial phase of assistance and are expected to result in a decline in mortality and morbidity. To be accurate and timely, initial assessments and the follow-up surveys and surveillance protocols must:

1. Be evidence-based
2. Incorporate valid indicators
3. Derive verification from epidemiological studies
4. Build a data foundation by which one measures relief effectiveness

By this process initial assessments build the foundation by which the humanitarian community gains the knowledge and understanding of causes and consequences of the particular complex emergency and how it compares and contrasts to others.

The process of assessment of complex emergencies has advanced considerably, and standards now exist for the process and the indicators. The humanitarian community has learned a great deal, but much needs to be done. Spiegel emphasizes that to ensure an evidence-based assessment environment more research is needed, especially in a grading system for existing indicators (type and levels that lead to improved health outcomes) that address the different phases of complex emergencies and the level of development of the country in which the conflict occurs. This would provide "credibility and a strong foundation" for decision-makers and future research. He specifically sees indicators as being evaluated in four areas:[86]

1. Type of indicators
2. Manner in which they are implemented and interpreted
3. Standardization within and between different NGOs and settings
4. Their effects on program implementation

Experience over the last decade has shown that complex emergencies are longer lasting and more complex, dangerous, and widespread than previously thought. This information, to a great degree, has come through a variety of assessment and monitoring events, both political (e.g., economic, social) and medical. The violence perpetrated against the civilian population in complex emergencies has caused unprecedented mortality and morbidity as well as the destruction of vital public health lifelines. Societies have ceased to function, govern, or protect their citizens. Arguably, complex emergencies are appropriately referred to as catastrophic public health and human rights emergencies that often require the total rehabilitation and reconstruction of the entire country. Assessments have been critical in painting this epidemiological picture for decision-makers.

Unfortunately, attempts to intervene in a complex emergency by the humanitarian community are often severely restricted by a claim of sovereignty by the country in conflict. With health indicators deteriorating, healthcare providers frequently become "peacebuilders" by negotiating and mediating cease-fires to immunize and feed children and other vulnerable groups. The assessment data are used in these negotiations as a public health argument and as an educational tool for the warring factions to realize the extent of the destruction caused by the continued warring.

Currently, the humanitarian community is interpreting that in complex emergencies, human rights takes precedence over sovereignty, and that civilian victims have the "right to assistance" and the humanitarian community "has the duty to provide it." Health is considered a fundamental human right, and in recent complex emergencies (e.g., East Timor) the UN Declaration of Human Rights functioned as the guiding principle for aid programs. In the future, the humanitarian community, both civilian and military, must ensure that disaster and vulnerability assessments, their indicators, and the operational responses, reflect and protect health as a human right.[87,88]

4

Concern Worldwide's Approach to Water and Sanitation and Shelter Needs in Emergencies

Tom Arnold

PROVIDING ADEQUATE WATER, sanitation, and shelter are high priorities in emergency operations. Various United Nations agencies, military, governments, and international humanitarian groups will respond with different mandates. In this chapter I will present the approach of a voluntary nongovernmental organization that, by choice, works among the world's poorest people.

Generally, the criteria for Concern Worldwide's engagement in a country is that it must be among the bottom forty countries listed on the Human Development Index (HDI) produced annually by the United Nations Development Program (UNDP). However, some of the countries in which Concern is operational do not appear on the index because the UNDP is unable to access reliable information for the indicators used in developing the ranking. Amongst these countries are Afghanistan, Somalia, Liberia, East Timor, and North Korea.

To be most effective, Concern grounds its programs in the social and economic realities of the countries in which it works. Having a presence in these countries has been, and continues to be, an important factor in doing this. Concern prefers to work through civil society and in particular with local government and local groups who accord with the Concern ethos as this approach represents the most efficient use of our resources.

Given the widely differing situations of the poor in different countries, our country teams are encouraged to develop strategies and plans guided by organizational policies but relevant to national and local contexts. Our emergency programs are primarily intended as measured responses to bring quick relief with dignity. We seek to utilize and enhance local capacities so as to maximize effectiveness and to ensure a rapid return to normality. Consideration is given to the causes of the emergency so that our activities can contribute to their elimination.

Even in emergency situations we proceed based on a belief that the poor have the best knowledge of their own experience and current capacity, what change they hope to achieve, and what efforts they will make to achieve it. They should therefore be fully involved in decision-making about initiatives taken to meet their aspirations and in decision-making during the preparation, implementation, and monitoring of development projects. Special care is taken to give opportunities to women to play key roles.

In terms of the programmatic approach, Concern places its water and sanitation interventions within the broader context of environmental health, which it considers to include the following:

- Water, waste disposal (including excreta), and health education
- Shelter/Housing
- Vector control (vector examples: flies, rats, mosquitoes, etc.)
- Control of pollution, focusing on indoor air pollution

We have chosen these components as the toll from communicable diseases is still very high as illustrated by the list of the top five diseases prevalent in the developing world:

- HIV/AIDS
  —It is estimated that some 33.4 million people are currently HIV positive. Eighty-four percent of AIDS-related deaths are in Sub-Saharan Africa, where there were 2.5 million AIDS-related deaths in 1998 alone. The impact of HIV/AIDS is one of the primary factors in the recent decline in life expectancy in many countries that appear in the lower reaches of the HDI. In some instances, life expectancy has been shortened by as much as sev-

enteen years. Concern has established health interventions in numerous countries that seek to reduce the transmission and impact of AIDS.

- Malaria
  —It is estimated that, globally, there are now more than a million deaths as a result of malaria, and something between 300–500 million cases a year. We seek to address the threat posed by malaria through our activities in vector control.
- Diarrheal Diseases
  —It is estimated that there are between 2.2 and 4 million deaths and countless "episodes" of ill health each year as a result of diarrheal diseases. Access to safe water can reduce the occurrence of diarrheal disease by 25 percent, and, as such, this is a primary component of our work in the area of water and sanitation.
- Acute Lower Respiratory Infections
  —It has been estimated that there are as many as 1.9 million deaths linked to acute lower respiratory infections each year that are caused by excessive exposure to indoor air pollution. We seek to address this problem through projects that enhance pollution control.
- Perinatal Conditions and Measles
  —Tackled in combination by all three components of our health team.

Water and Sanitation Program Responses

The *Global Water Supply and Sanitation Assessment 2000 Report* produced by WHO and UNICEF suggests that globally, more than a billion people, approximately 20 percent of the world's population, lack access to a safe drinking water supply, and that nearly 2.5 billion people lack access to adequate means of excreta disposal.

The absence of access to safe water and means of excreta disposal have an enormous impact on the incidence of diarrheal diseases. On average, as much as one-tenth of each person's productive time is lost as a result of their being affected by water-related diseases. There is an obvious effect in terms of people's economic productivity and capacity to generate income.

"Water and Sanitation" is classified as one of the basic needs of any population affected by a disaster as the transmission of disease as a result of inadequate sanitation or potable water is the most common cause of illness and death among people affected by disasters.

In all of its emergency responses, Concern seeks to reach the minimum standards outlined in the Sphere Project—The Sphere Project is the *Humanitarian Charter and Minimum Standards in Disaster Response.* The chapter of the Sphere handbook dealing with water and sanitation suggests that the main purposes of emergency water supply and sanitation programs are "to provide a minimum quantity of clean drinking water, and to reduce the transmission of faeco-oral diseases and exposure to disease-bearing vectors. A further important objective is to help establish the conditions that allow people to live and to perform daily tasks, such as going to the toilet, and washing with dignity, comfort, and security."

Concern's approach to water and sanitation programming covers the following areas:

1. Water supply
2. Excreta disposal
3. Waste management
4. Vector control
5. Hygiene education

WATER SUPPLY

Access to water is essential for survival. Water has many uses, including the irrigation of crops, the generation of electricity, and as a medium for transportation. In terms of protecting human health, we are mostly concerned with the use of fresh water for domestic purposes. WHO currently estimates that over 1.1 billion people worldwide still lack access to an adequate supply of clean water.

In the domestic setting, the principal uses of water include:

- Drinking
- Personal hygiene
- Cleaning, e.g., cooking utensils
- Food production—such as garden vegetables

Quantity

Generally speaking, a minimum of twenty to forty liters per person per day is needed for drinking, personal hygiene, and cleaning. The actual quantity of water required can vary enormously, depending on the climatic conditions, the sanitation facilities available, religious and cultural practices, the food people cook, etc.

Quality

The water should be free from chemical and biological contamination plus be acceptable in terms of color, taste, and smell. The quality of the water should comply with the guidelines laid out in the WHO *Guidelines on the Quality of Drinking Water* (1993).

Sources of Fresh Water

- Surface water: for example, streams, rivers, lakes, and ponds
- Ground water: for example, wells and springs
- Rainwater, as harvested off buildings

SURFACE WATER

Surface water is the most easily accessible source of fresh water, but also the source most prone to contamination. Human and agricultural activity nearby often contaminate surface water, and this has to be taken into consideration when using this as a source of water when responding to a disaster.

GROUND WATER

Ground water is more likely to be of a higher quality than surface water. However, ground water can be difficult to access as complicated forms of extraction such as submersible pumps may be needed. Ground water comes from springs, shallow wells, or deep wells.

Shallow wells: The water is collected from above the first impervious layer, and they may be hand dug or drilled. Shallow wells may be open or fitted with a hand pump, common examples of which are the India Mark III or Afridev. Shallow wells are often less than ten meters in depth and are potentially prone to contamination such as when a latrine is built within thirty meters of the well.

Deep wells: The water is sourced from below the first impervious layer, and deep wells may be up to one hundred meters deep. The depth of such wells excludes the use of manual extraction systems, and mechanical systems are needed. Such systems are costly to install, run, and maintain.

RAINWATER

In some countries it is culturally acceptable to collect rainwater, and this may provide a source of good quality water if the surface areas on which it is collected are kept clean. Rainwater also needs to be stored safely.

Protection of Sources

Obviously surface water sources need a great deal more protection than ground water sources. Each source still needs protecting from contamination, and in developing countries, the main types of contamination from which it needs to be protected are human feces and animals. Excreta from small children is particularly hazardous because the level of excreta-related infection among children is frequently higher than among adults.

Protection can be achieved through the construction of physical barriers such as fences and walls and/or through hygiene promotion. Good planning is also another important means of protection by, for example, ensuring pit latrines are not constructed within thirty meters of a shallow well.

Storage

Water from a clean and well-protected source may still become contaminated during storage. Storage containers should be well protected from outside contamination, be used for no other purpose other than the storage of clean water, have an opening that is small, and a tight-fitting lid. Storage containers, such as water jars used in Cambodia, may also serve to promote the proliferation of disease vectors such as *aedes agypti*, the mosquito that transmits dengue fever. Hygiene promotion efforts are necessary to ensure storage containers are used properly.

Treatment

In many instances some form of treatment will be necessary to ensure the quality of the water. The degree of treatment will depend on the quality of the raw water sourced. Surface water sources tend to require the greatest level of treatment, whereas spring water may not require any treatment at all. Treatment may be as simple as boiling in the home, or a series of activities resulting in water fit for human consumption. Depending on the quality of the raw water, here are the stages of treatment that may be followed.

FLOCCULATION AND SEDIMENTATION

The purpose of flocculation and sedimentation is to remove as much solid matter, such as suspended particulates, from the water as possible thus aiding the stages of filtration and disinfection. Flocculation normally involves the addition of alum (aluminium sulphate), which acts as a coagulant, allowing suspended particulate matter to sink and settle out of suspension. The removal of such particulates is important, as their presence interferes in the disinfection process as well as giving water an unacceptable physical appearance. The aim is to reduce the turbidity to less than 5 NTU, which facilitates the disinfection process.

FILTRATION

The best-known method of filtration is the passing of water through a combination of small stones and sand, a method that is often described as "slow sand filtration." Filtration is a means of removing both particulate matter and pathogenic organisms and may also be used to remove chemical contaminants in water.

DISINFECTION

The most common form of disinfection is chlorination. Disinfection is the last stage in the treatment process and is aimed at killing pathogenic organisms in the water. In municipal treatment plants, chlorine gas is often used, but on a small scale other forms of chlorine are used such as granules or tablets. One of the most common forms is granules of calcium hypochlorite containing a 70 percent concentration of chlorine.

Chlorine is consumed by organic matter, and it is therefore important to remove as much organic matter as possible from raw water before disinfection. The stages of flocculation, sedimentation, and filtration are all aimed at removing organic matter allowing administered chlorine to act on the pathogens that remain. When water is disinfected, the aim is to leave a residual of chlorine in the water to deal with additional contamination once the water leaves the point of treatment up to the point of consumption. A normal residual chlorine level is 0.2–0.5 mg/l. This compares with the residual chlorine level found in swimming pools of 1.5–2 mg/l.

Distribution

Once a supply of water fit for human consumption has been achieved, the next challenge is to distribute that water in an equitable manner while maintaining the quality of the water. Basically there are two options:

Individual water points are the ideal solution if reasonably practicable. They allow families to obtain water easily, thus improving their opportunities for greater hygiene. Individual water points are common in the developed world, but less so in the developing world.

Public water points are most common in developing countries, where the delivery of water directly to individual houses cannot be afforded. Such public water points may provide water of sufficient quality, but this does not mean that, when consumed, the water will still be safe. There are a number of important issues to consider around the provision of public water points. One of the most crucial issues is that of access.

Access means that people should not have to travel too far from their home to any public water point, and that they should not have to queue for a long time waiting to access a tap. The Sphere Project minimum standards state that people should not have to walk more than 500 meters in order to reach a water point, that there should be one water point for every 250 people, and that the flow rate from each tap should be no less than 0.125 liters per second.

In addition to access, families also need containers for the hygienic collection of water. Without such containers—and others for storage—the good work of providing water fit for human consumption at the point of distribution is likely to be lost. Normally, two twenty-liter jerry cans per family is considered sufficient.

Other issues around public water points concern the drainage of waste water, the maintenance of such water points, and the protection of such from contamination or pollution.

End Use

The critical point at which water supplies need to be safe and free from pathogenic organisms is at the point of consumption. All the work in providing water in sufficient quantity and of high quality will be lost if consumers do not display hygienic practices and behavior. This is the point where hygiene promotion/education plays a vital role.

Testing of Water Supplies

When a new source of water supply is provided, the water from that source should be tested for physical, biological, and chemical parameters. A sampling program for periodic testing should also be established for the purpose of continuous monitoring. The frequency of testing will be largely determined by the size of population served.

The physical parameters to be looked at in determining a water supply's suitability are its color (turbidity), smell, and taste.

The key indicator of biological contamination in a water supply is the presence of *fecal coliforms*. The presence of coliforms in numbers greater than 10 coliforms/100 ml as determined in the Sphere Project's minimum standards indicates an unacceptable level of contamination.

There is whole range of chemical contaminants one can test for, including nitrates, phosphates, fluoride, arsenic, and iron.

All water tested should be tested with reference to the WHO *Guidelines on Drinking Water Quality* (1993).

EXCRETA DISPOSAL

The main objective of the International Drinking Water and Sanitation Decade 1980–1990 was to substantially improve the standards and levels of services in drinking water supply and sanitation by the year 1990. Sanitation is taken to mean excreta disposal. As of the year 2000, an estimated 2.4 billion people still lack access to an adequate means of excreta disposal (WHO 2000). Most urban centers in Africa and Asia have no sewerage system at all, including many cities with a million or more inhabitants (WHO 1992).

Human excreta is an important source of pathogenic organisms, especially the causative agents of diarrheal diseases. In addition, feces are attractive to flies, which not only spread pathogenic organisms contained in the feces but also breed in them. As a consequence, the disposal of human excreta is of primary importance to any public health program and in most emergency situations should be accorded as high a degree of priority as the establishment of a reliable water supply. Appropriate facilities for defecation are one of a number of emergency interventions essential for people's dignity, safety, health, and well-being.

The objective of any latrine or toilet should be to dispose of potentially dangerous excreta, and to prevent the proliferation of vectors that might breed in such waste. In the tropics, there are two basic choices of excreta disposal—pit latrines or pour flush toilets.

The choice of system will depend on a number of factors including adequate site planning, the availability of water, the soil type, skills present in the community, the level of the water table, existing culture of excreta disposal within the community, and the availability of material and financial resources.

Whatever system is chosen, there are a number of principles that should be adhered to, but the overarching principle to which Concern adheres in providing latrines in emergency situations is that the program beneficiaries have access to a sufficient number of toilets, sufficiently close to their dwellings to allow them rapid, safe, and acceptable access at all times of the day and night to toilets which are designed, constructed, and maintained in such a way as to be comfortable, hygienic, and safe to use.

The key indicators established by the Sphere Project for the attainment of this principle are as follows:

- There is a maximum of twenty people per toilet
- The use of the toilets is arranged by household(s) and/or segregated by sex
- Toilets are no more than fifty meters from dwellings, or no more than one minute's walk

• Separate toilets for women and men are available in public places (markets, distribution centers, health centers, etc.)

Principles of Excreta Disposal Structures

1. They should be safe. For example, it should not be possible for small children to fall into a latrine pit
2. They should be built using hygienic and easy to clean materials. For example, the floor of latrines should be made from a hard and durable material such as concrete, rather than compacted soil
3. They should be accessible to all sections of the community, including the young and the old
   Note: Excreta from children is particularly hazardous because the level of excreta-related infection among children is frequently higher.
4. They should be designed to minimize the proliferation and harborage of disease vectors such as flies and mosquitoes
5. They should provide a degree of privacy to the users
6. They should be located in such a way as to avoid the potential of contaminating water sources. For example, they should be a minimum of thirty meters, and preferably downhill, from a water source
7. They should avoid the need to handle fresh feces

Pit Latrines

Pit latrines are the most basic of excreta disposal systems and are further divided into two main types, the simple pit latrine and the VIP (Ventilated Improved Pit) latrine.

PIT LATRINES

Pit latrines are characterized by their simplicity of design (see fig. 4.1) (DFID 1998). Unfortunately, they are often also characterized by the presence of a foul smell and huge numbers of flies.

The simple pit latrine is usually dug to a depth of two meters and is between one and 1.5 meters in diameter. In ideal condi-

Figure 4.1

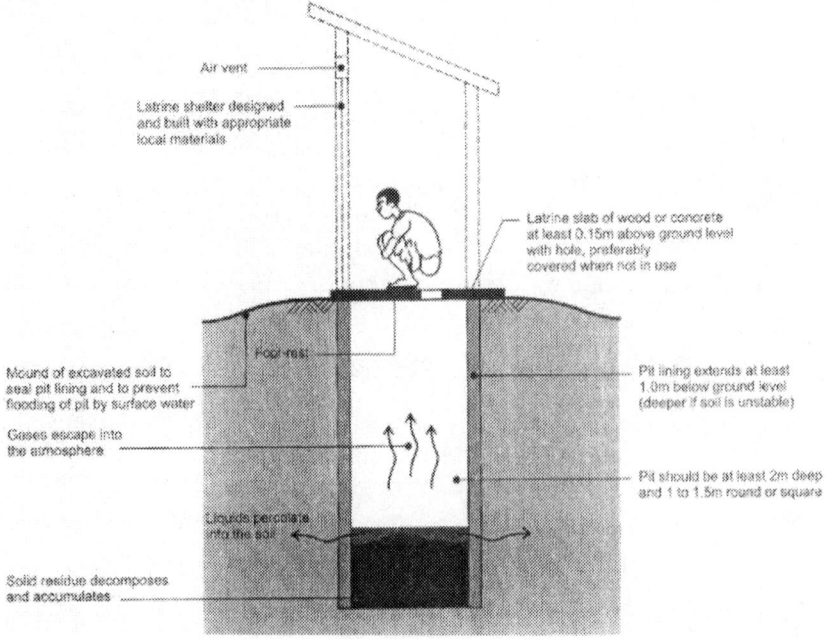

Air vent

Latrine shelter designed and built with appropriate local materials

Latrine slab of wood or concrete at least 0.15m above ground level with hole, preferably covered when not in use

Foot-rest

Mound of excavated soil to seal pit lining and to prevent flooding of pit by surface water

Pit lining extends at least 1.0m below ground level (deeper if soil is unstable)

Gases escape into the atmosphere

Pit should be at least 2m deep and 1 to 1.5m round or square

Liquids percolate into the soil

Solid residue decomposes and accumulates

A simple pit latrine

tions, the liquid part of the waste percolates out through the surrounding soil, leaving the solid matter behind. However, heavy clay soils will prevent the percolation of liquid, resulting in a shorter lifespan for the latrine and more conducive conditions for the vectors of disease. Sandy soils, although providing good percolation, are prone to collapse. When constructing pit latrines in sandy soils it is necessary to line the pits to prevent their collapse. The floor slab is often made from concrete or timber but in some cases is compacted soil over sticks. The floor should be raised up 150 mm above ground level to prevent the possibility of surface run-off water entering the latrine pit. The drop hole in the floor slab is sometimes provided with a cover to prevent the escape of foul smells and to prevent access/escape for disease vectors such as flies. The superstructure is usually made from local materials such as mud and wattle, bamboo and sugar palm thatch, or timber and tin sheeting.

VENTILATED IMPROVED PIT (VIP) LATRINES

The ventilated improved pit (VIP) latrine is designed to eliminate the common problems associated with the simple pit latrine—namely, the foul smells and the presence of conditions that encourage the proliferation of disease vectors.

The principal difference from the simple pit latrine is the addition of a ventilation pipe, which is normally placed outside the superstructure. The vent pipe should be 110–150 millimeters in diameter and extend at least 0.5 meter above the roof. The top of the vent pipe must be fitted with a fly-proof screen with a mesh size of one millimeter and should be made from a noncorrosive material. The superstructure must also be kept dim. The VIP latrine works because of the passing of wind over the top of the vent pipe, which acts like a conventional chimney. The wind creates a draft of air up the vent pipe and down into the pit through the drop hole. The effect of this air flow is twofold—first, the direction of air flow prevents foul smells emanating from the pit, and second, flies present or breeding in the pit, attracted by the light at the top of the vent pipe, are drawn up the vent pipe and become trapped by the fly-proof screen. The airflow keeps them trapped at the top of the pipe until eventually they die. In addition, female flies looking for an egg-laying site are drawn to the smell at the top of the pipe, and the fly-proof screen prevents them from gaining access to the pit.

Cairncross (1993) quotes an example of the difference between the simple pit latrine and the VIP latrine. During controlled experiments in Zimbabwe, 13,953 flies were caught during a seventy-eight-day period from an unvented pit latrine, but only 146 were caught from a vented pit latrine.

There are other types of latrines that loosely fit within the category of pit latrine. These include the twin pit latrine, bucket latrine, trench latrine, and the borehole latrine. Trench latrines are often used at the beginning of an emergency, where large numbers of people have become displaced.

Pour Flush Toilets

The alternative to the pit latrine is the pour flush latrine, which has the added advantages of preventing foul smells and removing easy access for the vectors of disease. However, pour flush latrines are dependent on an ample supply of water all year-round and a population who know how to use them properly.

Figure 4.2 (DFID 1998) illustrates two types of pour flush latrines. The offset type, with the pit located to the rear of the superstructure, allows for easy access when it comes to the emptying of the latrine. The pour flush latrine works when a seal of water is maintained in the U-bend, thus preventing smells coming out and preventing flies and mosquitoes from getting in or out.

Disposal

When latrines become full, one has a number of possible options. For pit latrines, it is often possible to simply dig a new hole and build a new superstructure, or to move the existing superstructure over the new hole. In some countries, a system exists whereby two pits are used alternatively, allowing the contents of one pit to be removed and used as compost/fertilizer. These latrines are often described as "compost latrines." The two pit system allows the contents of one pit to be rendered harmless over time (often up to six months) before removal. In other circumstances, excreta is removed by hand and disposed of into another hole, which is then filled in. Pour flush latrines in particular may need a vacuum truck to pump out the waste and dispose of it in another location.

Sewerage

Although not common in the tropics, even in cities, excreta may also be disposed of by a water carriage system, also known as sew-

Figure 4.2

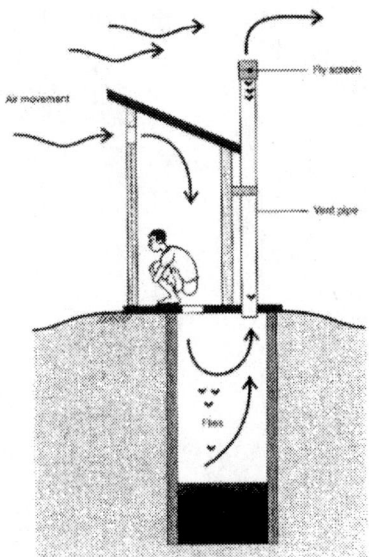

A VIP latrine

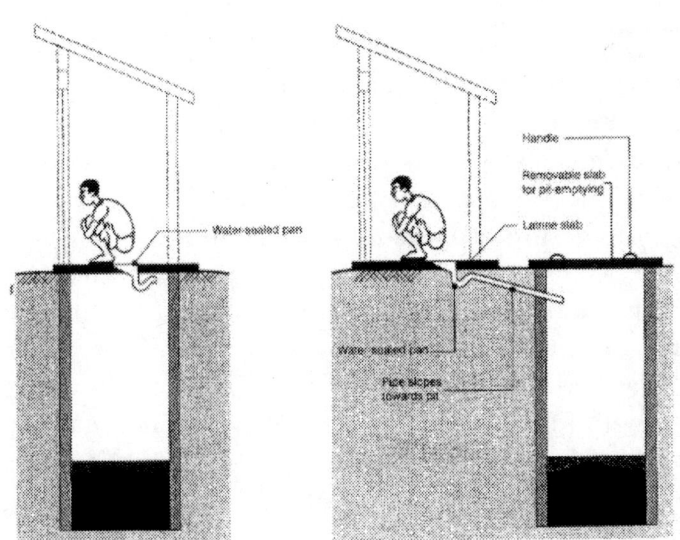

Pour-flush latrines

erage. Toilets connected to sewers are of the pour flush variety commonly known in the northern hemisphere as the water closet (WC). The water used in flushing (up to nine liters per flush in the United Kingdom) is used to transport excreta through a network of sewers or pipes to a treatment plant, a collection point for additional transport, possibly out to sea, or may discharge directly to a water course.

WASTE MANAGEMENT

The management of waste is a key element in the protection of public health. Different types of waste pose different problems, but in general, failure to manage and dispose of waste properly exposes people to increased risk of infectious disease.

Apart from excreta, the other types of waste common to the tropics include the following:

Domestic Waste

The management of domestic waste or refuse may be broken down into storage, collection, recycling, and/or disposal. Domestic waste normally consists of organic material such as food waste and inorganic objects such as bottles, tins and packaging, etc.

Storage: Domestic waste accumulates continuously, and the first stage in its management is storage prior to collection and disposal. Sufficient containers or bins have to be available to collect the waste and limit opportunities for vectors of disease such as flies and rats to feed on and breed in it. They must be convenient to access both for the user and the collector. Organic waste may be composted directly without the need for storage and collection. Inorganic waste such as paper, tins, and glass may be recycled.

In developing countries, people tend to dispose of waste once it is produced. Good practice in this regard entails the placing of waste in a pit and, depending upon the moisture content, it can either be burned or buried.

Collection: Where the collection of domestic waste is possible, collections should be at regular and consistent intervals. The frequency of collection will often depend on the capacity and quality of the storage containers used. Collection workers need protective clothing and education in order to reduce the risk of infection to themselves.

Disposal: The correct disposal of waste is very important, and there are a number of options available. The system of disposal needs planning from the very beginning and must consider the types and volume of waste being produced, and the best disposal method within the circumstances. Common disposal methods include:

- Landfill—probably the most common method of domestic waste disposal, usually consisting of four steps:
  1. Depositing waste in a planned, controlled manner
  2. Spreading and compacting it in layers to reduce its volume
  3. Covering the material with a layer of earth
  4. Compacting the earth cover

  Landfill areas are often located on the periphery of large cities. Great care is needed in the selection of landfill sites as domestic waste can be highly polluting.
- Burning—possible where the moisture content of the waste is low. Burning is generally carried out at a localized level in the absence of adequate collection services. Burning has a number of disadvantages, particularly if it occurs in close proximity to domestic dwellings (particularly if made of highly flammable materials such as bamboo and thatch) as it creates an additional fire risk and atmospheric pollution
- Composting—best suited in situations where waste high in organic matter content is produced

Market Waste

Most market waste can be treated in the same way as domestic refuse, although waste deriving from an abattoir or slaughter house tends to need special treatment, particularly for the liquid wastes produced, and to ensure slaughtering is carried out in hygienic conditions.

Waste Water

Waste water from bathing and domestic washing can present public health problems if not dealt with properly. If not drained away, waste water can accumulate, creating conditions conducive to the proliferation of disease vectors, particularly mosquitoes. In addition, washing water containing phosphates may cause problems if discharged into water courses in excessive quantities.

In the absence of a sewerage system to carry waste water to a treatment plant, the common solution at the individual household level is the use of a soak pit, sometimes referred to as a soakaway (see fig. 4.3, taken from *Engineering in Emergencies*, RedR 1995). The purpose of the soak pit is that it should contain the waste water and protect it from vectors (mosquitoes and flies), allowing time for percolation into the surrounding soil. The pit is filled with stones to prevent it from collapsing and is topped with a plastic or tin sheet prior to being covered with topsoil.

Medical Waste

Medical waste, by its very nature, is potentially harmful and poses a special threat to health and safety. As a general principle, special provision must be made for the safe disposal of medical waste, generally within the perimeter of a medical facility, cholera isolation center, feeding center, etc. Medical waste should not be mixed in with the general settlement refuse.

Medical waste can be divided into two types:

SHARPS

Syringes, needles, and similar sharp medical waste should be placed in sealed containers, such as tin boxes and filled with dis-

Figure 4.3

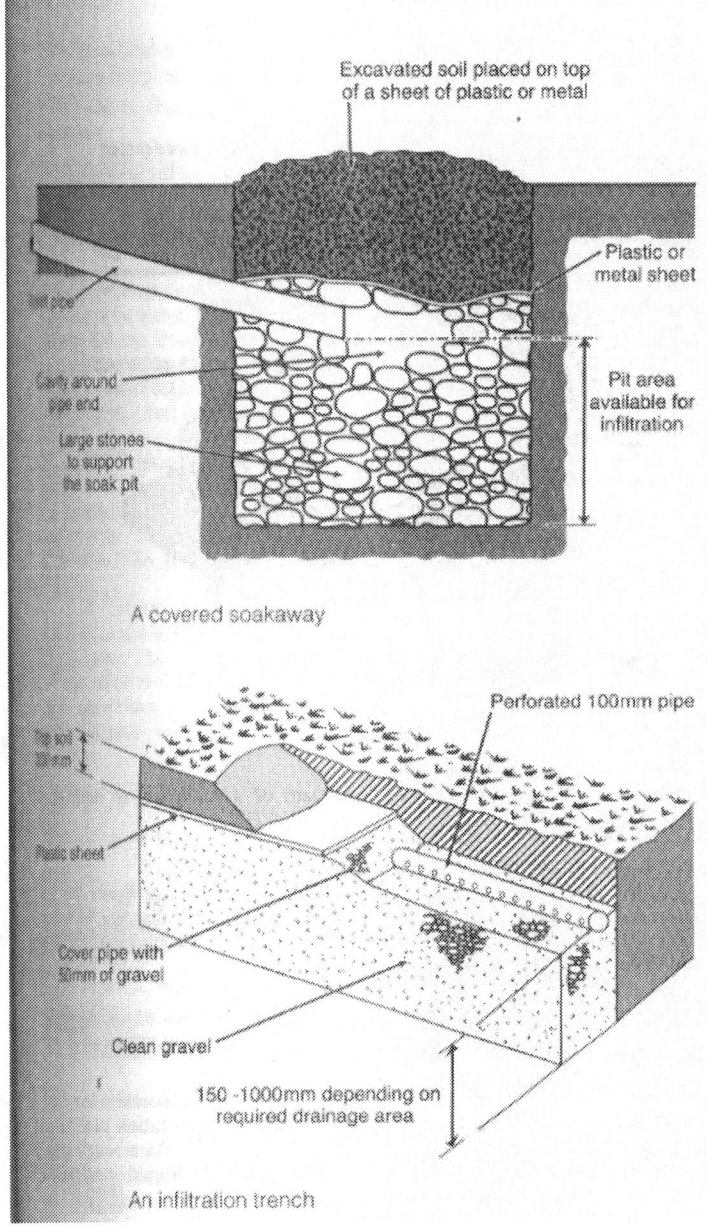

Excavated soil placed on top
of a sheet of plastic or metal

Plastic or
metal sheet

Pit area
available for
infiltration

Cavity around
pipe end

Large stones
to support
the soak pit

A covered soakaway

Perforated 100mm pipe

Plastic sheet

Cover pipe with
50mm of gravel

Clean gravel

150 -1000mm depending on
required drainage area

An infiltration trench

infectant when possible. When full, these containers should be buried to a depth of at least one meter (Davis and Lambert 1995).

PATHOLOGICAL WASTES

All nonmetallic wastes that have been in contact with body fluids need separate collection and disposal. Disposal should be in the form of incineration, and there should be a correctly designed, constructed, and operated incinerator, with a deep ash pit, within the boundaries of each health facility.

THE DEAD

Generally, dead bodies pose minimal health risk unless they have died from a highly infectious disease such as cholera in which case they need to be disposed of as soon as possible. The form of disposal is normally dependent on the cultural practices of the population concerned. Some opt for burial (Christians and Muslims) whereas others opt for cremation (Buddhists and Hindus). If the method of disposal is burial, sufficient space needs to be allocated and a suitable site found which considers soil conditions and the depth of water table. If cremation is the preferred option, sufficient fuel must also be available.

VECTOR CONTROL

Vector-borne disease remains a substantial problem in the tropics. Malaria, which is transmitted by the *Anopheles* mosquito, remains one of the top five killers in the developing world (source: WHO) and, alongside diarrhea, is considered a major danger for refugee or displaced populations. In addition to death, malaria is also responsible for an estimated 300–500 million episodes of the disease each year, which has a huge economic effect.

The common vectors and their associated diseases are listed below:

Vector-Associated Disease

Flies	Eye infections such as conjunctivitis and diarrheal diseases
Mosquitoes	Malaria, Dengue Fever, Filariasis, and Yellow Fever
Rats	Leptospirosis, Salmonellosis
Fleas	Typhus and Plague
Mites	Scabies
Lice	Epidemic Typhus and Relapsing Fever
Ticks	Relapsing Fever and Spotted Fever

What is a vector of disease?

A vector may be any arthropod or animal that carries and transmits infectious pathogens directly or indirectly from an infected animal to a human or from an infected human to another human. (Lacarin and Reed 1999)

The key to vector control is to work on the following principles:

1. Know as much about the vector as possible

Know where it breeds, where it likes to rest, where it likes to feed, what it likes to feed on, what time of day it is active, what it does not like, etc. Knowledge of the vector and its habits is crucial to its control and elimination as a transmitter of disease.

2. Prevent the vector from breeding

Ideally, vector-borne disease can be prevented if the vectors do not exist in the first place. If breeding sites are eliminated, then they can no longer proliferate. For example, mosquitoes breed in water, and a prevention program would fill in holes and provide good drainage, thereby preventing the formation of pools of water in which mosquitoes could breed. Other examples include the routine collection of rubbish, denying flies a suitable environment for the laying of eggs.

3. Control/Eliminate the vector at the earliest point in its lifecycle

In most cases, the total elimination of breeding sites is not possible. As a result, it is preferable to target vectors in their "infant" stages before reaching maturity. For example, mosquitoes emerge from eggs as larvae, where they are confined within water until reaching the adult stage. Targeting of these water sources with a larvacide such as *Temephos* (also known as *abate*) can eliminate the larval stage of mosquito vectors such as those responsible for malaria and dengue fever.

4. Control/Eliminate the vector to prevent disease transmission

In many circumstances, and particularly during an epidemic, the most suitable control measure is to target adult vectors to reduce or prevent transmission. A number of options are available and include the use of chemical control methods including space spraying and/or residual spraying of insecticides with regard to mosquitoes or the laying of poison/traps with regard to rodents. Other actions include the removal of potential resting sites, for instance, the removal of vegetation from around homes where mosquitoes may be found resting.

5. Personal protection

In addition to each of the other control measures mentioned in principles 2, 3, and 4, is the option of personal protection. Personal protection is best described in relation to mosquitoes and may include the use of chemoprophylaxis, wearing long-sleeved clothing and socks to reduce opportunities for mosquitoes to bite, and using insecticide-impregnated bednets while sleeping. The use of such bednets has been shown to reduce childhood deaths from malaria by as much as 20 percent (UNICEF). In relation to leptospirosis, a personal protection measure would be the use of rubber gloves if working in an area that may have been in contact with rat's urine.

In summary, each of the principles described above needs to

be considered in the design of any program intending to control/eliminate vector-borne disease. In some instances, treatment of cases is also considered a prevention measure. Treatment of people with malaria removes reservoirs of infection, preventing the transmission of disease from one human being to another.

HYGIENE EDUCATION

The promotion of hygiene is an integral component of environmental health activities and is often included as a component of water and sanitation programs. Although it is difficult to measure the impact of hygiene promotion programs in most emergency situations, properly designed interventions that focus on a small number of important practices that can be influenced can have a considerable impact. While important, the promotion of hygiene (often described as the "software" side of an intervention) is no substitute for the "hardware" components—the provision of clean water and the safe disposal of excreta—if one is to achieve an impact in the reduction of water-related diseases.

> Too often health/hygiene education is perceived as being essentially a simple matter of telling people what they ought to do to be healthy. Dangerous oversimplifications of this sort have gone hand in hand with a tendency for health education to be treated as an "instant expert" subject. (Downie, Fyfe, and Tannahill 1990)

Hygiene education is not an "instant expert" subject. It is a specific component to health education, which, in turn, forms a part of health promotion. Hygiene education cannot work unless the enabling factors (i.e., the "hardware") are in place in order for people to engage in positive behavior change associated with the messages they receive in hygiene education.

Health promotion can be defined in the following way:

> Promoting health is more than just providing health services. Peace, housing, education, food, income, a sustainable environ-

ment, social justice, and equity are all necessary for achievement of health. It calls for people to act as advocates for health through addressing of political, economic, social, cultural, environmental, behavioral, and biological factors. (Hubley 1994)

Health promotion covers a very broad range of issues, but many of these issues are necessary if hygiene education is to achieve success as part of a wider public health program.

Hygiene or health education can be defined as "a process with intellectual, psychological and social dimensions relating to activities that increase the abilities of people to make informed decisions affecting their personal, family and community well being" (Hubley 1993).

Hygiene education allows people to become better informed or more aware of the influences affecting their health and, when combined with some of the other components of health promotion, enables people to make positive behavior changes. The types of behavior change generally associated with hygiene education in the tropics include:

1. Washing your hands with soap before preparing food and after going to the toilet
2. Knowing how to collect and store water hygienically
3. Boiling water if you are unsure of its source

For example, hygiene education may deliver messages on the importance of washing hands after going to the toilet to prevent diarrheal diseases. However, such a message on its own cannot work unless there is a source of water accessible nearby and people have enough money in their pockets to pay for soap. A wider health promotion program will work toward ensuring a supply of clean water is available and that people have opportunities to earn an income that would allow them to buy the soap.

Hygiene education can be disseminated in one of two broad ways:

1. Face-to-face channels

The face-to-face channels of communication include person-to-person contact on an individual basis, and contact with larger numbers of people through talks or focus groups. They are slower for spreading information and the use of different senders may distort the message being delivered, but they have a number of advantages over the mass media:

- One can selectively reach specific target groups
- The communication can be tailored to fit local needs
- Direct feedback is possible at the time of message delivery through two-way dialogue
- A greater chance of achieving behavior change is possible through the use of face-to-face communication (taken from Hubley 1993).

2. Mass media

The dissemination of hygiene messages through the mass media is a common mechanism used to achieve behavior change and to disseminate information. One must stress that this role is only as a supportive role to other interventions such as improving the physical and social environment. In the tropics, populations are generally more susceptible to mass media interventions due in large part to the fact that the messages are not as negative as we have received in the West, and the changes that the messages seek are relatively simple (Tones, Tilford, and Robinson 1990).

The mass media can do the following:

- Raise consciousness about health issues
- Help place health on the public agenda
- Convey simple information
- Change behavior if other enabling factors such as the following are present:
  —Existing motivation
  —Supportive circumstances
  —Advocating simple one-off behavior change

Using media is more effective if:

- It is part of an integrated campaign including elements such as one-to-one advice

- The information is new and presented in an emotional context
- The information is seen as being relevant for "people like me"

The media cannot:

- Convey complex information
- Teach skills
- Shift people's attitudes or beliefs
- Change behavior in the absence of enabling factors

Generally speaking, a well-planned hygiene education program will involve some combination of both face-to-face and mass media approaches, utilizing the advantages inherent in both.

SHELTER

Access to adequate shelter is a basic and fundamental need, and its provision is a key component in the protection and promotion of health. It is estimated that by 2025, 60 percent of the world's population will be living in cities, and that between one-third and two-thirds of these people will live in inadequate housing units. Overcrowding and poor ventilation contribute hugely to the spread of diseases, particularly air-borne diseases such as tuberculosis, which kills three million people a year. Shelter carries equal priority with nutrition, health care, and water and sanitation interventions because of its importance to people's health and the degree to which it can afford a sense of security, social status, and a base from which those with access to adequate shelter can seek to establish means of production without having to worry about putting a roof over the head of their families.

However, the provision of adequate shelter is a difficult problem to solve—one for which the international community as a whole has few satisfactory answers. It is an area of intervention that is potentially highly capital intensive, and one in which the cost per beneficiary can be extremely high. Although cheap alternatives are available—through the provision of plastic sheeting or tents, for example—these solutions are neither durable nor necessarily socially appropriate. Such solutions, generally used in warmer climates, can only be a temporary measure and must be replaced with more durable and appropriate solutions.

High-cost responses—that is, permanent or semipermanent structures—targeted at the poorest in the affected area do not necessarily solve the problem either, as people lacking access to means of production may, because of its enormous value, sell or rent out their house. This would lead to a dilution of the benefits of the intervention to the intended target group and a further erosion of its assets.

Similarly, more durable and costly physical structures take time to establish and need large quantities of donor funding and clear planning processes and stability of land tenure—aspects that are often absent in transitory situations.

In this section we will consider only the temporary shelter options that are generally used by international organizations when dealing with the displacement of communities on a scale that necessitates the establishment of temporary settlements. The camps in which Concern usually works can be divided into two basic types:

Reception or Transit Centers

The purpose of reception or transit centers is to receive and register arrivals, to screen medically, and distribute food and non-food items to them. It is intended that people remain at such a center for a relatively short period, two to three days, before being moved to a refugee camp. The camps can also be used in a similar manner to host families prior to their return to their homes. Such camps may cater for up to five hundred families or three thousand individuals (assuming that the average size of a family is six).

Refugee Camps

These are the main camps in which the displaced settle and may be established for an undefined period of time, possibly for weeks or even years. Regardless of UNHCR guidelines (which state that refugee camps should be at least forty kilometers from the border of the country from which people are seeking refuge), many refugee camps established in recent years have been much closer to the border of the countries from which people have sought refuge, especially when the site of such camps has been self-selected by the displaced, rather than identified and established beforehand by relief organizations. Properly established camps will ensure that the refugees will have access to adequate water and sanitation facilities, and to medical and community services.

One constant that applies to all of the types of settlements indicated above is the need to ensure that whatever locally available resources exist are carefully managed to ensure that the displaced and local populations have access to water, fuel, and construction material, but that the increased demand for these resources does not damage the local economy or environment.

There is often a degree of tension between displaced and host populations, and one of the most common sources of discontent is the perception of the negative impact of displaced camps on the local environment. Any such interventions should seek to ensure that the establishment of camps has the slightest possible impact on the host population and its environment. However, the need to be sensitive to local impact has to be balanced against the fact that the primary purpose of any interventions in the area of shelter or camp establishment is to meet the needs of displaced individuals, families, and communities and to ensure that they have access to safe and appropriate living conditions.

In terms of the appropriate establishment of camps, two distinct areas of concern must be taken into consideration:

1. Site selection and planning. In the tropics many housing developments are built without due consideration for site selection and planning. Many urban slums, for example, are built in locations prone to environmental health risks such as flooding, are close to discharges of potentially harmful industrial waste, or at risk from landslides. Many such developments are also planned without due consideration for the following issues:

- *Water*—WHO recommends that 20 liters is the standard minimum per person per day
- *Security*—Displaced people should be removed from the situation that has resulted in their displacement and should not be placed in the firing line
- *Space*—Some publications estimate that an average of 45 square meters per person is needed, excluding land for agricultural purposes. The 45 square meters would cover all space needed in the camps to include roads, public buildings, recreation areas, market places, etc.
- *Access*—Both for the receiving of services such as food or waste collection, and to markets
- *Soil type and Water table*—These will have a direct bearing on the type of excreta disposal system chosen
- *Drainage*—Vital for the removal of storm water and preventing the formation of pools of water which might assist the breeding of mosquitoes, for example
- *Availability of fuel*—Most households in the tropics depend on biomass fuels for cooking and heating
- *Vegetative cover*—Necessary to provide shade and prevent soil erosion

2. *Shelter.* In establishing shelter, the following issues need to be taken into account:

- *Space per person*—The Sphere standards in relation to emergencies state that each person should have a covered area of between 3.5 and 4.5 square meters
- *Suitable materials for construction*—Construction materials need to be appropriate to the climate and culture, and to be environmentally friendly. Such materials may need to reflect excessive heat away during the day and/or retain heat indoors at night. Conversely, in cold climates shelters must be well insulated and offer protection not only from low temperatures, but also from chill factors—airflow and conduction of heat through the floor. In cold climates it is preferable to help people to make one

room habitable, rather than providing collective accommodation

- *Ventilation*—Enough ventilation is needed to provide a fresh throughput of air and the removal of harmful particulates produced by cooking or heating
- *Cooking facilities*—Space needs to be provided for cooking facilities and if possible the use of non-flammable construction materials
- *Storage*—For items such as food to ensure that they are protected from vectors such as rodents and flies
- *Excreta and other forms of waste disposal*—Latrine facilities need to be accessible and nonpolluting of water sources
- *Access to potable water*—Water also needs to be accessible, preferably within one minute's walk, in adequate quantities and of sufficient quality
- *Vector control*—As indicated in the water and sanitation section above, it is essential to ensure that there is adequate vector control to prevent infestation by vectors such as mosquitoes, rats and flies, and pests such as snakes and scorpions

Concern's policy with regard to emergencies is based not only on its commitment to addressing the causes and effects of absolute poverty, but also on a recognition that acting alone, the organization's ability to make a significant difference is less than it would be if working in concert with partners. As such, Concern will seek linkages with national and international partners, including Alliance 2015, and will ensure that we acknowledge and utilize the capacity of local communities to enhance our ability to make a difference.

In responding to emergencies, Concern has agreed to be bound by international codes of conduct and practice, including the *Code of Conduct of the International Red Cross and Red Crescent Movement and NGOs in Disaster Relief*, the *Humanitarian Charter*, the People in Aid *Code of Best Practice in the Management and Support of Aid Personnel*, and the Sphere Project's *Minimum Standards in Disaster Response*. In addition, our interventions should be informed by international humanitarian law, refugee law, and, particularly in conflict situations, the Geneva Conventions.

There is an ongoing debate about the politicization and militarization of aid, and the practical difficulties inherent in operating in emergencies. The following principles govern Concern's work, irrespective of the type, speed of onset, or duration of the emergency:

- The *humanitarian imperative* to save lives and reduce suffering comes first and will be given precedence. However, we also recognize that the organization's primary objective is the *elimination of extreme poverty,* and that this may require the adoption of a robust interpretation of humanitarianism based on human rights, and designed to enhance the protection of civilian populations. This means that we have to make greater efforts to identify and challenge the underlying causes of poverty—including the causes of conflict—with *advocacy* becoming an increasingly important tool in this struggle. In doing this we need to ensure that the benefits of an advocacy strategy are balanced against the potential impact on our ability to deliver an appropriate program response. Programmatically, the focus on *saving lives* has to be expanded to include the wider objective of *protecting livelihoods*
- *Impartiality*—Aid priorities are calculated on the basis of need alone, and our responses should be *proportional* to the level of need
- *Accountability* to the program's intended beneficiaries, counterparts, and the donors, whether governmental or public
- Independence from political, military, or religious agendas
- Recognition *of the capacity of affected communities and of the need for beneficiaries, both men and women, to be engaged in the management of aid to their communities*
- *Targeting*—Whether in response to an emergency, or in establishing a longer-term development program, Concern programs will work with those who need us most, rather than with those who can benefit most from our intervention
- *Transparency*—Concern's programs will be transparent in their dealings with all stakeholders, including beneficiaries, partner organizations, and donors

Concern's current emergency interventions cover a broad spectrum from emergency preparedness and disaster mitigation, through conflict resolution, to response and rehabilitation. Our approach to the water, sanitation, and shelter needs of the enormous number of refugees and internally displaced persons is consistent with our goals to be an increasingly effective, highly professional, but sensitive and compassionate NGO.

The organization recognizes that there is a strong link between poverty and the impact of emergencies. Most disasters exacerbate inequity within a country, affecting the poorest to a greater degree insofar as they have fewer resources to aid their recovery from the impact of renewed crises. Disasters also impact differently on men and women, changing social and economic norms, and increasing vulnerability, not least of all to HIV infection.

Increasing numbers of people are being marginalized—inter- and intra-state conflict and the frequency of extreme climatic events are on the rise and, combined as they are with rapid economic, institutional change, and declining donor budgets, this pattern of increasing marginalization seems set to continue.

Part 2

Conflicts, and the resultant victimization of innocent civilians caught in the cross-fire of battles they often do not understand, is a perverse phenomenon of modern times. The UN Secretary-General's Representative for Internally Displaced Persons details the scope of this global problem and the organizational arrangements developed to help alleviate the suffering.

There is a great danger in viewing a complex emergency solely as a physical assault, forgetting that there is almost always a population where basic human rights have been violated, and mere sustenance does not offer adequate protection to traumatized and oppressed populations. The long-time Director of Emergency Response for the IRC considers this critical dimension of relief operations. In every disaster the most vulnerable are the very young, very old, and women. Even in supposedly safe refugee camps, sexual exploitation and child abuse are tragically common. Judy Benjamin has worked in all the hell-holes of the world and offers, with passion, her assessment of the problem and possible solutions.

Finally, I review the malnutrition extremes one can find, too often, in refugee camps. The clinical picture of starvation is a vivid reminder of the stark reality seen in emergency relief operations.

5

Internal Displacement: A Challenge of Peace, Security, and Nation Building

Francis M. Deng

OVER THE LAST DECADE, the international community has been confronted with the new global crisis of internal displacement, involving some twenty-five million people in over forty countries around the world. These are people who have been forced to leave their homes by internal armed conflicts, communal violence, and egregious violations of human rights but have not crossed international borders. Had they moved across the borders, they would be considered refugees for whom the international community has well-established legal and institutional frameworks and mechanisms for their protection and assistance. And yet, they remain exposed to severe threats to their physical and psychological security, gross violations of human rights, and denial of basic needs to shelter, food, medicine, sanitation, potable water, occupation, and education.

There is a fundamental contradiction in the assumption that protecting and assisting the internally displaced is primarily the responsibility of the state or national authorities. In most cases, state authorities may not only cause displacement but may lack the will or the capacity to address the needs of the victim population. With such large numbers of people exposed to extreme suffering and maybe death as a result, it is paradoxical for the international community to continue to rely on the states to provide protection by their national authorities. And yet, with the narrow and negative definition of state sovereignty acting as a barricade against external intervention, what practical alternatives are available to the international community?

The way out of this dilemma is to reaffirm the emergent notion of state sovereignty as a normative concept of state responsibility for its citizens and those under its jurisdiction, without discrimination on the basis of race, ethnicity, religion, language, culture, or gender. For the concept to be meaningful, responsibility must be backed by national and international accountability, with incentives and disincentives, including various forms of intervention, ranging from diplomatic persuasion to economic sanctions, and, in extreme cases, military actions, sometimes accorded through peacekeeping operations. The extent to which this normative framework is realistic or idealistic is a reflection of where the international community stands in developing a global sense of human security, humanitarian response to tragedy, and durable solutions in pursuit of the universal norm of human dignity.

This chapter will first outline the magnitude of the crisis and the challenge, then explain the approach that I have adopted in the work of my mandate as Representative of the UN Secretary-General for Internally Displaced Persons, with an emphasis on the interpretation of sovereignty as a positive concept of state responsibility for protecting and assisting its citizens, rather than a negative concept of insulating the state against international solidarity with the needy population. This will be followed by a section on the activities of the mandate and another on the need to address the root causes that underlie internal conflicts and the violation of human rights, which generate displacement. The chapter will conclude with a call for a strategic vision for action.

The Magnitude of the Crisis

The tendency in the international community is to respond to the crisis with humanitarian relief assistance, with little or no attention given to protection. Internal displacement is indeed a humanitarian issue, but it is also a human rights concern. If we are to avoid the paradox of the "well-fed dead," it is critical that assistance be closely linked to protection.

Although the internally displaced are particularly vulnerable and have distinctive needs, they often represent a sample, or a microcosm, of the wider community affected by the conflict. Under certain circumstances they may even fair better than the resident communities that have not escaped the looming threat of death and perpetual harassment by the warring parties or factions. The goal, therefore, must be to provide comprehensive protection and assistance, and at the same time address the specific needs of vulnerable groups. Even among the displaced populations, certain categories of people that constitute the overwhelming majority of the displaced, notably children, women, the elderly, and the disabled, are more vulnerable and deserve special attention.

Many of the displaced women become heads of households because their husbands have gone to war, have been killed, have chosen to remain behind to protect their land and other properties, or have moved to areas where they can avoid recruitment into armed forces, avoid arbitrary detention, or seek employment. Displaced populations, as a result, have among them disproportionate numbers of widows with children, as well as unaccompanied minors separated from their guardians, or whose guardians have been killed. Sadly, war itself cripples many fighting men who are then abandoned and left without care.

What is involved in most, if not all, cases of internal displacement resulting from conflicts and systematic violations of human rights is an acute crisis of national identity that goes to the heart of social, ethnic, cultural, and religious cleavages within a country. These cleavages determine who is "in" as a recognized citizen and who is "out," denied a sense of belonging on equal footing, with dignity and pride in the national identity framework. The challenge this situation poses for the affected countries is profound. It demands a fundamental restructuring of the equations of power sharing and resource allocation. What is required is a framework of peace with justice and a mutual sense of belonging and participation on equitable bases, without discrimination based on divisive factors of identity. Such factors as gender and age also often figure as grounds for discrimination that merit special attention and remedial action. Beyond the pressing need for protection and assistance, this is a long-term challenge of human security and nation building that ultimately must be confronted by the nationals of the country in question, but in which the international community can and should play a constructive role.

THE RESPONSIBILITY OF SOVEREIGNTY

Perhaps the approach that has emerged as the most powerful in my dialogue with governments, whether on a bilateral basis or in the pertinent bodies of the UN system and other regional organizations, is to recognize the problem of internal displacement as inherently internal and therefore under state sovereignty, to affirm respect for the sovereignty of the state and its policies, but to uphold sovereignty positively as a concept of responsibility for ensuring the protection and the general welfare of the citizens.

It was because of the need for sensitivity to the issue of sovereignty that the Commission on Human Rights decided in 1992 to appoint a Representative of the Secretary-General rather than the Rapporteur or Working Group mechanism normally created for such thematic issues. Indeed, the first task assigned to me in this role was to prepare a study to advise the Commission whether this was an area in which the United Nations should be involved and, if so, through what mechanism. Bearing in mind both the sensitivity of the issue and the crosscutting nature of the problem, that should involve humanitarian and development agencies, in addition to the Commission, I recommended continuing with the mechanism of the Representative of the Secretary-General.

As already noted, in carrying out my work under the mandate, I approach sovereignty not as a negative concept by which states barricade themselves against international scrutiny and involvement, but rather as a positive concept entailing responsibility for the protection and general welfare of the citizens and of those falling under State jurisdiction.

Under normal circumstances, States are expected to, and do in fact, discharge those responsibilities. If they cannot discharge those responsibilities for lack of capacity or resources, they are expected to seek, or at least welcome, international assistance. If, on the other hand, they fail to meet their obligations or to welcome international assistance, and masses of their people suffer humanitarian and human rights tragedies as a result, then they must expect the international community to show concern and perhaps even threaten intervention. Such intervention could range from persuasive diplomatic intercession, to more assertive political and economic measures in the form of sanctions, to coercive military intervention in extreme cases. It is obvious, therefore, that the best way to guarantee state sovereignty is to discharge the responsibilities of sovereignty toward the citizens and those under State jurisdiction. In my dialogue with governments—one of the requirements of my mandate—the first five minutes with the head of State or relevant Minister is crucial to assure them of my recognition of the problem as internal and therefore under State responsibility. Having emphasized my respect for their sovereignty, I quickly move on to present the positive interpretation of sovereignty and the supportive role of international cooperation. Once I establish a cordial climate, candid and constructive dialogue can follow with little or no constraint in the name of sovereignty.

The reality is, of course, less congenial or harmonious than this picture of seeming civility conveys. As noted earlier, internal conflicts, especially those connected with acute ethnic, religious, or cultural contradictions often create sharp divisions between the victim population and their government or other controlling authorities. Instead of being seen as citizens who merit protection and humanitarian assistance, these people are often perceived as part of the enemy, if not the enemy itself. Therefore, they are neglected, and perhaps even persecuted. The problem is compounded by ineffective government authority and control, limited capacity for economic growth and distribution, and, above all, tensions between centralized political and economic forces and various local and ethnic constituencies seeking greater autonomy and equitable participation in the political and economic life of the country. Dispossessed by their own national authorities, their only source of protection and assistance becomes the international community. The critical issue becomes how the international community can intercede to overcome the obstacles of negative sovereignty and ensure access to the needy population.

THE ACTIVITIES OF THE MANDATE

When the mandate was created by the Commission on Human Rights with the support and encouragement of nongovernmental organizations and concerned governments, the need was glaring. Yet it was not clear what the international community could do about it. My mandate was both specific and open-ended, which allowed considerable room for creativity and innovation. Importantly, however, what we did under the mandate was requested, authorized, or sanctioned by the Commission, the General Assembly, and related organs of the UN system.

Over the years, the role of the mandate crystallized into that of advocacy, raising the level of awareness about the displacement crisis worldwide and acting as a catalyst for international response. Specifically, the activities of the mandate focus on four areas:

- Developing an appropriate normative framework for responding to the protection and assistance needs of the internally displaced
- Fostering effective institutional arrangements at the international and regional levels to these same ends

- Focusing attention on specific situations through country missions
- Undertaking further research to broaden and deepen our understanding of the problem in its various dimensions

Developing a Normative Framework

With respect to the first area of work, there was from the start a wide recognition of the fact that, unlike refugees who are governed by the 1951 Convention on Refugees, there is no international legal instrument for protecting and assisting the internally displaced. At the request of the Commission on Human Rights and the General Assembly, I began to work with a team of international legal experts to study the extent to which international law provides adequate protection for internally displaced persons (IDPs). In a two-part *Compilation and Analysis of Legal Norms* they found that although existing law covers many relevant aspects to the situation of internally displaced persons, nonetheless significant gaps and gray areas exist where the law fails to provide sufficient protection. The team recommended compiling all the legal provisions relevant to internally displaced persons in one document to restate the law and to address the identified gaps and gray areas. The Commission on Human Rights and the General Assembly welcomed the compilation and, on that basis, requested that I develop an appropriate normative framework for the internally displaced. In response to that request, I continued to work with the legal team, and we developed the "Guiding Principles on Internal Displacement" (Guiding Principles). The process was broad-based, bringing together legal experts from all different parts of the world, including representatives of international and regional organizations, nongovernmental organizations at the international and national level, and research and academic institutions. The Guiding Principles were finalized in January 1998.

Although not a binding instrument, the Guiding Principles restate the existing norms of human rights and humanitarian law, as well as refugee law by analogy, that are relevant to the internally displaced. They set forth the rights of internally displaced persons and the obligations of governments, insurgent groups, and other actors toward these populations in all phases of displacement. They provide protection against arbitrary displacement, protection and assistance during displacement, and protection during return or resettlement and reintegration. Their aim is to provide practical guidance to all those with a role in addressing the plight of the internally displaced. The idea was that, as a restatement of existing legal norms, the Guiding Principles would provide only guidelines for the implementation of existing standards with a focus on internal displacement and would not require formal adoption by the relevant UN agencies.

Since their presentation to the Commission on Human Rights in 1998, the Guiding Principles have been acknowledged widely by UN bodies. The UN Secretary-General has cited them as a major achievement in the humanitarian area and recommended to the Security Council that in cases of massive displacement, it encourage States to be guided by the Guiding Principles. The Council has begun to refer to them in regard to specific situations. Even earlier, the Inter-Agency Standing Committee (IASC), composed of the heads of the major humanitarian, human rights, and development organizations, welcomed the Guiding Principles and called upon its members to disseminate them and have their staffs apply them, especially in the field. The General Assembly and the Commission on Human Rights requested that I make use of the Principles in my dialogues with governments and intergovernmental and nongovernmental organizations.

The General Assembly and the Commission also encouraged the wide dissemination and application of the Principles by international, regional, and nongovernmental organizations (NGOs). Several regional organizations, among them the African Union (formerly the Organization of African Unity), the Inter-American Commission on Human Rights of the Organization of American States, and the Organization for Security and Cooperation in Europe have indeed begun to disseminate the Principles, to use them as a basis for measuring conditions on the ground, and to sponsor workshops featuring the Principles. In October 1998, the OAU co-sponsored with UNHCR and the Brookings Project a workshop on Internal Displacement in Africa. Subsequent workshops have been held in Bogotá, Colombia, in May 1999; in Bangkok, Thailand, in February 2000; in Tbilisi, Georgia, in May 2000 (in cooperation with OSCE); in Jakarta, Indonesia, in June 2001; in Yerevan, Armenia, in October 2001; Tbilisi, Georgia, in February 2002; and Baku, Azerbaijan, in February 2002. Plans for a number of additional country and subregional workshops are underway. In addition, NGOs such as the Norwegian Refugee Council have held training workshops on the Guiding Principles in Burundi, Colombia, India, Liberia, and Sierra Leone. Following the workshops, projects are undertaken to help strengthen local capacities, with the support of partner organizations.

The Brookings Project on Internal Displacement together with OCHA and the Inter-Agency Standing Committee have produced two additional publications on the Guiding Principles: *Handbook for Applying the Guiding Principles* and *Manual on Field Practice in Internal Displacement,* which spell out the Guiding Principles in more understandable language and explain their practical application in the field. Furthermore, the Brookings Project, in collaboration with the American Society of International Law, has produced Professor Walter Kaelin's *Annotations* on the Guiding Principles, which explain their sources in human rights law, humanitarian laws, and analogous refugee law.

To assist in the promotion, dissemination, and application of the Guiding Principles at the national level, and indicative of their increasing use and relevance in different parts of the world, the Principles continue to be translated into an increasing number of languages. Initially made available in all the official languages of the United Nations (Arabic, Chinese, English, French, Russian, and Spanish) for their submission to the Commission in 1998, the Principles have since been translated into many local languages relevant to particular situations of internal displacement: Albanian, Armenian, Azerbaijani, Bahasa (Indonesia),

Burmese and Sgaw Karen (Myanmar), Dari and Pashtu (Afghanistan), Georgian, Macedonian, Portuguese (Angola), Serbo-Croat, Sinhala and Tamil (Sri Lanka), Tagalog, and Turkish. Their translation into Abkhazian (Georgia), Chin (Myanmar), and Tetum (East Timor) is planned, and interest has been expressed to translate them into Dinka (Sudan), Gulu (Uganda), and Kurdish. Efforts to translate and publish the Principles have been undertaken at the initiative of a variety of actors—the United Nations and its agencies, international and local NGOs and governments, often working in partnership.

In addition to the translation and dissemination of the Principles, efforts are also focusing on the translation of the *Handbook for Applying the Guiding Principles*. While the *Handbook* was originally published in English only, the importance of further empowering local NGOs and displaced communities and the need to develop outreach strategies has underlined the need also to translate it into the United Nations' official languages and other local languages.

At a colloquy on the Guiding Principles convened in collaboration with the Government of Austria in Vienna, September 2000, national NGOs throughout the world reported on their use of the Principles in their dialogue with local and national authorities. Regional intergovernmental organizations also cited the Principles as an effective protection tool; and in Asia, national human rights commissions acknowledged the utility of the Guiding Principles, both in their monitoring activities and in advising government officials and legislators on the content of draft legislation. Furthermore, the Principles have been cited by UN treaty bodies in their interpretation of the law relevant to internally displaced populations.

Governments also have found the Guiding Principles a useful guide for the development of laws on internal displacement and as a yardstick for measuring conditions in their countries. For example, in Angola, the Principles form the basis of the Norms on the Resettlement of the Internally Displaced, and in Burundi they have been used as a base for a permanent framework for the protection of internally displaced persons. In Colombia, a Presidential Directive of November 2001 recalls two decisions of the Constitutional Court citing the Guiding Principles, and elaborating the responsibilities of government authorities for protecting and assisting the internally displaced. The Government of Georgia has informed the UN that it is committed, through a special parliamentary commission, to bringing its electoral laws in line with the Guiding Principles. The Ugandan Government is also engaged in developing a national policy for IDPs and an implementation plan, both of which draw heavily on the Guiding Principles on Internal Displacement.

Meanwhile, it must be said that there is a small number of governments that has begun to question the innovative process by which the Guiding Principles was developed. At the July 2000 session of the UN's Economic and Social Council (ECOSOC), a number of governments expressed the view that principles not drafted or formally adopted by governments cannot have real standing. In the Third Committee of the General Assembly of 2000, the same group of governments tried to prevent the reference to the Guiding Principles in the "omnibus" resolution on the work of the UNHCR, despite the fact that such reference had been part of the resolution adopted unanimously by the General Assembly for the preceding two years. In the end, at the insistence of Egypt, the resolution was voted on and adopted by a majority of 118 with none against and thirty abstentions. The same governments raised similar concerns during the 2001 General Assembly and argued for the submission of the Guiding Principles for the formal consideration by the General Assembly. After intensive and extensive consultations, the resolution on internal displacement was adopted by consensus. The Representative of the Secretary-General in collaboration with the Emergency Relief Coordinator has since continued to carry out informal consultations with these and other delegations to promote understanding and develop a common ground on the Guiding Principles.

Ironically, these governments that are now expressing reservations were among those that had voted for the Commission and General Assembly resolutions encouraging the development of the Guiding Principles over the years, recommending their wide dissemination and requesting me to use them as the basis for dialogue with governments. On a positive note, the outcome of the vote itself testifies to the increasing recognition the Guiding Principles are receiving, which in turn reaffirms that they indeed fill a normative vacuum.

Developing Institutional Arrangements

With respect to institutional arrangements, the gaps in the international system relating to the internally displaced have always been obvious. Again, in contrast with refugees for whom UNHCR has responsibility for their protection and assistance, there is no one specialized agency for the internally displaced. In my first report to the Commission, I suggested a number of remedial options ranging from the creation of a specialized agency for the internally displaced, to the designation of an existing agency to assume full responsibility for them, to a collaborative arrangement that would utilize existing capacities and enhance the effectiveness of the international system.

Regarding the first option, it soon became clear that there was no political will in the international community to create a new agency for the internally displaced. Designating a single agency to assume full responsibility for the internally displaced is an idea that resurfaces periodically, as it did again in January 2000 when Ambassador Richard Holbrooke of the United States made that proposal, while serving as President of the Security Council. However, a broad consensus emerged that the problem is too big for one agency and requires the collaborative capacities of the international system.

Nevertheless, there is a need to strengthen the collaborative approach to overcome the challenging problems of coordination and response gaps that frequently arise under the present arrangement, especially in the realm of protection. The Secretary-

General's reform program drew special attention to the gaps in the international system in responding to the protection and assistance needs of the internally displaced and gave the Emergency Relief Coordinator (ERC) the responsibility for ensuring that these needs are addressed adequately within the interagency framework.

In an effort to focus greater attention on the protection of internally displaced persons, I consulted the ERC and the UN High Commissioner for Human Rights. We concluded that it would be useful to draft a joint policy paper on what precisely protection means and how protection might be ensured by the international system. The resulting paper, adopted by the IASC in December 1999, notes the need to give practical effect to the responsibilities of international agencies in regard to protection as a principle of security, physical integrity, and respect for all human rights. The paper sets out a number of strategic areas of activity through which the international community can seek to fulfill those responsibilities. These include promotion and dissemination of the Guiding Principles; active and assertive advocacy for the rights of the internally displaced; strengthening local and national protection capacities; promoting protection in the design of assistance programs, including those regarding return or resettlement and reintegration; and operational monitoring and reporting.

The IASC also adopted supplementary guidance to UN resident and humanitarian coordinators to facilitate carrying out their protection and assistance responsibilities in relation to internally displaced persons. The resident and humanitarian coordinators are deemed responsible for coordinating the UN's response to both the protection and assistance needs of the internally displaced in a given country, and for ensuring that response gaps are addressed systematically. The IASC subsequently appointed a Special Coordinator to lead an Inter-Agency Network to examine situations of internal displacement with a view to ensuring both an effective response to the protection and assistance needs of internally displaced persons and an appropriate coordination mechanism.

In April 2001 the Special Coordinator issued a report on the activities and findings of the Network. The report found that the United Nations, the international organizations, and nongovernmental organizations all need to increase their focus on, and support to, internally displaced persons. To ensure increased focus, the Special Coordinator recommended the establishment of a nonoperational, internally displaced persons office within the Office for the Coordination of Humanitarian Affairs (OCHA). Based on the Special Coordinator's recommendation, the Emergency Relief Coordinator proposed to the Secretary-General the establishment of such an office. The proposal was endorsed by the Secretary-General and the Unit became operational as of January 2002.

Parallel to the process of supporting greater collaboration at the international level, and pursuant to the resolutions, my mandate is in the process of developing cooperation with regional organizations. The importance of regional approaches to the problem of internal displacement should be underscored. Indeed, regional organizations are beginning, in varying degrees, to devote attention to issues of conflict prevention and mass displacement. The mandate is forging partnerships with the Council of Europe, the Organization for Security and Cooperation in Europe, the African Union, and the Organization of American States, as well as with subregional organizations, such as the Economic Community of West African States, and cross-regional organizations, such as the Commonwealth.

In September 2000 the OSCE's Office for Democratic Institutions and Human Rights, in conjunction with the Government of Austria in its capacity as Chairman-in-Office of the OSCE, convened a Supplementary Human Dimension Seminar on Migration and Internal Displacement. The seminar sought to elaborate ways in which OSCE institutions, field operations, and participating States could enhance their response to internal displacement, particularly through the practical application of the

Guiding Principles. Among its recommendations, the meeting called for the integration of internal displacement into the activities of the OSCE, using the Principles as a framework for doing so. The recommendations of the Vienna meeting were revisited in September 2001 at the OSCE's Human Dimension Implementation Meeting, held in Warsaw. During the meeting, a statement delivered on my behalf recalled the recommendations of the Vienna meeting and noted the importance of the Warsaw meeting as an opportunity to reaffirm those recommendations and to call for their translation into practical measures to ameliorate the plight of Europe's internally displaced.

Country Missions

Country missions are the most tangible means for assessing both the conditions on the ground and the effectiveness of the national and international response to specific situations. To date, I have undertaken twenty-one such missions, including recent visits to Indonesia and Sudan. Invitations for missions have recently been received from the Philippines and Turkey.

These country missions offer the opportunity for dialogue with governments and other concerned actors on ways to improve the conditions of the internally displaced by bridging the gap between principles of protection and assistance and the actual conditions of the internally displaced on the ground. They also help advance understanding of the generic problems of internal displacement and the responses needed to alleviate the dire conditions to which the displaced often are subjected.

Country missions, ironically, also raise the stakes involved in the needed response. Merely undertaking a mission conveys to the displaced populations that the international community cares about their plight. Although one should not promise too much in meetings with them, it is inevitable that one gives them hope for international cooperation with their government to address their needs. Yet, unless these missions in fact result in improved responses to their needs, their hope can turn to despair and leave them worse off than they were before the mission. This is why I plead with all concerned, both national and international actors, to do what is within their capacity to respond to the needs of the displaced and prove to them that the world genuinely cares about their plight.

Research Agenda

Finally, as part of the mandate we have been involved in the preparation of studies on internal displacement, the most significant of which is the comprehensive study, composed of two volumes, *Masses in Flight: The Global Crisis of Internal Displacement* and *The Forsaken People: Case Studies of the Internally Displaced,* respectively co-authored and co-edited with Roberta Cohen and published by the Brookings Institution in 1998. An illustrated, abridged version of these two volumes entitled *Exodus Within Borders: An Introduction to the Crisis of Internal Displacement* was also published by Brookings in 1999. The objective of the study was to probe into such issues as the numbers and distribution of internally displaced persons globally, their needs, how these needs are being met, what gaps exist in meeting these needs, and how these gaps can be bridged by the international community, including regional organizations and NGOs. In particular, the study identifies the tremendous gap in the area of protection and makes a series of recommendations for increasing attention to the physical security and human rights of displaced populations. It was our hope that the study would contribute to a more in-depth understanding of the global crisis of internal displacement, and of the steps needed to address it. And, indeed, the response we have received indicates that the study has achieved much of our intended objective.

ADDRESSING THE ROOT CAUSES

An effective response to the crisis of internal displacement beyond the challenge of humanitarian assistance and protection must go to address the deeper, root causes that lie in the structural problems of nation building: mismanagement of identity conflicts, gross inequities in the shaping and sharing of power, national wealth, opportunities for development, and chronic abuse of power resulting in egregious violations of human rights.

During the Cold War, these internal problems were overshadowed by the larger global confrontation of the superpowers and their proxy conflicts between and within nations. The tendency was to see conflicts largely in terms of this global ideological divide. Internal and regional crises were addressed, contained, or covered up through this bipolar control mechanism of the cold war global order.

With the end of the Cold War and the strategic withdrawal of the major powers, crises are perceived now in their proper national and regional contexts, instead of being distorted as part of the proxy confrontations of the cold war era. This is indeed a positive development. However, commensurate to this is the need to reapportion responsibility, with the state concerned assuming the primary role, countries of the region that are affected by the overflow of internal crises coming next. But the international community is still needed to play a supporting role as the ultimate guarantor of universal human rights and humanitarian standards.

The tragic events of September 11, 2001, changed the world in a dramatic way. The United States successfully mobilized a united international front against terrorism, not only by staging a massive attack on the Taliban and their Al-Qaeda allies in Afghanistan, but also by setting in motion a global antiterrorism campaign. This new dynamic presents two potential directions for the world. The unity of purpose against terrorism, which the United States is championing, could bring the world together around fundamental values and principles of security, stability, and global law and order. Pursued in close collaboration with allies around the world and within the framework of the United Nations, this could be a monumental accomplishment for global governance and public order. On the other hand, there is the potential that the world could revert back to the cold war divide between ideological camps, those committed to the war against terrorism and those outside this circle. What is even more ominous is that such a division could lead to accepting and supporting those who are, or purport to be, allies in the war against terrorism, irrespective of their domestic record in terms of democracy and respect for human rights.

The challenge for the post-September 11 world order is whether the United States and allies, indeed, the international community, beyond welcoming the alliance of all nations against terrorism, will define terrorism universally and fight it wherever and by whomever it is practiced, even when it is inflicted by a state against its own citizens, as was the case in Afghanistan.

Ironically, displacement often exposes the affected rural population to the opportunities that citizens in urban centers enjoy and that they have been denied. It can have the effect of increasing their resentment and hostility. Unless effectively remedied, this may sow the seeds of further conflict in the country. Indeed, the crisis of displacement should be seen as a wake-up call and an opportunity for addressing the deeper, structural ills of the country to forge a national common ground and collective vision for nation building.

As a symptom of the structural problems that generate conflict, displacement is a national challenge that ultimately calls for creating an environment where all citizens feel a sense of belonging on equal footing: an environment where their human rights and fundamental liberties are respected without discrimination on the grounds of race, national origin, ethnicity, religion, culture, gender, or other grounds; where the state will respond effectively to their needs for protection and humanitarian assistance; and where, in the end, they are guaranteed lasting solutions to return to their homes, or are resettled and assisted to resume self-reliant and integrated development.

This new focus on the challenges posed by displacement will require a more strategic approach to in-depth studies of specific country situations, sharing the results with opinion shapers and policy-makers, national political and administrative authorities, and international partners. The Guiding Principles could provide a conceptual framework for analyzing the country situations in terms of prevention, response, and solutions.

Several questions corresponding to this approach would provide the appropriate framework for research and dialogue, and outreach activities, involving concurrently both analysis and advocacy.

First, what, in both ideal and practical terms, is needed to create a national political, economic, social, and cultural framework with which all citizens can identify and that would provide them with a sense of belonging with pride and dignity as citizens and on more or less equal footing with national or other groups?

Second, should a conflict or a crisis occur that displaces populations or otherwise affects civilian populations, what humanitarian and human rights principles should the government and other parties to a conflict observe to ensure that innocent citizens and civilian populations are protected and assisted without discrimination based on the identity factors behind the conflict?

Third, what constructive measures could the parties to the conflict take to facilitate immediate solutions for the displaced and other affected populations to ensure for them alternative options, including return to areas of origin in safety and with dignity, be resettled in other areas of their choice with appropriate protection and assistance, or otherwise integrate themselves into the communities where they happen to be according to their wishes?

Fourth, what are the deeper issues in the conflict that need to be addressed, the positions of the parties in conflict that need to be reconciled, and the principles that are likely to be accepted as the basis for a constructive system that guarantees peace with justice, as prerequisites for long-term security and stability?

The search for answers to these questions could be the objective of the research agenda, teaching programs in academic institutions, intellectual and policy oriented discussion groups, and outreach activities in which policy recommendations are widely disseminated and advocated. This would be an important complement to the work by the Representative of the Secretary-General and other UN bodies in responding to what may well be one of this century's greatest challenges to the international community.

6

Protection Strategies in Humanitarian Interventions

Gerald R. Martone

HUMAN RIGHTS VIOLATIONS and the abuse of civilian populations are at the core of most of today's crises. The physical and legal protection of civilians is at times, however, a subordinate intervention to the enormous logistical demands of humanitarian assistance. The primary mandate of relief agencies operating in humanitarian emergencies is to provide urgent material assistance to affected people. These initial activities typically involve the provision of food, shelter, water, medical services, and other essential services.

The character of humanitarian action tends to position itself to alleviate the effects of human rights violations rather than addressing the violations in themselves. Most relief organizations do not direct substantial effort or resources toward addressing human rights abuses and legal protection issues.

There is a conspicuous compartmentalization peculiar to the field of humanitarian action that distinguishes the activities of assistance and protection as almost entirely distinct guilds. In some cases, relief organizations have deliberately avoided an institutional proximity to the public protest of human rights abuses fearing a compromised presence in that country.

When one considers the frequency, duration, and severity of human rights abuses in today's emergencies, it is not a question of whether relief agencies should address the issue of human rights and protection, but rather to what degree and through which methods. The continuum of options varies from the strict neutrality, discretion, and nondisclosure of the International

Committee of the Red Cross (ICRC) to the public denounce-ments and vocal political advocacy of the human rights organiza-tions.

As the attention paid to human rights and protection issues by relief nongovernmental organizations (NGOs) increased signifi-cantly in recent years, the United Nations High Commissioner for Refugees (UNHCR) has published a practical field guide for nongovernmental organization staff, *Protecting Refugees*,[1] that out-lines the basics of protection issues. Several nongovernmental or-ganizations have even established institutional departments charged with a mandate to address advocacy, public policy, and protection.

In the IFRC/NGO Code of Conduct, the single unifying cove-nant governing humanitarian conduct, there is not a single code that delineates the commitment to the ideal of protecting vulner-able civilian populations.[2] The practical dimensions of political advocacy, community mobilization, and public denouncements are conspicuously absent.

Protection interventions are the spectrum of activities de-signed and undertaken to ensure the rights of refugees and other vulnerable groups. Protection has faced greater challenges in re-cent years, as the rights of war-affected populations are regularly violated. The issue of enforcing protection has presented the in-ternational community with a number of legal, ethical, and prac-tical dilemmas. The new challenge is to address the needs of refugees, IDPs, and war-affected populations in a way that up-holds humanitarian principles and humans rights simultane-ously.

Given the strong field presence and local knowledge, aid work-ers are particularly well placed to promote and protect the rights of refugees, internally displaced persons (IDPs), and other vul-nerable populations. Aid workers are often in direct contact with the effects of human rights abuses. Aid organizations should, log-ically, be prepared to respond to the protection needs of the pop-ulations they serve. Without a vigorous campaign of advocacy, mobilization of public opinion, human rights monitoring, reporting, and information sharing, the provision of relief assistance without protection becomes merely palliative. Agencies must review their roles and responsibilities in the areas of human rights and protection. It is no longer acceptable for the protection of human rights to be a secondary or subordinate aspect of the work of assistance agencies. There are effective and practical approaches that aid organizations can successfully graft into their field programs that will protect the rights of the populations that they serve.

MEDICALIZATION OF HUMAN RIGHTS

With increasing frequency, relief agencies find themselves in situations where they are, in fact, responding to the consequences of blatant human rights abuses, war crimes, and other atrocities. The crises in Sierra Leone, West Timor, Bosnia, Afghanistan, Somalia, Sudan, Rwanda, Liberia, and countless other conflicts have forced relief organizations to reconsider their missions, their responsibilities, and the ethical principles that guide their efforts.

Some of the highest profile crises of the past decade, Bosnia and Kosovo, for example, did not consistently result in mortality statistics that would qualify these conflicts as emergencies, for example, crude mortality rates greater than one death per ten thousand people per day. These crises were, in fact, "epidemics" of human rights abuses.

Perhaps if human rights abuses were tracked as medical indices and regarded with equal relevance to morbidity and mortality statistics, the integration of protection and assistance efforts would gain a foothold. The "medicalization" of human rights abuses—tracked with the voracity of competent disease surveillance, vaccination coverage studies, and communicable disease prevalence—might evoke a new level of involvement from the assistance community. It would have to.

RIGHTS-BASED APPROACH

A rights-based approach presumes that the rights to material and nonmaterial assistance are inseparable. Those affected by calamity have fundamental and universal rights or claims. Life with dignity, freedom from cruel, inhuman, and degrading treatment or punishment is a right. All people are entitled to it.

The rights-based approach switches the motive of assistance from the feelings or the compassionate urges of the giver to the fundamental or universal rights of those affected by a crisis. Relief assistance is a right. Humanitarian agencies have a moral duty to provide these services. Compassion in this interpretation, is not a feeling, it is a professional obligation.

The conventional notion of a humanitarian "impulse" to deliver services implies a sanctimonious urge, above reproach and critique. This anachronistic and outmoded conceptualization of humanitarianism must evolve. It should no longer be understood as a charitable whim or quality of mercy that compels an agency to bestow its gifts. The inherent rights and claims of disaster victims must be part of the altruistic equation. They are not merely objects of pity.

A rights-based approach is not about charity, largesse, volunteerism, and beneficiaries. Rather, a rights-based approach is about duty, legal obligation, claimants, and rights holders. A needs-based approach patronizes people; a rights-based approach dignifies them. A rights-based attitude moves beyond the emotional moral appeal of the charity mentality to a technical, calculated altruism.

The Sphere Project *Minimum Standards in Disaster Response*[3] opens with a Humanitarian Charter that moves this beleaguered and outdated paradigm to a rational, calculated, and ultimately more humane assumption. The Humanitarian Charter promotes a rights-based approach in the provision of humanitarian assistance unambiguously delineating claimants rather than beneficiaries in its opening principle.

The rights-based approach emphasizes the relative position of an individual or group within society rather than exclusively their situation. The perspective is broadened to include an analysis of power, governance, and legally entitled rights of people in crisis.

PROTECTION AS HUMANITARIAN INTERVENTION: FOUR CATEGORIES

Presence Is Protection

The over-zealous critique of the unintended negative effects of aid over the last few years has been unbalanced. Missing from this analysis is a balanced look at the simultaneous unintended *positive* effects of assistance. There are many noteworthy examples where distressed populations implored international staff not to leave—and in some cases have even physically barred their departure—fearing the loss of their protective presence regardless of whether or not direct services were provided.

The mere presence of international relief workers in the field, a secondary protection effect, is considered by some to have a deterrent effect on abuses simply by the witnessing role that that presence connotes. The legitimacy of this intervention is demonstrated by the mandate of certain organizations to employ a deliberate tactic of providing international volunteers to live within at-risk communities or alongside targeted human rights activists as a "Protective Accompaniment" strategy to deter attacks or aggression.

The Representative to the UN Secretary-General for Internally Displaced Persons has advocated strongly for the increased presence of international organizations in Colombia's humanitarian crisis: "The presence of international personnel . . . has served to provide protection to civilians at risk in outlying areas . . . both international and nongovernmental organizations could expand their presence and programs. . . . International support is imperative."[4]

This presence, however, must be proactive; not passive, inadvertent, or accidental. Humanitarian staff must be engaged with the community and actively participate in protection activities if they are to truly offer protection assistance to the surrounding population.

It must be said that presence alone is insufficient to confer protection. The concept of preventive protection has been called into question during the crises in Bosnia and the refugee camps in Goma, Zaire. Gross violations of human rights continued in these examples despite the presence of humanitarian workers and peacekeeping forces. In order for preventive protection to be truly effective, it must be enacted with a broader field-based strategy that includes not only humanitarian assistance but also discrete protection activities, even beyond the mere monitoring and reporting of human rights violations.

In addition to the indirect deterrent effect of international attention and the witnessing role, this secondary prevention may also come in other forms. Humanitarian agencies demonstrably model an ethos of distinction between combatants and noncombatants and an implied ethical message of the sanctity of civilians. As Madame Ogata stated in her May 21, 1997, statement to the UN Security Council, "Humanitarian action is not just about relief . . . but also ensuring physical protection. . . . The challenge must be to bring safety to the people rather than people to safety."

This protective presence must be conspicuous, forceful, and courageous. Unaccompanied by action, the silence of international staff in an abusive context conveys the wrong message, that is, that violations will be tolerated or condoned.[5] A passive, resigned presence not only fails to deter violations of civilians but also inoculates perpetrators to the presence of international witnesses.

Assistance as Protection

The life-saving interventions of providing food, potable water, sanitation services, shelter, and basic medical care may, in themselves, be considered legitimate key protection activities. The very fact that war-affected populations have been forced from their homes with reduced access to the necessities that sustain life is, after all, a gross violation of their basic rights.

In addition, there are other relief activities that deliver, at times unintentionally, proven protective effects. Refugee education programs for children, for example, have demonstrated a measurable decrease in the number of minors conscripted into fighting forces in conflict settings. Access to micro-lending and micro-enterprise projects has provided legitimate alternatives for women and girls, thereby reducing sexual bartering and prostitution. The provision of firewood in camp settings, thereby reducing the need for foraging far off from the safety of the camp surroundings, has been felt to reduce the incidence of rape to women and girls traditionally gathering wood at increasingly greater distances.

Relief organizations are in a unique position to capitalize on the grassroots connection to the people they serve. From this vantage, aid workers can perform assistance activities that will ultimately improve the status of physical and legal protection of refugees and war-affected people, even if the effect is an indirect one.

Self-protection

Many activities that have been the domain of human rights and protection interveners occur at a governmental, intergovernmental, or high-level policy fora. Extraordinary efforts are at times exerted to persuade disinterested governments and war profiteers to adhere to international conventions that have no relevance or meaning to them. Attempting to apply the rule of law in situations that are essentially lawless will yield little result. There is an inherent futility in appealing with a moral duty to the amoral profiteers that are largely responsible for today's wars.

The Geneva Conventions were drafted assuming that there was little military advantage in the deliberate targeting of civilians.[6] In addition to the diversion of precious combat resources, civilian casualties would have resulted in moral outrage and protest of civilized governments. This, of course, has not been the case. It was also assumed that the conduct of combatants would also yield to a "warrior's honor."[7] The implication is that this code of honor would describe the soldier's moral and ethical conduct on the battlefield. The concept of a warrior's honor has existed throughout military history and throughout many societies in the world.

Consistently it appears, however, that combatants comply more vigorously with a soldier's code of honor than to any civilian rule of law. Legal consequences have proved poor deterrents for adherence to the conventions of rules of engagement in combat. Perhaps the most illustrative of this point is the Yugoslav National Army's (JNA) behavior during the war in Bosnia. The JNA was known for being well trained in the Geneva Conventions.

In an effort to persuade human rights violators, mass publication and dissemination of factual information are used in an attempt to stigmatize or embarrass these perpetrators. This "mobilization of shame" is hoped to affect a cessation of hostilities. The cruel despots that are guilty of these flagrant abuses of human rights are hardly chastened by this type of adverse publicity.

Missing from this approach is the involvement and edification of the very people that are intended to be "protected." The individual refugee, IDP, or person affected by war must be made aware of his or her basic human rights and entitlements by law. They should not be approached as passive, helpless, or violated objects. A mobilized and informed community is the best deterrent to outside abuse and neglect; refugees and IDPs approached as claimants or rights holders rather than beneficiaries. They must participate in their struggle to protect themselves.

Direct Protection Activities

Finally, direct protection interventions can, and should, become a critical part of the overall impact of a humanitarian intervention responding to political violence and war. To do otherwise would be shortsighted.

Direct protection activities should be a sine qua non of an assistance strategy rather than assistance substituting for protection. In the jargon of some aid workers, direct interventions that promote protection have been referred to as, "non-assistance assistance."

In order to support the collection, documentation, and compatibility of information on the status of protection in an affected community, a standardized protection assessment form should be developed. To measure progress toward addressing protection dimensions in relief activities, output indicators might be created that directly measure and document these interventions. Although many organizations pay tribute to the importance of protection in their rhetoric, this activity remains without reference or standards, prevailing best practices, and universally recognized indicators. As the aphorism of evaluation observes, "what gets measured is what gets done."

If direct protection activities were quantified and monitored with the same vigilance as other relief deliverables, a cascade of evolutionary changes in the way humanitarian action is delivered would inevitably result.

Below is a list of examples of protection initiatives and the key activities that can be adapted to respond directly to the protection dimensions of populations in extremis:

1. Development of an NGO Technical Advisor for Protection
    a) Create the function of a full-time NGO community-wide Technical Advisor role dedicated to the specific dimensions of physical and legal protection
    b) Pursue collective involvement and buy-in from the NGO coalitions—national and international—for the role and function of an NGO Technical Advisor for protection
    c) Seek funding for this position from among the NGO members themselves and their particular donors
    d) Encourage communication, coordination, and direct collaboration with the UNHCR Reach-Out Program in the design and implementation of this function

e) Promote and participate in all in-country inter-agency coordination forums

f) Develop an NGO Focal Point for protection concerns

g) Organize a technical/sectoral working group to address protection concerns

h) Create a regular schedule of information/coordination meetings on the issues of protection among all participating humanitarian agencies

i) Support efforts to disseminate the Guiding Principles on Internal Displacement

j) Assist NGOs in designing "rights-based" programs and train NGOs in "rights-based" programming and activities

k) Assist NGOs to identify specific at-risk populations

l) Instruct and refer NGOs to appropriate avenues to report and document human rights abuses or neglect

m) Assist NGOs to take into account the unique and special needs of vulnerable individuals

n) Assist NGOs in ensuring hiring practices of national staff that optimize the protective effect of assistance projects

o) Work with NGOs to assess location of relief activities that ensure maximum access for refugees and IDPs

p) Refer NGOs to the Sphere Project *Humanitarian Charter* and its "rights-based" orientation in all activities

q) Assist NGOs to develop and integrate Protection Indicators and Protection Standards in relief assistance projects

r) Provide examples of specific and concrete protection activities that can be integrated into the design of all relief assistance activities

s) Collect and disseminate examples of good relief assistance projects that emphasize protection activities and indicators in their design

t) Encourage NGOs to use protection indicators in all sectors of relief assistance

u) Work with UNHCR, when appropriate, in establishing a "Framework Agreement"

v) Provide informal and voluntary "audits" of NGO projects to assess presence of protection indicators, potential negative impacts, and neglected rights of refugees and IDPs *w)* Advocate for additional monitors for special needs of children, adolescents, elderly, and/or women

2. Establish IDP Information Centers in Areas of Large Displaced or Refugee Populations

  a) Support data collection that provides accurate information on numbers of people, their location, needs, condition, and unique circumstances

  b) Determine what legal rights and laws already exist in support of refugees and IDPs

  c) Provide a venue for refugees and IDPs to learn about their entitlements under law

  d) Make available host government frameworks for refugee and IDPs rights

  e) Provide specific details regarding access to the justice system and legal recourse

  f) Develop a "What Are My Rights?" pamphlet for distribution

  g) Provide basic legal assistance and practical advice and counsel

  h) Develop referral options for medical assistance

  i) Develop referral options for additional legal assistance and access to justice system

  j) Provide referrals to "safe houses" or other secure living alternatives for extremely vulnerable cases

  k) Provide referral for, or opportunities to, report incidents and collect details of harassment or abuse

  l) Track and report trends of abusive incidents against refugees and IDPs

  m) Ensure information exchange with UNHCR Protection Officers and other appropriate human rights monitoring mechanisms

  n) Devise a mechanism to receive and send messages and forward letters to separated family members of refugees and IDPs

  o) Provide referral options to assist refugees and IDPs in acquiring personal documentation and identification papers such as birth and death certificates

  p) Provide referral options to assist with notarizing and validating documentation

  q) Provide referral options for special cases, such as unaccompanied children (UACs), to preselected foster family arrangements

3. Establish a Legal Aid Center

a) Establish a center for refugees and IDPs to seek free legal advice, assistance, and referrals against discrimination, harassment, abusive treatment, and/or arbitrary arrest

b) Provide easy access to basic legal information to all refugees, IDPs, and returnees

c) Mandate a schedule of regular, consistent, and routine field visits to all sites

d) Emphasize outreach and visitation, that is, bring legal aid to refugees and IDPs, not the reverse

e) Advise refugees and IDPs on basic rights and how to register complaints

f) Determine which legal rights or laws are already in existence

g) Support data collection providing accurate information on unmet needs, condition, and unique circumstances of refugees and IDPs

h) Coordinate with the host government and local authorities the establishment of national civil registries

i) Assist provincial committees to provide structures for seeking political representation

j) Provide a venue for people to learn about their entitlements under law

k) Provide specific details regarding access to the justice system and legal recourse

l) Provide basic legal assistance and practical advice and counsel

m) Provide, when appropriate, "accompaniment" arrangements for witnesses or plaintiffs

n) Provide referrals to "safe houses" or other secure living alternatives for extremely vulnerable cases

o) Provide input to UNHCR Protection Officers for recalcitrant cases that may be appropriate for asylum in a neighboring country

p) Offer a place to document and follow up on reports of situations where IDPs are not receiving relief assistance

q) Collect and make available all legal standards applicable in the region *r)* Track and report trends of human rights violations and abusive incidents

s) Provide a place to report unlawful incidents of restricted movement or travel

t) Inform refugees and IDPs of who is responsible for investigation of crimes

u) Provide information on ramifications of legislation on mixed marriages

v) Ensure information exchange with UNHCR Protection Officers and other appropriate human rights monitoring mechanisms

w) Provide referral options to acquire personal documentation and identification papers and obtain notarization or validation of documentation

x) Research information on inheritance laws and entitlements

y) Provide information and updated laws of burial practices and proper disbursement of personal belongings

z) Assist with acquiring/validating land-use rights and property entitlements

aa) Provide information on obtaining copies of property titles for assets other than land, for instance, cars, businesses, shops, equipment, etc.

bb) Assist with dealing with issues related to confiscated property

cc) Provide referral for special cases such as UACs, complicated medical cases, and other vulnerable individuals

dd) Provide training and sensitization to local authorities on the rights of refugees and IDPs

ee) Help refugees and IDP settlers in mobilizing and advocating for social responsibility and justice in host community

ff) Assist with lobbying efforts of refugee and IDP community to advocate for themselves

4. Develop a "What Are My Rights?" Brochure for Distribution

a) Provide a simply written information pamphlet for refugees and IDPs to learn about their entitlements under law

b) Determine what legal rights and laws already exist

c) Provide specific details regarding access to the justice system and legal recourse *d)* Include basic legal information and practical advice and counsel

e) Include referral options for additional legal assistance and access to justice system

f) Translate the pamphlet into the appropriate local language and vernacular

g) Arrange oral presentations of the pamphlet by community leaders for illiterate refugees or IDPs

h) Label and date each revision of the pamphlet to keep pace with changing legislation

i) Provide written documentation regarding the status of an individual's rights in issues related to restricted movement or travel, personal documentation and identification, inheritance laws and entitlements, burial practices and proper disbursement of personal belongings, confiscated property, land-use rights and property entitlements, and other rights related to assets such as cars, businesses, shops, and equipment

5. Develop Emergency "Safe Houses" for Extremely Vulnerable Cases

a) Design a sheltered "safe house" program for the temporary referral of extremely vulnerable cases and UNHCR-referred protection cases, that is, unusual situations involving harassment, domestic violence, complicated child custody disputes, severe trauma, complicated interethnic marriage circumstances, unaccompanied and incompetent elderly persons, etc.

b) Provide twenty-four-hours a day on-site experienced staff

c) Ensure confidential services and document handling

d) Provide referrals for complicated cases, medical intervention, and psychological care

e) Provide input to UNHCR Protection Officers for recalcitrant cases that may be appropriate for asylum in a neighboring country

f) Provide easily accessible in-house counseling and assistance

g) Refer appropriate cases or longer-term situations to foster family options

h) Offer access to free legal advice, assistance, and referral

i) Provide easy access to basic legal information and counsel *j)* Provide a monitoring mechanism to ensure that residents of safe house are free from further abuse or mistreatment by staff or local residents

6. Develop Foster Family Networks for Extremely Vulnerable Cases

a) Provide safe community-based living alternatives for UACs, unaccompanied elders, victims of domestic abuse, severely traumatized individuals, mixed marriages, etc.

b) Pre-select appropriate foster family arrangements

c) Train and sensitize foster families in the special needs of extremely vulnerable individuals

d) Determine appropriate and sustainable compensation and retainer-fee structure for foster families

e) Assist referred cases to other community supports besides foster family placements for individual cases when required

f) Provide a monitoring mechanism to ensure that fostered children are free from further abuse or mistreatment by foster family or from neighbors

7. Develop an Ombudsman Liaison for Refugees and IDPs Seeking Recourse for Unmet Needs or Aggrieved Rights

a) Identify or develop a respected and independent entity, organization, or individual to act on behalf of refugees or IDPs

b) Ensure nonpartisan demeanor and beneficiary/claimant orientation of Ombudsman functions

c) Mediate between relief agencies and local authorities representing the concerns of the refugee or IDP community

d) Offer a place to document and follow up on reports of situations where people are not receiving relief assistance

e) Ensure a highly visible and easily accessible representation to register complaints, seek legal recourse, or document abusive situations, conditions, or persons

f) Emphasize an outreach or visitation methodology in being available to refugees and IDPs

g) Develop a routine and predictable schedule of field visitation and monitoring

h) Collect factual information on abuses or neglect

i) Track reported incidences and analyze trends for dissemination for all relevant authorities

j) Ensure information exchange with UNHCR Protection Officers and other appropriate human rights monitoring mechanisms

8. Promote Use of Social Marketing for Awareness and Sensitization of Communities

   a) Develop appropriate radio programming and information messages for public dissemination about the situation and rights of refugees and IDPs

   b) Test appropriateness, relevance, and potential impacts of developed radio messages for public broadcast

   c) Contract for radio airtime during periods of high usage for dissemination of sensitization messages

   d) Design, test, and contract for appropriate print media messages (newspaper, sign board, posted notices, etc.) sensitizing the public about the circumstances and rights

   e) Develop and test radio and print messages that can raise awareness of the unique circumstances of refugee and IDP children leading to increased vulnerability to forced conscription and child prostitution

9. Organize IDP Leadership Committees in Various Camp Settings

   a) Organize and encourage initiative and self-governance in addressing the needs and rights of refugee or IDP communities

   b) Facilitate indigenous leadership, when appropriate, among the communities

   c) Provide training in representational leadership and consensual decision making to leadership committee members

   d) Ensure gender balance and representation among leadership committees

   e) Mobilize the community to take action and advocate for change when faced with abuse or neglect by local authorities or local community

   f) Work closely with church groups and other national human rights groups

   g) Lobby local authorities for adherence to basic rights and justice for communities

   h) Provide access to UNHCR Protection Officers for the reporting and tracking of incidents and trends among the community *i)* Assist community leaders, when appropriate, in developing civilian patrols

    j) Provide community support when bringing violators to justice

10. Support and Creation of Women's Committees

    a) Ensure representation of women and girls' needs in camp activities

    b) Ensure participation in of women in the design of programs and distribution schemes for food and nonfood items

    c) Involve women's committee in site-planning for water points and latrine placement

11. Provide Presence or "Accompaniment" for Witnesses, Aggrieved, or Plaintiffs Seeking Legal Recourse

12. Capacity Building for National NGOs, Church Groups, Justice Workers, District Authorities

    a) Determine the need, and appropriate audience for, a brief and focused training program in basic human rights and the circumstances of refugees and IDPs

    b) Ascertain current level of knowledge of intended national NGOs, justice workers, and/or district authorities regarding human rights and displaced populations

    c) Sensitize participants to the complex issues of displaced populations, disruption of civil society, and personal rights

    d) Develop a training curriculum specifically designed to raise awareness and technical knowledge about the basic human rights

    e) Expose participants to the Guiding Principles on Internal Displacement

    f) Discuss importance of access to justice and legal recourse

13. Organize Human Rights and Legal Entitlements Training for District-Level Police Force

    a) Determine current level of knowledge regarding displaced populations

    b) Sensitize local police to complex issues of personal rights of displaced persons

    c) Develop a training curriculum specifically designed to raise awareness and technical knowledge about basic human rights. Instruct police in basic human rights framework

    d) Expose police to the Guiding Principles on Internal Displacement

    e) Discuss importance of access to justice and legal recourse

    f) Teach questioning and assessment techniques

14. Provide Sensitization and Support to Traditional Authorities and Civilian Administration Representing the Hosting Communities

15. Assist with Efforts Regarding the Dissemination, Integration, and Understanding about the Guiding Principles on Internal Displacement

    a) Support training programs and translate Guiding Principles documents into relevant local language

16. Assist in the Preparation of NGO/Nonprofit Laws for Registration/Accreditation of National and International NGOs to Facilitate Work

17. Implement Active Tracing and Reunification

    a) Provide input to and assist with the ongoing efforts of ICRC, UNICEF, and UNHCR in tracing and reunification of UACs

18. Assist with Efforts to Provide Information to Refugees and IDPs about the Conditions of Their Homes

    a) Organize "look-see" advance visits, when appropriate, to homes of origin

    b) Provide personal "accompaniment" in special cases

    c) Assist with determining recoverable assets of families and other property from homes of origin

    d) Assist with determining status of illegally occupied homes

    e) Determine availability of seed and animal stock in returnee areas

19. Organize Advance "Look-See" Teams to Returnee Areas

    a) Organize "advance teams" prior to full return to returnees' homes

    b) Assist returnees with preliminary home repairs

    c) Assist in the determination of the status of illegally occupied residences

    d) Facilitate initial planting cycle if seasonally appropriate

7

Issues of Power and Gender in Complex Emergencies

Judy A. Benjamin

Introduction

THIS CHAPTER addresses two key issues that dramatically affect the lives of women and children caught in the chaos of complex humanitarian emergencies. Gender concerns for refugee and internally displaced women living in camp[1] settings primarily relate to two core issues: protection and equal access to relief goods and services. Equal access means that women and girls have the same access and rights to relief items and services that men have in the camps: food and nonfood items, shelter, health services, access to clean water, sanitation facilities, training, employment, and education opportunities. Protection's role includes safeguarding displaced people—women and girls, in particular—from rape, abduction, forced sexual slavery, genital mutilation, forced marriages, exploitation, torture, and murder.

The objectives of the chapter are to simplify the concept of gender in complex emergency situations in order to foster awareness of the main issues that affect the lives of women and children. Gender-based violence is defined and illustrated and, it is hoped, explained in ways that help the reader identify potential problems that might lead to violence against women and children. The chapter identifies important measures and initiatives needed to ensure the rights of women and children in emergency situations. Key terms are defined within the text as appropriate and in the glossary found in this chapter's Glossary of Terms section at the back of this book. The author makes recommendations for international agencies, donors, and aid workers. The list of recommended additional reading (found in this chapter's References section at the back of this book) should prove useful to both experienced and less experienced field workers interested in improving their understanding of the gender issues addressed in this chapter.

The material presented here largely pertains to people who have been forced by either conflict or natural disasters to flee their homes and become either refugees outside their country of residence, or are displaced within their own borders as internally displaced people (IDPs).

THE FUNDAMENTAL RIGHT TO BASIC HUMAN NEEDS

Conflict is the main reason people become refugees or internally displaced. Women and children comprise an estimated 80 percent of displaced populations. In situations of complex humanitarian emergencies, women assume primary responsibility for the survival of their families. Women keep the social fabric intact by maintaining cultural practices and traditions even during conflict and displacement.

The basic human needs embody the fundamental rights of all people. Basic needs include food, water, shelter, nonfood items (blankets, clothes, cooking pots, etc.), health care, sanitation, education, and opportunities for self-support, as well as freedom from persecution.

Access to Food, Power, and Gender-Based Violence

The entry point for preventing abuse and violence against women is the food distribution line. It is there that gender-power relationships are manifested in harmful ways. Food ranks as the most valuable commodity in a refugee camp. Food can be readily sold, traded, or bartered for cash or other items. Power rests with those who control access to food. Women do not enjoy equal access to food in nearly all of the hundreds of refugee and IDP camps I have visited during the past ten years. The recently exposed sex exploitation scandals[2] in West Africa in the camps in Guinea, Sierra Leone, and Liberia point to food as the main resource exchanged for sex. Food and other humanitarian relief items provided by the international community fall under the control of men. Poor monitoring by relief agencies permits the sexual exploitation of women and girls. Other men, including international peacekeepers, military forces, and UN and relief agency employees exploit the severe poverty conditions suffered by the refugees by offering to women and young girls small sums of money or "gifts" in exchange for sex. The majority of the victims of exploitation are females under the age of eighteen—the most vulnerable recipients of humanitarian assistance.

Equal participation in relief programs and services will not guarantee that women will not be pressured into providing sexual services or that they will not be cheated on their rations as they pass through the distribution lines, but the chances of blatant abuse will be lessened with women in decision-making roles and actively engaged.

The highlighted issues raised in this chapter—protection and equal access to resources—relate to the physical abuse and violation of women and to exploitation by men with some degree of power over vulnerable members of the assisted community. The vulnerability of women relates to their role in society and the specific circumstances in which they find themselves. Women are perceived as having natural tendencies to protect and nourish their young regardless of the risks to themselves. Women are adept at survival and will go to extreme lengths to ensure the survival of their children, members of their family, and themselves.

Refugees versus Internally Displaced Persons

Most conflicts today occur inside the boundaries of the affected country, therefore, the global number of IDPs exceeds that of refugees. In the writer's experience, refugee and IDP camps are much the same. Some IDPs receive less international assistance than refugees do for several reasons. IDPs fall under the jurisdiction and responsibility of their own government, although in many situations the government may be the cause of the displacement, or may not have the means to offer support to its displaced citizens. The UNHCR's mandate does not normally include responsibility for IDPs although in some cases they take on the task when requested to do so by the UN Secretary-General. International relief agencies may not be operational in IDP camps unless the conflict has high visibility or has gained international attention.

APPLYING A GENDER ANALYSIS IN HUMANITARIAN ASSISTANCE

This analysis employs a gender perspective to examine several key questions: What are the major issues of concern to refugee and displaced women and girls? What steps can the assistance community take to address and ensure the rights of women in emergency situations? How can the gap between policy and practices be closed? What can individual humanitarian workers do to ensure the protection of the rights of vulnerable refugees and displaced persons?

Gender analysis requires a basic understanding of the premise upon which gender theory rests. Gender refers to the female and male roles within a given culture. These roles and the expected behaviors of men and women are based on cultural practices formed over time. We cannot study gender by focusing on females or males to the exclusion of the other sex because gender involves dynamic interactions between women and men—to understand gender-power relationships we must examine those interactions.

Gender may be defined simply as the culturally prescribed and learned roles of women, girls, men, and boys.

As a concept gender often raises more questions than answers. In many cultures the word gender does not translate into local languages and dialects. Although understanding of gender and the idea of gender equity has evolved in the last decade, and has become part of the global development and relief vocabulary, in situations of forced mobility, whether caused by conflict or natural disaster, people tend to behave according to the gender norms in their society. Extraordinary events, however, may result in behavior that deviates substantially from social norms or personal standards.

Gender as a Social Construct

How gender is constructed explains the position of women in society. Women in developing countries negotiate their lives within a gender framework set by their particular cultural groups. As Caroline Moser[3] has rightly noted, when lives drastically change, as in the case of forced migration and conflict, women often lose their negotiated positions of strength and revert to less equitable social statuses. If gender is about a socially constructed concept that describes how men and women interact within a particular society and how they define their roles in that culture, then gender constructs are brought with refugees in exile along with other remnants of their culture.

The Gender Dimensions of Refugee Life

Several main theoretical frameworks underpin discussions on the integration of gender issues into humanitarian and development work. A review of refugee literature points to a gap in classifying refugees in gendered roles. Development anthropologist Elizabeth Colson called the gap "biased toward undifferentiated people without gender, age, or other defining characteristics." References to refugees in international agency and media reports often omit reference to gender, age, or other defining characteristics except ethnicity. Media accounts merge refugees into one mass of starving, malnourished people wearing the same bitter, hungry expressions. Such ethnocentric attitudes add to the problems women and children face in the camps. The representation of women refugees[4] has been that of passive, dependent homogeneous victims treated as nameless faces in masses of humanity—individuality and personal identity missing. Harrell-Bond (1996) rejected the idea that women refugees are helpless and dependent. Rather she saw their vulnerability stemming from their lack of participation in humanitarian aid upon which their lives so much depended. The categorization of women as helpless victims marginalizes them in the sense that they are not afforded respect and, therefore, not afforded the opportunity to become leaders and decision-makers in the camps.

The term "victim" evokes images of helplessness and weakness. Images of resourcefulness, stamina, and fortitude must replace the negative depictions of women to support their becoming important members of their societies.

Tools for Gender Analysis

UNHCR uses a planning tool that they promote in field locations for staff training called the People-Oriented Planning (POP) method. POP examines, among other things, who does what, who owns what, and who controls what within a community. In other words, to better understand the gender roles within a given society one seeks to understand how the division of labor, economics, and control over resources are broken down by gender. Several international NGOs have adopted POP methods, and at least one other UN agency has borrowed certain aspects of POP for their gender training portfolios.

The POP method uses a simple framework to analyze gender. The three components are (1) Refugee Population Profile and Context Analysis, (2) Activities Analysis, and (3) Use and Control of Resources Analysis. Each analytical component can be charted in simple tables (see table 7.1).

Table 7.1   Activities Analysis (use for the pre-refugee experience and present situation)

Activities	Who (Gender/Age)	Where	When/How long
Production of goods for example, carpentry, metal work, etc.			
. . . and services for example, teaching, domestic labor, etc.			
Agricultural tasks for example, land clearing, planting, weeding, harvesting, etc.			
Household production for example, childcare, home garden, water collection, etc.			
Protection for example, of unaccompanied children, of fighting-age boys, of single women, of elderly, etc.			
Social/Political/Religious for example, community meeting, ceremonies, etc.			

GENDER VIOLENCE ASSOCIATED WITH CONFLICT AND FORCED DISPLACEMENT

Conflict-imperiled women have been subjected to gender-specific abuses, including rape, sexual slavery, and forced marriages to members of various fighting forces. Systematic and widespread rape and other sexual violence have been a hallmark of many internal and external conflicts around the globe. Sexual violence has been directed against women of all ages, including very young girls. Thousands of cases have been reported, including individual and gang rape, sexual assault with objects, and sexual slavery. All parties to armed conflict have committed human rights abuses, however, the international community has paid little attention to gender-specific violations to date.

Gender violence in conflict situations violates the fundamental human right to mental and physical integrity as protected under the Universal Declaration of Human Rights,[5] the Convention on the Elimination of All Forms of Discrimination against Women (CEDAW),[6] and the Convention Against Torture and Other Cruel, Inhuman or Degrading Treatment or Punishment.[7] Violence is the chief source of fear for displaced women and girls. Researchers have begun to focus attention on the long-term effects of living under the threat of violence.[8]

Conflict situations greatly increase the violence inflicted upon women and girls—at no other time are they more vulnerable. Frequently during conflicts women not only lack the protection of their families and spouses, but also are under threat by armed soldiers, who may regard them as spoils of war. Even when abuses are not aimed at them personally, women suffer violations of their human rights disproportionately when the normal codes of social conduct are ignored because of conflict. Teenage members of the ruthless rebel group in Sierra Leone, the RUF, ignored custom and social mores by raping women old enough to be their grandmothers.

When Short-Term Coping Equals Long-Term Risks

Both unequal access to food and gender-based violence lead to coping strategies that may endanger women including increasing their exposure to harmful diseases such as HIV/AIDS and other sexually transmitted infections. These two concerns are among the most critical problems women and girls face when uprooted by circumstances that force them from the relative safety of their homes and villages into temporary living situations fraught with danger and high risk.

WHAT IS GENDER-BASED VIOLENCE?

Gender-based violence refers to violence targeted to people because of their gender, or because of their special roles or responsibilities in their society. In many cases women have sole re-

"In humanitarian emergencies, the virus spreads even more rapidly than in nonconflictual situations. Yet rarely in situations of conflict or even postconflict or demobilization, is attention focused on the symbiotic relationship among violence, displacement and brutality, their psychosocial effects, and the spread of the HIV epidemic." Elizabeth Reid, *Challenge of the HIV Epidemic*

sponsibility for their households. Certain responsibilities of women's gender roles put them at greater risk of injury. Crossing landmine fields or walking near military encampments in the course of their gender-defined task of searching for water and firewood subjects women to maiming, crossfire injuries, and sexual attacks. Gender-based violence may be manifested in several ways: domestic violence, rape, and forced prostitution and marriages. Although rape and other sexual abuses are recognized as serious crimes in humanitarian laws, only recently has the international community addressed these forms of violence as serious infringements of fundamental women's rights.

Rape is a deliberate tactic used in war not only to dehumanize and dishonor women, but also husbands, families, communities, or ethnic groups. The humiliation and degradation of rape are only compounded by the impunity of the perpetrators. The incidence of rape against refugee and internally displaced women is higher than what is actually reported. Women IDPs are often reluctant to report rape for fear of retribution from the perpetrators. Other forms of sexual coercion are rife in refugee and IDP settings where young girls may be abducted and forced into marriage or prostitution. Awareness of the problem and special programs are needed to reduce the likelihood of such occurrences.

WHAT CONSTITUTES VULNERABILITY?

In general, the greater the mobility of displaced women and girls, the greater their vulnerability. Program interventions in emergency situations need to pay special attention when women become highly mobile. War-affected women often find themselves without male household members who under normal circumstances would provide protection to them and their children. When people are forced to flee their homes and seek refuge they often escape with only the clothes they are wearing. Women are usually the ones who must secure the household's necessities including food, water, and cooking fuel.

In situations of forced migration women without husbands or fathers in their households are more vulnerable to abuse than women with male adults present in the home. Since most emergency situations today are the results of conflict, in many refugee settings women outnumber men. In war zones many men die in conflict, become prisoners, or actively engage in ongoing fighting. Vulnerability also increases during periods of food shortages and scarcity.

WHO IS RESPONSIBLE FOR PROTECTION?

In the case of refugees, the host state is responsible for the protection of refugees (under the 1951 Refugee Convention obligation). However, the responsibility for protection is also an international one that calls on assistance from UN agencies and NGOs as well as host communities. UNHCR is the primary UN agency with a mandate to provide for the protecting of refugees. Other UN agencies who have taken on protection issues for both refugees and internally displaced people are UNICEF, WFP, WHO, UNDP, and OCHA. Likewise, implementing partners are expected to maintain the same principles. The International Rescue Committee formed a protection unit that provides some protection services to UNHCR in some locations (in IDP camps in Afghanistan, for example).

WHY IS RESPONSE TO SEXUAL AND GENDER-BASED VIOLENCE SO INADEQUATE?

Implementing agencies often lack of clear and coherent policies regarding gender issues. Even when international organizations' headquarters endorse strong gender policies, the field often does not implement programs. This can be due in part to the high rate of staff turnover that makes it difficult to provide sufficient training on critical issues. The tendency to compartmentalize sector activities in the field leads to vertical programming that does not integrate well into other sectors. Gender issues crosscut through all sectors.

Inexperienced Western field workers are sometimes intimidated by unfamiliar cultural practices. Their ignorance creates fear to the extent that they may not respond to events they would not tolerate in their Western environments. Domestic violence is a huge problem in camps. Women are seriously injured and even murdered, but relief workers are reluctant to interfere in household conflict. They may not recognize cases of child abuse or exploitation of child labor. Large poor families sometimes send their older children out to fend for themselves in order to reduce the number of mouths to feed. Some of those children become virtual slaves for their employers.

CULTURAL RELATIVISM

"It's cultural, there is nothing we can do" is a response often heard from aid workers to excuse themselves from responding to cases of human rights abuse. Aid workers have used the "cultural practice" response to excuse their inaction in the following documented cases involving displaced persons:[9]

- In Guinea, a male school headmaster was caught after repeatedly raping his young female pupils
- In Afghanistan, a fourteen-year-old girl's family members received death threats, and were assaulted and shot at, when they tried to protect the girl from a forced marriage to a militia member
- In Sierra Leone, over one thousand young internally displaced girls in a West African IDP camp were forcefully circumcised

Humanitarian organizations that work with refugees or IDPs in various cultural settings must be prepared to address misconceptions regarding cultural practices when dealing with issues such as those in the cases mentioned above. Assistance agencies must take action to educate their local and international staff about human rights, refugee laws, UN conventions and resolutions (such as the Convention on the Rights of the Child and CEDAW; see Appendix 1), agency policies, and operating practices in order to combat harmful practices that violate international standards. "It's cultural" is not an acceptable excuse to ignore the protection needs of refugees and IDPs. Agencies must clearly state their policies, and staff must be held accountable for carrying out their agencies' policies and intended practices. One of the founding principles of human rights law is that it is not culturally relative—basic human rights are universally applicable as a matter of law.

Most NGOs working in refugee or IDP camps do not consider protection to be their responsibility. UNHCR admits they do not have the capacity to protect individual refugees. Their mandate directs them to provide overall legal protection related to asylum in the country of refuge. Women and girls are insecure and at risk of sexual abuse and exploitation from the time they leave their homes, during their exodus, and ongoing during their refuge in camps. Border guards, police, and military factions demand sexual favors of women in transit. Once inside refugee camps women may fear venturing out of their shelters because of harassment or sexual assaults. In a large IDP camp outside of Herat, Afghanistan, women are afraid to visit feeding centers or health posts because of the number of sexual assaults that have taken place.

What Steps Can Be Taken to Increase Protection?

Structural

Changes in camp layout and structures will increase protection and reduce the risk of violence against women and girls living in camps. Such measures include lighting, especially around water collection points and latrines; locating latrines safe distances from shelters or setting up smaller latrines to be shared by four to five families; changes in camp layout of latrines and water pumps;

employing women as guards; establishing women's "safe haven houses;" and setting up community night watches.

Protection overlaps into all sectors within camp settings—health, education, income generation, shelter, water, and sanitation. Because of severe water shortages, women at the Ngara, Tanzania, refugee camps stood in line for hours both before dawn and after dark. Many were attacked or forced to provide sex in exchange for water. At the same camp, young girls were raped when they visited the latrines. The incidents were so frequent that the design and location of latrines was changed from large communal areas to small, four-family latrines located nearer residences. In most refugee camps electricity is not available, which creates a high-risk factor after daylight hours.

Awareness-Raising

Humanitarian agencies can support women and help build their capacity to survive with dignity. Agencies can help prevent gender violence by raising awareness about gender-based violence within the affected community by providing rights-based programming and by working to prevent physical and psychological abuses associated with forced displacement. The UNHCR *Guidelines on the Protection of Refugee Women* and *Sexual Violence against Refugees: Guidelines on Prevention and Response*[10] are excellent resources. These guidelines should be more widely implemented by international and local agencies.

Basic everyday chores become risky when women have to venture outside camps in search of firewood or water. These activities greatly increase the risk of physical attacks. Some refugee and IDP sites provide truckloads of firewood within the camps. Another approach engaged the labor of refugee men to cut wood to supply roadside wood depots. These solutions can be expensive and require donor funding but do provide some protection. Alternative energy sources such as solar ovens should be explored.

Local Organizations Fight Gender-Based Violence

Women's organizations such as Forum for African Women Educationalists (FAWE), the Sierra Leone Association of University Women (SLAUW), the National Displaced Women's Organization, and Legal Access for Women Yearning for Equal Rights (LAWYER) are active women's associations that provide assistance and training for women and girls in West Africa. Women's groups can be powerful advocates for the rights of women.

Displacement Brings Rapid Social and Gender-Role Changes

The loss of social support systems and community solidarity experienced when people become displaced and move to crowded camps may cause families to break up. Families that lose their social networks of support often lose everything. Men may be unable to find work or may become involved in the conflict, leaving the woman responsible for the household—often an unaccustomed role for which she may be ill prepared. Women separated from their husbands or widowed must take on the responsibilities of providing for the household.

Loss of Social and Cultural Ties

Displaced women generally lack community support. In many instances, the community is fragmented. Key opinion holders, respected elders, and important role models are frequently absent. Displaced women in former Yugoslavia reported feeling unwelcome in the areas where they had fled and suffered discrimination at the hands of local people.[11] The disintegration of community unity increases the vulnerability of women and children and weakens their coping mechanisms. Women and adolescent girls become easy targets for abuse when they are separated from normal support systems, husbands, and other male family members. Internally displaced women continue to require protection against further displacement and abuses even after they return home. Women especially need support from their communities to defend their rights and cope with their plight. When families lose support networks they may fall victim to crime and violence.

Unequal Access to Food: Exploitation of the Weak by the Powerful

The most powerful people in refugee or IDP camps are the ones in control of resources—usually men. They take advantage of those less powerful—usually women.

Relief specialists have often pointed out that the issue is not lack of food in the world but the control over food and its distribution that counts. Having control over food resources represents power. Those in control of food resources at refugee and IDP camps have the capacity to exploit those needing the food. The greatest source of abuse and exploitation in emergency settings stems from unequal access to food and other distributed items.

Women and children represent a higher percentage of camp residents than do men. Because of inherent gender inequities in less-developed countries, women in traditional societies are less educated than men and more likely to be illiterate. Their illiteracy adds to their vulnerability by making them more dependent on authorities in the camps and less able to learn about their entitlements. In my nearly two decades of field experience working in complex emergencies and refugee camps I have yet to see food distributions free of exploitation.

SKILLS TRAINING AND INCOME GENERATION ACTIVITIES

After basic needs are met and protection ensured, people need assistance to get them on the road to self-sufficiency. Women especially need opportunities to learn how to support themselves so they do not have to resort to harmful and degrading practices. Well-intended agencies set up skills-training programs in camps; however, many skills-training programs and income-generation activities are ill planned and do not meet the practical needs of women. This happens most often because programs are planned by international agencies without adequate input by the women the programs are meant to serve. Women may sacrifice their limited time to participate in training only to become more frustrated when the training does not result in job opportunities.

The desperate need of refugee women heads-of-households to secure food for their children can push women into prostitution. Humanitarian agencies should be aware of the coping strategies of women without male household contributors and help women make healthy choices. The most important help organizations can provide to women is to ensure equal access to all resources offered in the camp. Skills training and income generation are vitally important to improving conditions and in helping to empower women and decrease vulnerability.

PROTECTION UNDER THE LAW

International and local organizations cannot protect the rights of people under their care without understanding the basics of international human rights and refugee laws. Several international bodies of law pertain to the activities of humanitarian actors concerning refugees and internally displaced persons. Laws are fundamental to rights-based programming—the teeth that provide enforcement and the cement to fill the gap between policy and practice that many programs lack.

The Universal Declaration of Human Rights (UDHR) was approved by the General Assembly in December 1948, and for the first time the concept of human rights had a definition. The UDHR is a declaration, not a treaty, and there is no mechanism to review or enforce compliance.

The International Committee of the Red Cross is the principal humanitarian law monitoring organization. The Geneva Conventions are the core of international humanitarian law and were put into effect in 1950. Humanitarian law is also referred to as the law of armed conflict and covers the wounded and sick in the armed forces, treatment of prisoners of war, and protection of civilians in time of war—Article 3 of the Geneva Conventions.

Refugee law: separate from human rights and humanitarian law, international refugee law covers aspects of protection and assistance that are related to the rights afforded to refugees. The 1951 Convention Relating to the Status of Refugees describes a refugee as any person who "owing to a well-founded fear of being persecuted for reasons of race, religion, nationality, membership of a particular social group or political opinion, is outside the country of his nationality and is unable, or owing to such fear, is unwilling to avail himself of the protection of that country."

The 1951 Refugee Convention establishes the fundamental principle of *nonrefoulement*, which forbids states from expelling or returning a "refugee in any manner whatsoever to the frontiers of territories where his life or freedom would be threatened on account of his race, religion, nationality, membership of a particular social group or political opinion."

Refugee law does not clearly spell out protection for internally displaced persons. UNHCR's mandate does not normally extend to cover IDPs although the UN Secretary-General may specifically request UNHCR to do so. To help address the specific needs of IDPs the Secretary-General created the position of Representative for IDPs and appointed Francis Deng to that post. Deng has carried out numerous fact-finding missions to countries with IDP populations. In 1998, Deng introduced thirty guiding principles for the treatment of IDPs that are consistent with international human rights law and international humanitarian law. The Guiding Principles highlight the need for protection as well as assistance. The problem, as with many guidelines and manuals, lies in the implementation and enforcement.

"Civilian casualties outnumber military nine to one. Civilians are targeted, used as 'shield,' raped, and forcibly conscripted." William G. O'Neill, *A Humanitarian Practitioner's Guide to International Human Rights Law*

The Rome Statute of the International Criminal Court makes explicit that rape and other gender-based violence are among the most serious crimes of concern to the international community by specifically defining them as constituent acts of crime against humanity and war crimes.

The Convention on the Elimination of All Forms of Discrimination against Women (CEDAW) was adopted by the General Assembly in 1979 and took effect in 1981. Also known as the Women's Convention, CEDAW seeks to do away with discrimination against women. In spite of CEDAW, discrimination against women continues. (A slightly abridged text of the CEDAW is printed in Appendix 1 at the back of this book.)

How it works: The Convention obliges state parties to submit to the Secretary-General a report on the legislative, judicial, administrative, or other measures they have adopted to implement the Convention within a year after its entry into force and then at least every four years thereafter or whenever the Committee[12] on the Elimination of Discrimination against Women requests.

The Convention on the Rights of the Child (CRC) went into effect in 1990 (ratified by every UN member state except the United States and Somalia at this writing). The CRC definition of a child is "every human being under the age of eighteen."

Both CEDAW and CRC merge civil and political rights with economic, social, and cultural rights, including the rights to life, nationality, expression, association, assembly and thought, conscience, and religion.

Convention on the Elimination of All Forms of Discrimination against Women

"Discrimination against women violates the principles of equality of rights and respect for human dignity, is an obstacle to the participation of women on equal terms with men in the political, social, economic, and cultural life of their countries . . . and makes more difficult the full development of the potentialities of women in the service of their countries and humanity." *Preamble* to the Convention

The following legal instruments address the right to food for refugees:[13]

- Universal Declaration of Human Rights, Art. 25
- 1951 Convention Relating to the Status of Refugees, Art. 23
- International Covenant on Economic, Social, and Cultural Rights, Art. 11
- Convention on the Elimination of All Forms of Discrimination against Women
- Convention on the Rights of the Child, Art. 27
- African Charter on Human and Peoples' Rights, Art. 16
- African Charter on the Rights and Welfare of the Child, Art. 14

INTERNATIONAL RESPONSE TO GENDER VIOLENCE

United Nations

The UN Special Rapporteur on Violence Against Women's post was created in 1994 in the wake of crimes committed against women in Bosnia and Herzegovina. The post involves fact-finding missions around the world and reporting findings to the UN High Commissioner on Human Rights, but the post has no enforcement power. The UN can only expose and use diplomatic measures against such practices.

International NGOs and Committees

Several international NGOs have initiated programs to address gender-based violence and human rights issues. The International Rescue Committee (IRC) with support from their advocacy department, the Women's Commission for Refugee Women and Children, have made progress in preventing gender violence by raising awareness. IRC was among the first organizations to start sexual and gender-based violence (SGBV) programs in refugee camps. The programs conduct awareness training for men and women in refugee and IDP camps and help set up gender violence centers inside camps and safe havens for abused women and girls. A number of other NGOs now have programs to address gender-based violence, including the Reproductive Health Consortium, which is a collaborative endeavor with members drawn from several NGOs with a common purpose of improving the reproductive health of refugees and IDPs worldwide.

In the case of the Rwandan Hutu refugees who fled Rwanda following the genocide to camps in Ngara Tanzania and former Zaire, the population was fairly balanced with approximately the same number of men and women. However, there were a number of female-headed households and even some children-headed households because during the exodus many families became separated—some went to former Zaire and some went to Tanzania. The Rwandan refugee camps were highly insecure and overpopulated. Considering the events in Rwanda from April 7, 1994, until the mass exodus around July 18, 1994—the gruesome hundred days of violence during which an estimated 800,000 people were slaughtered—the atmosphere in the camps seemed laden with violence and hatred. Violent behavior continued in the camps. Men and women were accused of disloyalty to commune leaders who had participated in the genocide. Some of those accused were murdered. Women and girls were raped in alarming numbers, and domestic violence was persistent. The NGOs and UN agencies responded by setting up Crisis Intervention Teams (CITs) to assist survivors of rape with a comprehensive support program that included medical treatment, counseling, legal help, new clothing, and new shelter if warranted.

A number of organizations are implementing programs to combat gender-based violence and to promote better understanding of gender issues in emergency situations. CARE launched a Human Rights Initiative in January 1999, which seeks to raise awareness and promote shared understanding of human rights by training, conducting research, and promoting a rights-based approach to programming in CARE's global work. Oxfam has provided leadership in developing gender training and theoretical material. The International Committee of the Red Cross initiated the Impact of War on Women Project. Save the Children U.S. developed a series of field guides to address the needs of children in emergencies that includes a Gender-Based Violence Prevention and Response volume.

REPATRIATION AND REINTEGRATION

Women from the affected communities should be involved in determining the postconflict needs of women and girls, and must be fully taken into account in the formulation of repatriation and resettlement plans, as well as during the demobilization and disarmament process.

Rehabilitation and reintegration programs must take into account the wide extent of sexual assault and rape and formulate programs to address the specific needs of survivors. Special initiatives must be developed to ensure that the security and subsistence concerns of war widows and other female heads-of-household are addressed.

NGOs and UN agencies can provide valuable assistance by sharing their program reports, lessons learned, and experiences of working with refugee and IDP populations with agencies dealing with repatriation and reintegration of the same population. To date such collaboration and cooperation have not occurred effectively.

Governments in IDP countries and all parties should abide by and ensure enforcement of the Guiding Principles on Internal Displacement. Governments must adopt effective measures to guarantee that the particular security concerns of women and children displaced by the conflict are met, including measures against rape and other gender-based violence. Governments and the international community should take immediate action to ensure that IDPs have access to basic services, particularly in regard to food, shelter, health, education, and protection.

REFUGEE AND IDP CAMP GENDER-BASED VIOLENCE MANAGEMENT

Promote use of the UNHCR Guidelines on the Protection of Refugee Women to address gender-based violence and to guide the

organization of both refugee and IDP camps. The physical structure and design of camps should be done in consultation with
the displaced with input and guidance from women. Full participation of refugee women in planning and providing services is
essential. Special consideration should be given to providing protection for vulnerable groups. Female community leaders should
play significant roles in camp management, especially regarding
protection, the allocation and layout of shelter, and in setting
up safe havens for at-risk women and girls. Women beneficiaries
should be involved in setting up mechanisms to meet the needs
of unaccompanied adolescents, the elderly, and the disabled.

Women should be properly registered and should carry their
own documentation. Camp management must ensure their
equal access to camp services and essential goods such as food,
fuel, and water. Distributions should be monitored and staffed by
females and males. Female-headed households should be regularly spot-checked to assess food security and shelter.

Latrines, water sources, clothes washing, and bathing facilities
should be central, secured with locks, and well lit. Female security guards should be stationed at locations frequented by women
and children.

ENSURING COMPLIANCE BY LOCAL NGOS AND REFUGEE CAMP OFFICIALS

International NGOs and UN agencies should not assume that
local NGO partners understand gender equity or international
human rights and humanitarian laws. Therefore their services
should be monitored and their activities spot-checked to ensure
that women have equal access to entitlements and that no
gender-based violence or exploitation of vulnerable people
occur. Monitoring, supervision, and training must occur at the
point nearest to service delivery because that is where violations
occur. Visual, unannounced, spot-checking by experienced staff
is the best deterrent to abuses that occur during food and nonfood item distributions, at wood and fuel distribution points, and
at water collection sites. Large illustrative posters strategically

placed at distribution points are also very helpful in reminding women and other beneficiaries of their rights but also in reminding male staff to respect the rights of women and the rules and policies of the organization they work for.

International NGOs and UN agencies can promote gender equality by requiring local NGO implementing partners to hire gender-balanced staff. International organizations should insist that women are represented on refugee management teams in appropriate percentages based on the population of the camps. Unless women participate in camp management their voices and concerns will not be heard. Neither literacy nor the ability to speak English should be requirements for active participation in camp management. Those skills would not be required for women to participate in civil society in their home villages and towns.

Coordination among NGOs and UN agencies

Protection issues and gender-based violence cut across every sector of humanitarian assistance and should not be relegated to "women's interests." These issues should be included general coordination meetings and in health, protection, food distribution, and community services meetings.

SUGGESTIONS FOR FIELD-BASED RELIEF WORKERS

All field workers need training in gender awareness, human rights laws, and the convention on the rights of the child. Field staff—international and national—must be able to recognize exploitation and abuse of women and children and know what correct actions to take.

Field workers are well positioned to make tremendous differences in the lives of women and children in emergency situations. Once field workers understand the issues and know how to recognize the signs of gender-based violence and child abuse they can be the best advocates for change. Unfortunately, most workers are not aware of abuses. Unless people know what to look for they might not notice abuses in the food distribution line, for example.

RECOMMENDATIONS

The length of the following list of recommendations is indicative of the distance yet to be covered by all agencies and actors involved in humanitarian assistance in order to end gender-based violence and exploitation of women and children in complex emergencies.

- Conduct regular comprehensive assessments of needs, risk factors, and capacities of beneficiaries—particularly of women, children, adolescents, disabled, and the elderly
- Guarantee equal access for women to relief items and services
- Provide gender sensitivity and human rights training for all relief workers, with periodic frequent reviews for relief rations distribution staff

Gender Checklist for Field Workers

1. Training for all staff working in field location sites serving displaced populations on:
- Gender awareness and preventing gender-based violence
- Geneva Conventions and Protocols (especially Pro. 1, Art. 75, Sec. 3)
- Convention on the Elimination of All Forms of Discrimination against Women (CEDAW)
- Convention on the Rights of the Child (CRC)
- Universal Declaration of Human Rights
2. UN and international NGOs to provide written policy statements to all field workers and provide guidance in how to carry out policies under difficult circumstances.
3. Field workers' guidelines and manuals:
- The Sphere Project Manual
- UNHCR Guidelines for the Protection of Refugee Women
- UN Guiding Principles on Internally Displaced Persons

- Improve the quality, quantity, appropriateness, and variety of food distributed
- Standardize accountability reporting for all implementing agencies
- Monitor relief item distribution with follow-up household livelihood analyses including use of distributed goods
- Expand participation of women, elderly, disabled, and adolescents in operational programs by seeking constructive inputs on design and implementation
- Improve coordination and collaboration among operational agencies
- All parties to take measures to protect women and girls from rape and other forms of sexual violence
- State publicly that rape in the conduct of armed conflict constitutes a war crime and may constitute a crime against humanity under defined circumstances, and that anyone who commits rape will be brought to justice
- Investigate all reports of rape and other forms of gender-based violence; prosecute those alleged to have committed such crimes
- Those who have survived sexual violence need to be protected from further attacks and receive appropriate treatment for the physical and psychological consequences. The treatment must be given confidentially and in a manner that is sensitive to the local culture
- Ensure appropriate training is provided to prosecutors, judges, and other officials in handling cases involving rape and other forms of gender-based violence in times of armed conflict and in peacetime, in accordance with current standards of international law
- Ensure that the training of armies and police includes training on international human rights and humanitarian law and that those dealing with women's cases have expertise addressing violence against women and gender-based crimes

CONCLUSION

The source of much of the suffering of women and children in emergency situations stems from their lack of access to food and

other entitled resources and services provided for refugees and
IDPs. When refugee women heads-of-households receive the
basic items to which they are entitled—food rations, plastic sheeting, pots and pans, blankets, equal job and training opportunities—they are much less likely to enter into sexual bartering or
to accept exploitative and abusive living arrangements with inappropriate partners. Not only are such coping measures harmful
to women but also they represent violations to the rights of
women. The denial of equal access to food and other entitlements goes against the policies of United Nations, international
NGOs, and donors who provide assistance to refugees and IDPs.

Women refugees' voices are seldom heard. They have little say
in camp management, design, or operations, and yet women and
children make up approximately 80 percent of the population in
most camps. Women in refugee and IDP camps are less likely to
be selected as camp managers, leaders, or community educators
and trainers than men because fewer women speak English (hiring English speakers is a convenience to international workers—
not a requirement for efficiency).

In the interest of space, this chapter did not address a number
of important issues that affect the lives of women and children,
such as health and safe motherhood. The reader is encouraged
to consult the reading list for more comprehensive information.

Greater participation of women refugees in decision-making
roles that influence camp management—especially in food distribution—will reduce the abuse and exploitation of women and
will greatly improve the living conditions of children and adolescents. Women must be involved in food distribution and monitoring to prevent men from making demands on women
recipients. Moreover, the responsibility to monitor closely the actions and comportment of actors at the point of delivery of goods
and services rests with the organizations receiving funding for
the operation—normally international NGOs or UN agencies.
Donors can put pressure on the organizations they fund to be
more accountable for the actions of their staff and the staff of
their local partners. Agencies responsible for overall refugee and

IDP camp management must assume responsibility for protecting the rights and the physical security of the people under their
oversight. The agencies most likely to be responsible for refugees
and IDPs are the UNHCR, UNICEF, and the International Office
of Migration (IOM). Agencies are urged to take proactive stands
to protect women and children from gender-based violence.
Agencies' staff need to know what to look for regarding gender-
based violence and will require training in order to recognize
and prevent gender-based violence.

A gender perspective must pervade all activities in humanitarian assistance. International and local organizations' staff need
to be trained in gender principles so they may be sensitive to
and understand the different roles, rights, and obligations men,
women, and children hold in the cultural groups with which they
work. The "gender-blindness" of refugee aid must end.

8
Clinical Aspects of Malnutrition

Kevin M. Cahill, M.D.

A FUTURE VOLUME in this international humanitarian books series will consider the multiple facets of food relief during and following natural and man-made disasters. It is a complex topic with significant philosophic, agricultural, and economic, as well and nutritional, implications. In this book on the operational response to an emergency, it is important to include at least a partial clinical presentation of malnutrition. A medical chapter focusing on a common health problem gives a human face to a crisis, allowing us to appreciate the extent of the damage and suffering inflicted in complex emergencies, especially on children.

The majority of the world's population survives with hunger and infections as constant companions and lives in "accident-prone" nations where famine and epidemic diseases often complicate the civil conflicts and natural disasters that are, unfortunately, regular events. Television pictures of the skeletal starving are the tragic, terminal images in a complex cycle of progressive malnutrition, especially in victims already burdened by an incredible array of dangerous parasitic, bacterial, and viral organisms. Since widespread hunger and the existence—or even threat—of contagions are the most common reasons offered to justify international humanitarian interventions, it is important that all involved in determining and effecting foreign policy be familiar with the evolving face of famine.

Famines have occurred in all areas of the globe in every period of recorded history, but our era has the odious distinction of being the period when more people will die of famine than in any previous century. To appreciate this indictment fully, it is necessary to realize that today mass death by starvation is rarely due to the vagaries of nature alone but reflects, rather, human decisions. Today's famines are man-made, for we have the ability to control short-term food deficits.[1]

Many factors can cause a local crop failure—droughts, floods, locusts, the spread of the desert, toxins, the erosion or exhaustion of soil—but in our modern world of instant communications and rapid transport, there must be an almost calculated effort for famine to flourish. Political decisions—or indecision—ignorance, neglect, and economic and cultural conflicts cause famines today. During periods of peace, corruption and mismanagement may lead to famine. The need for foreign exchange may force food-rich nations to export essential nutrients, leaving the indigenous populations to waste away. Wars, however, are the major man-made cause of famines, disrupting populations and the patterns of planting and harvesting essential for fruitful agriculture. Food stores are looted and hoarded, and supply lines are cut.

The developed nations of the world control the critical surplus of food supplies and have the capacity to both make and resolve or, as is too often the case, simply ignore famines. Throughout the developing world, famines develop on a fragile nutritional foundation where dietary intake is usually woefully inadequate and parasites, such as blood-sucking hookworms, drain their human hosts of protein, vitamin, and iron stores. The physical effects of malnutrition can be readily measured: low weight, stunted growth, frail bone structure, high infant and child morbidity and mortality rates, and decreased work capacity and intellectual performance. Acute prolonged malnutrition also impairs mental development, leading to tragedies that last for generations. The ultimate irony is that the vulnerable poor who are most often affected are the ones who need both the maximum physical and mental health to survive with their meager resources and harsh environmental challenges.

Although I had managed isolated outbreaks of acute malnutrition in Somalia for over a decade, the Sahel famine in the mid-1970s was my introduction to the chaos that stalks large-scale starvation. The traditional supportive nomad society seemed to disintegrate as more than a million refugees overwhelmed the land. Confusion reigned as neither the government nor clan structures could sustain the flood of utterly dependent persons. Most families had become separated, and the individual daily search for food and water dominated the escalating desperation. Infants, children, pregnant women, and the elderly died in disproportionate numbers while the stronger adults prevailed. The apathy and lethargy of a refugee camp contribute to the impression of imminent disaster.[2]

Those people most severely affected can present a clinical picture of great variety. At one end of the spectrum are the walking ghosts with marasmus, the victims of rapid, extensive caloric deficiency or, in a single word, starvation. At the opposite end are those suffering from chronic protein deficiency, or kwashiorkor. As in most disease states, the majority falls between these classic poles.

The child with marasmus leaves the impression of an old man's face on an infant's body. There is obvious wasting of muscles with total loss of subcutaneous fat. The buttocks disappear and the skin is loose and wrinkled. Scrawny limbs seem incapable of supporting the typical swollen body. The bony skull appears disproportionately large, and the knees stand out as awkward knobs. Eye lesions and skin rashes, with infected "tropical ulcers," are frequent. Diarrhea is the rule, and complete rectal prolapse from weakness of the anal orifice is not uncommon. A simple measurement of height and weight on a growth chart will document marked stunting. Nevertheless, the marasmic child is almost surprisingly alert, showing constant indications of hunger such as sucking and grasping movements. They are, however, patently weak and they rapidly tire, becoming short of breath after the slightest exertion.

Fat stores are mobilized, glucose uptake by muscle is reduced, and the amino acids, released from tissue breakdown, are used for the resynthesis of other proteins. These adaptations are associated with increased cortisol and diminished insulin activity. Economy is required in the use of resources in order to maintain processes essential for life. There is a reduction in the basal metabolic rate, in cardiac output, in sodium and sweat excretion, and the immune system is compromised.

This clinical picture is not due solely to starvation but reflects the added burden of multiple parasitic and respiratory infections. Malaria is extremely common in the tropics, and measles and tuberculosis are rife. Marasmus is very often precipitated, and almost always accompanied by, infection, the clinical signs of which may be modified by the profound depression of immunity. Other frequent and often fatal infections include enteritis, monoliasis, generalized herpes simplex, pneumonia, and gram negative septicemia.

Kwashiorkor is the other major protein deficiency disease. It was almost unknown to the Somali nomads because their customary diet of camel's milk and occasional goat meat is very rich in protein. I cannot recall seeing a single case of kwashiorkor in Somalia before the Sahelian drought of 1976, and there is surely nothing subtle about the striking features of kwashiorkor in the black African.[3]

In 1933, Cicily Williams, working in West Africa, described a clinical syndrome characterized by edema, dermatosis, a fatty liver, discolored hair, and irritability in young children who had to be abruptly weaned from the mother's breast by the arrival of a new baby. She gave the syndrome the name "kwashiorkor," a Ga word that literally translated means "the sickness of the other child when the next baby is born."

Kwashiorkor is a complex abnormality of metabolism induced by malnutrition. The liver fails to synthesize export proteins such as serum albumin, lipoprotein, and prealbumin, resulting in hypoalbuminemia with generalized edema, gross fatty infiltration of the liver, and a fall in retinol binding protein that may precipitate vitamin A deficiency. There is cessation of growth, loss of tissue weight, sodium retention, loss of temperature control, and depression of the immune processes, the lymphoid pattern being rather similar to that seen in HIV infection. Kwashiorkor represents a failure of adaption to protein calorie malnutrition and is precipitated when the protein of the diet must be utilized for gluconeogenesis.

As mentioned earlier, there is nothing subtle about the striking features of kwashiorkor in an African child. Marked edema is usually first seen in the legs, but the face is also affected; the eyes become puffy and the cheeks droop to give the characteristic "moon face." Edema of the penis may be mistaken for phimosis. The children are apathetic and constantly whining. The hands and feet feel cold, and though obscured by edema, marked muscle wasting can be readily appreciated, especially in the upper arms and around the scapulae. The hair often turns a soft red or white and becomes straight and limp in contrast to the black, crisp, curly hair of the healthy African child.

An "enamel paint" or "cracked pavement" rash is characteristic; it starts as small, purple-stained areas that evolve into black, varnished patches with sharp edges. These coalesce, crack, and peel, leaving desquamated areas resembling burns. The rash is similar in appearance to that of pellagra, but differs in affecting pressure zones such as the napkin or the inguinal region, knees, elbows, trunk, and trochanteric area. The abdomen is prominent, the liver enlarged, and congestive heart failure is often the terminal complication. Xerophthalmia or even keratomalacia may be present. The serum albumin ranges from 0.4 g to 2.0 g per 100 ml and levels below 0.8 g per 100 ml carry a poor prognosis.

Micronutrient deficiencies also contribute to the clinical spectrum of famine. Ancient scourges such as scurvy, pellagra, and beriberi—due to lack of vitamin C, niacin, and thiamine, respectively—are common problems in the severely malnourished. Inadequate vitamin A is recognized as a frequent cause of serious eye problems in refugee camps. Iron-deficient diets can produce profound anemias, especially in the most vulnerable groups—pregnant women and young children.

There were no laboratories in the Somali refugee camps I directed. Fortunately, there was little need for scientific confirmation to permit a working diagnosis for either marasmus or kwashiorkor. Therapy can be extremely challenging, and deaths can be caused by inappropriate actions as well as neglect. Forced feeding can precipitate both diarrhea and aspiration pneumonia. Washing a child can exacerbate hypothermia, and it is better to have a dirty child than a dead one. The careful replacement of fluids, calories, and specific nutrients must be coordinated with the therapy for concurrent infections.

Tuberculosis is a rampant problem in most crowded refugee camps, and establishing isolation tents must be a priority since dissemination of contagious diseases among the immunocompromised malnourished is a lethal combination. The usual benign course of measles, for example, becomes a deadly scourge in the setting of a refugee camp; the greatest tragedy is to watch children who have managed to survive starvation and long treks to the relative security of a feeding station then succumb in epidemic numbers to an infection such as measles, which could have been prevented by a simple vaccine costing less than ten cents.

There is, however, evidence that the relationship of malnutrition and infection is not always synergistic; an appreciation of this phenomenon is essential for those charged with food relief programs. There have been many documented outbreaks of diseases only after food supplies are restored. Malaria, for example, appears to decline among those strong enough to survive starvation and then reaches fatal epidemic levels only after intensive refeeding efforts begin. Relief workers have long been aware that their well-meaning efforts may actually be causing unnecessary deaths, thereby defeating the whole purpose of international humanitarian intervention.

Recent scientific studies offer an explanation for the transient protective effect of malnutrition against malaria. As essential nutrients, such as para-aminobenzoic acid (PABA) and vitamin E, decline, the malaria parasite cannot develop in the deficient human red cell. As refeeding programs correct these imbalances, fatal malaria outbreaks occur. PABA and vitamin E are high in grain and low in milk and meat products. The implications for those charged with nutrition planning in famine situations such as in Somalia are obvious. The Hippocratic Oath begins with the phrase *primum non nocere*—the first thing is to do no harm. Poorly conceived refeeding programs after famines can kill; the vast mountains of surplus grain may prove fatal if not integrated with appropriate supplemental antimalarial efforts.

Even in optimal circumstances—which hardly describe a Somali refugee camp—the period of rehabilitation for a patient with marasmus is judged in terms of months rather than days, and the pressure of new problems for an overworked health team frequently results in inadequate attention during recovery, inevitably ending in a rapid deterioration and death.

The role of a physician in managing catastrophic famine is not limited to the traditional diagnostic and therapeutic approach of the profession. He or she must learn to organize truck convoys, establish basic camps, and develop a team that will enable the food donated or purchased to reach the hungry masses. The physician-leader in this situation must emphasize hope rather than disease, offering a future to those who have lost their past.

Medical school training rarely prepares one for such challenges. The essential qualities required to serve effectively in such situations are not built on technical details that can be memorized, but must be based rather on the broad traditions that once made medicine a noble and learned profession.

The clinical faces of famine in Somalia are seared in my mind. The picture of marasmus or kwashiorkor tells a tale that few can evade, for it stares into our souls.[4]

Figure 8.1

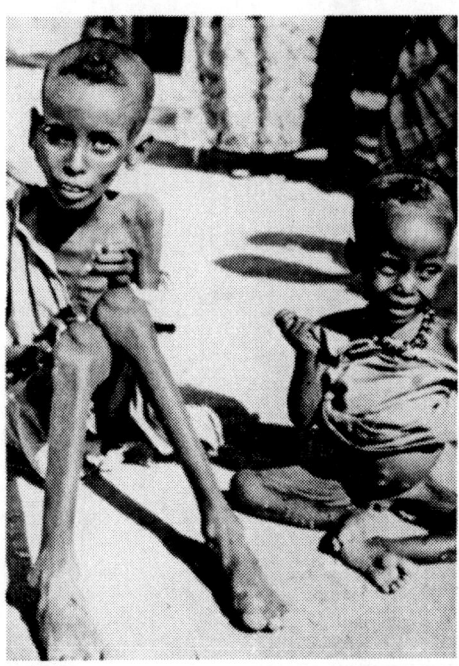

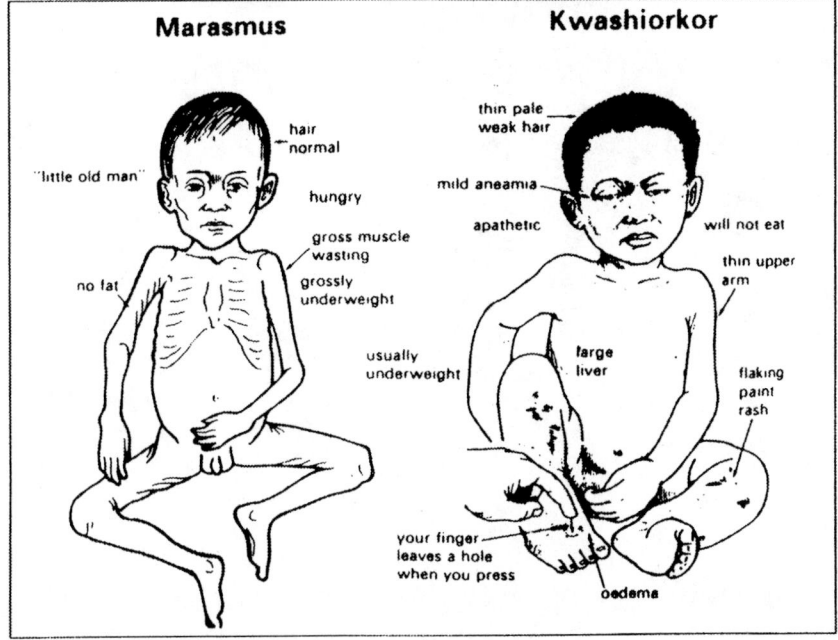

The tragedy of malnutrition in a Somali refugee camp is seen in classic marasmus (L) and kwashiorkor (R).

Part 3

The ability to deliver humanitarian assistance in the chaos that follows natural disasters and, especially, in the midst of armed conflict has always been a challenge. The International Red Cross movement was founded by a humanitarian shocked by horrendous conditions that faced the wounded and captured after a battle. Today, it is no longer only professional solders who are in danger in armed conflict; the vast majority of those wounded and killed in current conflicts are civilians caught in the cross-fire, and humanitarian workers trying to help. In recent decades, in UN relief operations, the armed Blue Beret peacekeepers have had fewer injuries than humanitarian workers. Many humanitarian relief operations require the logistical and armed support that can be provided only by the military. Yet there are inherent, almost cultural, differences between a military and a humanitarian organization. These are explored in a detailed chapter by a senior British Army General with exceptional experience in humanitarian crises. A dead or injured humanitarian worker does no good for anyone. The security measures that must be followed to maximize safety in a dangerous, volatile, complex emergency are also reviewed in this section.

9
Military/NGO Interaction

Major General Timothy Cross

INTRODUCTION

BY THE MID-1990s the International Committee of the Red Cross (ICRC)[1] judged that the human costs of conflicts and disasters of one sort or another were overwhelming the world's ability to respond. There were fifty-six conflicts in progress at that time, most reflecting the move away from both territorial disputes between states and wars of decolonization, to what some now call "wars of identity."[2]

Conflict has always been essentially tribal, but increasingly individuals seem to identify more with their ethnicity and perceived nationality than with their ruling governments; many seem prepared to fight for that identity. Sandwiched between the globe and the individual, the tribe or ethnic group looms larger, and there is an emerging sense that in the age of globalization, individuals increasingly feel a need to express their uniqueness; globalization leads people to ask "Who am I?" Most states are made up of more than one nation, which are themselves cultural entities of language, history, etc., and these nations seem to want recognition, whether that be Scotland or Kosovo.[3] The demise of the Soviet Union, and with it, ironically, the relative safety of the cold war, has certainly liberated those who had previously been constrained by super-power politics, and the results have been catastrophic. In the mid-1990s, while numbers vary from source to source, there were a conservative 17 million refugees and 26 million internally displaced homeless people (IDPs) around the world. Some conflicts, like those in Bosnia, have been very apparent to us; others, like that in Tajikistan, where the civil war resulted in an estimated 50,000 deaths, 500,000 economic émigrés, and 600,000 IDPs, went on almost unnoticed.[4]

Events over the last five years have served only to strengthen the ICRC's concerns. At the turn of the millennium, the Russian army mounted fresh assaults on Chechnya, and 200,000 refugees fled to the neighboring republic of Ingushetia; many still struggle to survive in makeshift shelters and old railway carriages. In Indonesia and East Timor, around the Great Lakes of Central Africa, in Sri Lanka, Sierra Leone, and the Sudan,[5] conflicts rumble on and millions more suffer and die. Operations continue in the Balkans, with Kosovo taking center stage for most of 1999, and British-led international forces (ISAF) are currently in Kabul, while the Americans, supported by British Royal Marine Commandos, continue to respond to the dramatic events of September 11, 2001, elsewhere in Afghanistan.

U.S. historian Barbara Tuchman once estimated that wars in the twentieth century killed 150 million people. Unlike earlier centuries, it is certain that the majority of those killed were noncombatant civilians; indeed, the percentage of civilian, as compared to military, casualties has increased from one in twenty (5 percent) 100 years ago to nine in every ten (90 percent) today; around 5 million civilian lives have been lost in the last decade alone.[6] Refugees, says Robert Fox, are now part of the culture of the criminality inherent in intra-state conflicts,[7] and women, children, and the elderly will continue to be indiscriminately and deliberately targeted by "rebel" movements as part of the asymmetric threat to unstable governments.

British military forces have been involved in the planning or execution of well over thirty separate operational deployments during the last dozen years: in the preceding forty-five years it was involved in only seven (see table 9.1).

Over the years of my service in the 1970s and 1980s, I served on U.K. operations in Northern Ireland and with the UN in Cyprus; in the 1990s I deployed with the "allies" in the Gulf and three times with NATO in the Balkans. Operation AGRICOLA, the deployment to Kosovo in 1999, was, however, the first time

Table 9.1 A Decade of British Military Operations

Location/Mission	Period
Northern Ireland—PE	Ongoing
Cyprus—UN monitoring	Ongoing
Gulf War—WF	1990–91
Kurdistan—HA	1991
S Iraq—No fly zone enforcement	Ongoing
Middle East (sp to SOUTHERN WATCH)	Ongoing
Bosnia—PK & HA	1991–95
Rwanda—HA	1994–95
Zaire—NEO (Planned)	1995
Bosnia—PE	1995–96
DRC—NEO (Planned)	1996
Monserrat Island—Evacuation	1996–97
Sierra Leone—Monitoring & NEO Planning	1997
DRC—NEO (Planned)	1997
ALBANIA—NEO (Planned)	1997
ALBANIA—NEO (Planned)	1997
Bosnia—PK	1997–98
Sierra Leone—Monitoring & NEO Planning	1998
Bosnia—PK	Ongoing
Brunei—Fire fighting (contingency role)	Ongoing
Honduras—DR/HA	1998
Georgia—UN monitoring	Ongoing
As above on standby	Ongoing
Kosovo—OSCE monitoring	1998–99
Kosovo—Extraction force (FYROM based)	1998–99
Kosovo—Air War, PE, HA & PK	1999
Albania—HA	1999

Table 9.1   (Continued)

Location/Mission	Period
East Timor—PK & HA	1999–2000
Mozambique—DR & HA	2000
Sierra Leone—NEO & PK	Ongoing
Afghanistan—ISAF PK	Ongoing
Afghanistan—WF	Ongoing

Note: See figure 9.6 for mission abbreviations.

that I came face to face with a large-scale humanitarian crisis. (See Appendix 2.) It was a challenging and demanding deployment for me, professionally and personally, but it was nonetheless "simply" another in a series of operations where U.K. Armed Forces have been faced with humanitarian action. Bosnia, Iraq, Rwanda, Angola, East Timor, and Sierra Leone involved armed conflict; Mozambique, Honduras, and Monserrat, natural disasters; Kurdistan and Albania, humanitarian assistance. All created widespread human suffering. On the evidence of the 1990s, such deployments are on the increase—and the first two years of the twenty-first century have done nothing to refute this.

Among the many challenges that these operations bring with them, the one that struck me the hardest was working alongside, and indeed for, large numbers of civilian agencies. These agencies can be international, like the UNHCR and WFP; governmental, like the United Kingdom's Department for Foreign International Development (DFID); or NGOs like the ICRC, the Oxford Committee for Famine Relief (OXFAM), and *Médecins sans frontières* (MSF). The reality of intra-state conflict and natural disasters is that such organizations are present in large numbers; they bring real strengths to bear and are key players in bringing relief to those who suffer. The military need to learn more about them, about how they operate, and about how we can work better with them.[8]

The "Humanitarian" Agencies

While relationships between the military and civilian humanitarians have certainly intensified over the last decade, they are by no means new. As Hugo Slim notes in a series of excellent articles,[9] the ICRC was born in 1863 out of the Battle of Solferiono, the Save the Children Fund (SCF) in 1919 out of the First World War, and OXFAM and the U.S. Committee for Aid and Relief Everywhere (CARE) out of the Second World War in 1942 and 1945, respectively. He points out that, to a large degree, "militarism and humanitarianism have represented two sides of the same coin—humankind's inability to manage conflict peacefully."[10]

There are three primary humanitarian forces: the NGOs, the UN, which Kofi Annan has come to personify perhaps more than any other official for generations, and the governmental agencies, most of whom have been born out of the liberal democracies of the northern hemisphere. NGOs exist primarily, if not solely, to provide relief from suffering and, in today's world, to try to bring about sustainable development, addressing the failures of governments and society as a whole. Slim defines them as "a wide range of primarily nonprofit organizations motivated by humanitarian and religious values, and that are usually independent of government, UN, and commercial sectors."[11] Ranging in size from large international and transnational organizations[12] to very small local groups who "send a cow" to Africa or Asia, there has been an explosion in their numbers over the last twenty years[13] (see fig. 9.1).

Worldwide, there are now over fifteen hundred international NGOs registered as "observers" with the UN. Nonetheless, of the hundreds in existence there remains a serious "1st XI," through which perhaps 75 percent of all emergency aid flows. They are a powerful force in the world, in many cases providing the dynamics for change, and the revolution in communications technology and in networking has only served to strengthen them further, especially in the last five years.[14]

Figure 9.1

"NGO Swarming"

Nongovernmental Organizations (in thousands)

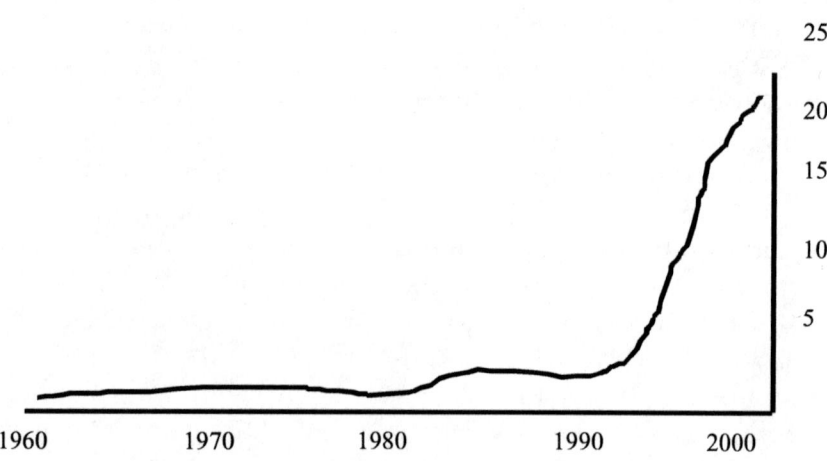

Source: *The Economist,* December 11, 1999.

These NGOs operate alongside, and often for, a wide range of governmental and international aid and relief agencies. The UN itself spawned a number in its early years, including the UNHCR and WFP, for although the UN Charter mentions the term NGO in Article 71, such organizations were, as noted above, relatively few and far between and were not the major players they are today.[15] International/governmental aid agencies can be "multilateral," like the UN or the World Bank, or "bilateral," like the U.S. Agency for International Development (USAID) or DFID. Funded by taxpayers to the tune of billions per year, these agencies have changed the shape of the world, for good or ill.

CULTURES

There are many who argue that these governmental and international aid and relief agencies do little good and often real harm,[16] but before looking in detail at my perceptions, particularly of the NGOs and the UNHCR, it is important to recognize that we are not talking about generic, impersonal bureaucracies, but people. All organizations, both military and nonmilitary, are comprised of unique, individual people. Molded in the womb, raised and nurtured by parents alongside siblings and peers, softened perhaps by family and friends but hardened and tempered by their environment and day-to-day life, through success and failure, rivalries and challenges, these individual people come together within organizations that themselves have identities. The UN agencies and the NGOs are not single organizations; they are a mix, in the same way that military forces around the world are a mix, of professional and amateur, effective and ineffective, efficient and inefficient.

In dealing with organizations we are inevitably dealing with their culture, ethos, and psyche, and in order to understand them it seems to me that one must at least have an understanding of their nature, and the nature of the people within them—what drives them. There has been a great deal of work done on cultural theory, and there are many models.

Geert Hofstede is arguably the most authoritative author on institutional culture; his well-known works include *Culture Consequences* and *Cultures and Organizations: Software of the Mind*. In these he stress that:

- Culture is learned, not inherited. It derives from one's social environment, not from one's genes. Culture should be distinguished from human nature on one side and from an individual's personality on the other, although exactly where the borders lie is a matter of discussion among social scientists
- It is the collective programming of the mind that distinguishes the members of one group of people from another

He identifies four ways in which different cultures may be seen to manifest themselves: through *symbols, heroes, rituals,* and *values.* The first three he describes as practices specific to a cultural group—and relatively unimportant. The fourth manifestation, however, is by far the most important and transcends all others. His "onion diagram," shown in fig. 9.2, illustrates this quite clearly and shows that *values* form the cultural core of an organization.

These manifestations, or outward cultural indicators, serve to identify different cultural groups, but Hofstede also proposed a method to measure degrees of cultural convergence or divergence between groups. He used four comparative metrics, each one of which may be considered in terms of a measurable (comparable) sliding scale from one polar extreme to another (see fig. 9.3).

Figure 9.2
Cultural Manifestations—Hofstede's "Onion Diagram"

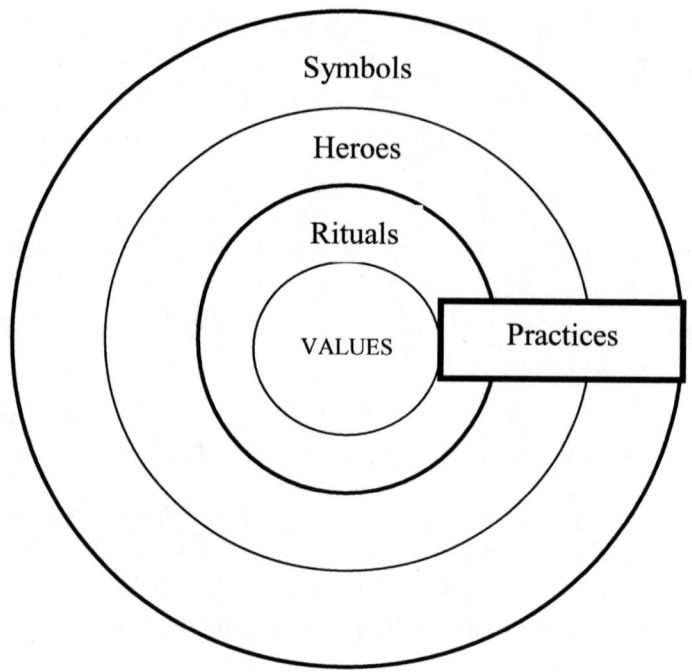

Figure 9.3

Hofstede's Cultural Dimension

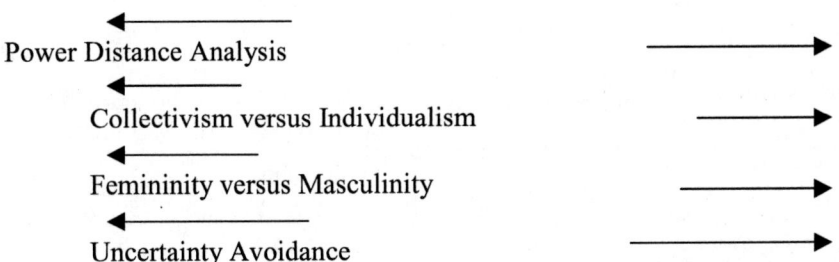

Tomlinson[17] has explored the cultural differences between the military and nonmilitary agencies in chapter 3 of his excellent dissertation. The key areas are shown in table 9.2. He rightly highlights that the British military, for example, are remarkably diverse in terms of appearance, rituals, symbols, heroes, etc., yet there is a core value of military culture; individuals must be willing to subordinate themselves to the common good, the team, and the task.

In his work, Tomlinson analyzed Hofstede's Cultural Dimensions, producing an interesting analysis that showed:

- A significant culture gap between the military and nonmilitary humanitarian agencies in the Power Distance indicators—the military displaying very strong traits
- A very wide culture gap in the area of Uncertainty Avoidance. The military's near obsession with order, clarity, conservation, and discipline sits very uncomfortably with the NGOs' more ambiguous, chaotic, abstract, overly democratic, and tolerant working environment

To reinforce these findings, Larry Minnear, in his post-Kosovo analysis, noted:

Western militaries are paid, trained, and equipped to use organized and regulated violence to accomplish objectives set by democratic governments. Military culture places high value on command-and-control, including top-down organizational structure, clear lines of authority, discipline, and accountability. The military gives high priority to logistics, with the necessary "force

Table 9.2 Cultural Dimensions

Cultural Dimension 1—Power Distance

	Small Power Distance (−)	Large Power Distance (+)
A	There should be interdependence between less and more powerful people.	Less powerful people should be dependent on the more powerful. Clear polarization between groups.
B	Decentralization is popular.	Centralization is popular.
C	Subordinates expect to be consulted.	Subordinates expect to be told what to do.
D	Organizational hierarchies are established for convenience only.	Hierarchies reflect the existential inequalities in people.
E	The ideal boss is a resourceful democrat.	The ideal boss is a benevolent autocrat or good father.
F	Privilege and status are frowned on.	Privilege and status for bosses are expected and popular.

Cultural Dimension 2—Collectivism vs. Individualism

	Collectivist (−)	Individualist (+)
A	Identity is based on the social network in which one exists.	Identity is based on the individual.
B	People taught to think in terms of "we."	People taught to think in terms of "I."
C	Seek harmony not confrontation.	Speaking one's mind is a sign of an honest person.
D	Employment relationships regarded as a family link—strong moral dimension.	Relationships based on contract and mutual advantage.
E	Management is of groups.	Management is of individuals.
F	Relationship prevails over task.	Task prevails over relationship.

Cultural Dimension 3—Femininity vs. Masculinity

	Feminine (−)	Masculine (+)
A	Welfare society ideal.	Performance society ideal.
B	The needy should be helped.	The strong should be supported.

C	Relatively high number of females employed.	Relatively small number of female employees.
D	Pacifistic.	Militaristic.
E	Peace and harmony through dialogue and example.	Peace through superior firepower.
F	Equal means granting equal status and rights to all.	Equality means being forced to admit nonconformists into the group.

Cultural Dimension 4—Uncertainty Avoidance

	Weak Uncertainty Avoidance (−)	Strong Uncertainty Avoidance (+)
A	Few and general regulations.	Many precise regulations.
B	If rules cannot be respected they should be changed.	If rules are broken, sinners should be punished.
C	Dissent is expectable.	Dissent is repressed.
D	Tolerance and moderation prevail.	Conservatism and good order prevails
E	One's values should not be imposed on others.	There is only one right way and it's ours.
F	High tolerance of ambiguity.	Low tolerance of ambiguity.

protection" to carry out tasks. The military invests heavily in human resources management, including training at all levels, leadership, redundancy of staff, and lessons-learning exercises.[18]

In contrast, Minnear believes that humanitarian organizations are less hierarchical, take a longer term view of their aid efforts, are more participatory in decision processes, invest relatively little in training—they simply cannot afford to maintain excess staff during noncrisis periods—and are less preoccupied with demonstrating their accountability or with learning from past experiences. Not surprisingly, he notes that, "Troops often have little patience for agencies that march to different drummers" and that "humanitarians often have little patience for the more coercive and directive approach of the military."

In support of Minnear—if it was needed—Thomas Wiess recently wrote, "It is hard to imagine two institutional cultures more different than the hierarchical military one and the more horizontal universe of the civilian humanitarian agencies. Interactions between these two cultures often present acute problems in complex emergencies."[19]

Notwithstanding this pessimistic assessment, Hofstede is clear that different cultures can work together, but only if they are forced to: "The most problematic are between groups that score very highly on Uncertainty Avoidance . . . and on Power Distance. In a world kept together by intercultural cooperation, such cultural groups will certainly not be forerunners. They may have to be left alone for some time until they discover they have no other choice but to join."

This is exactly the position the military and nonmilitary organizations now find themselves in: the reality is that we have no choice but to work together. Some time between 500 B.C. and 300 B.C., Sun Tzu wrote in his book, *The Art of War*, "If you know the enemy and know yourself, you need not fear the result of a hundred battles." Nonmilitary organizations are certainly not the enemy of the military, although it must be said that both sides sometimes portray them as such. Nonetheless, the principle holds true. To get the best results out of any relationship we must know both ourselves and those we work alongside. So, while recognizing that we can only brush the edges, it is worth at least assessing the psychology that lies behind nonmilitary organizations, setting it against the military ethos and psyche.

THE RAW MATERIAL: FIRED BY DUTY OR FIRED BY LOVE?

In discussions with Hugo Slim and others, and from my own observations, the development of individuals within the humanitarian community follows an intriguing progression. In early years, many pass through an "impetuous, altruistic" phase; some remain there! Wanting to alleviate suffering, they offer somewhat simplistic, if well-intentioned solutions. As a seven-year-old, Hugo Slim recalls wanting to hijack a jumbo jet, fill it full of food, fly out to Biafra, feed the hungry, and then be home in time for tea. Were that life was so simple! The twenties and thirties can often be "dysfunctional, chivalric, and politicization" phases. Wanting action and adventure, to be courageous and to demonstrate self-sacrifice, many within the humanitarian community drive around in 4x4s trying to change the world. They are "victim" orientated, and are often not really interested in the reasons for the conflict, or do not necessarily have a desire to find a solution, arguing that they are not a part of a "peace process."[20] Social justice and human rights drive them on; health, racism, poverty, gender relations, and the dangers of globalization are among the key issues.

While some remain rooted in that place, beyond these phases many, if not the majority, move into a "parental phase." Most, if not all, of the senior players I came across were intellectually and emotionally mature; they recognized the restraints and the reality of conflict. They, nonetheless, were driven to protect civilians wherever possible, providing security and relief, and to ensure human rights, equality, and dignity for all; they were also clear that the sovereignty of the individual and the sanctity of human life were not just academic phrases but important issues, and that war criminals, both military and political, should be prosecuted. They were, and are, impressive individuals.

These values are, to a large extent, universal, at least in the Western democracies, and most in the U.K. military would share them; we start in the same moral place, but take a different route to securing them. While within the U.K. military, most personnel would claim to be "humanitarian," the overall aim, nonetheless, is to bring the conflict to an end, through violence if necessary; military operational aims sometimes, by necessity, override suffering. In simplistic terms, the military are driven or fired by duty in the best sense of the word; they bring courage—both moral and physical—self-sacrifice, discipline, and order, with all the strengths that these bring in terms of output, structures, and control. Notwithstanding Hofstede's and Minnears's earlier comments, many military organizations are actually no more bound up with "authority" power than are comparable civilian organizations.[21] A military force is certainly large, centralized, and complex, but personalities matter, and mission command applies more today than ever in professional forces; commanders at all levels have the responsibility and authority to engage with everyone around them to achieve their mission. Not all are egotistic order givers, forcing compliance through threat—at best their directions flow smoothly like a natural stream, without harshness or aggression, but a relative gentleness that pulls people together naturally and focuses them on their respective tasks.

Any operational deployment has a number of "lines of operation;" the military line sits alongside the political, diplomatic, legal, economic, media, and humanitarian lines. To be effective, military commanders must face up to the challenges of shattered societies as well as direct military threats. They need to remain focused on their primary imperative, that of establishing a secure environment to enable the other lines to be developed, but balancing the various frictions is not easy. The British military in particular is rightly proud of its ability to work within these realities; decades of experience in many operational theaters have honed the skills necessary to balance and bring together the many players—in Northern Macedonia over the 1999 Easter weekend, those players included the tens of thousands of refugees, forty-five different NGOs, seven military contingents, Macedonian security forces, civilian contractors, media, and the many political and diplomatic pressures.

But taken to extreme the military can be too "task" orientated, becoming over-controlling, autocratic, and critical; the individual is held to be subservient to the greater good. State focused, with legitimacy coming from the state, the military are, by definition, political servants and are neither neutral, impartial, or independent. Too often we can forget individual needs and close our minds to others views; often our head rules our heart.[22]

The nonmilitary organizations on the other hand are driven or fired by love, again in the best sense of the word. They, too, bring courage and self-sacrifice, but also independence, individual nurturing, and encouragement; they are people, not state or task orientated. The NGOs exhibit softer, more manageable cultural traits than the military; traits that make them, generally, less confrontational and, generally, fairly effective in multicultural environments. There is rooted in their souls, a "blood-line" divide, which was often put there in their early years and which many struggle to cross in their search for moral and ethical virtues and a "what I stand for" doctrine. Nonetheless, taken to extremes, they can be self-indulgent, too focused on their particular human issue and, living within a "rights-based" culture, they can be resentful of control, morally arrogant, and blind to the dark side of individual human nature; often their heart rules their head.

Set within this context, and recognizing that I have skated over an extremely complex subject, we can now consider my perceptions of both the strengths and weaknesses[23] of the nonmilitary organizations, and draw out one or two conclusions.

STRENGTHS

Principled

Those who work for the humanitarian organizations are suspicious, if not scornful, of governments and institutions representing governments, including the military—often with good cause. It should not be forgotten that many NGOs were born out of the suffering caused not just indirectly but directly by military forces around the world, both ill-disciplined and unprofessional national armies and "rebel" or irregular forces. Nonetheless, the principles of independence, neutrality, and impartiality are usually tempered with a recognition that there is a "bottom line,"[24] as they face up to the conflicts between positive principles and negative imperatives—not to legitimize rebel movements, not to contribute to the war effort of either side, not to submit to government controls that interfere with their ability to fulfil their humanitarian mission. Recognizing that the very process of fulfilling the humanitarian imperative can mean that both neutrality and impartiality are compromised, and that their involvement does influence a conflict, their approach is to "minimize" rather than "do no harm." In an effort to match their principles, many take real risks and face real hardships.[25] They are prepared to work in dangerous areas and on both sides of a conflict, often moving between and across factional borders or boundaries to places where the cause may seem hopeless but where there is real need. MSF, for example, was one of the few organizations supporting the Chechen refugees over the winter of 1999–2000—no government dared to do anything more tangible than issue statements, registering their "grave concerns." Operating in areas where there may be no front lines, real security, or protection, and where access is difficult, they are often vulnerable to warlords and bandits; 140 of them were killed between 1992 and 1997.[26] Let no one, particularly those of us who work for heavily armed military forces, backed by all that NATO stands for, disparage or dismiss these people.

Knowledgeable

They know their business. Those who deploy on NGO/UN operations have often done so for many years. They have served in many countries, through many conflicts, and can bring their considerable skills to bear effectively. Most specialize in particular areas of the business. The OXFAM team who arrived in Northern Macedonia included experts in water and sanitation who had been through the mill on many occasions and knew what was required; we met members of the same team again in Southern Albania and in Kosovo, and they displayed equal energy in all three countries. WFP specializes in food; they were impressive, working quietly and efficiently, moving and distributing enormous quantities of food. Individuals within the UNHCR and CARE were equally as impressive. Other NGOs focused on health, children's work, registration, or camp management; whatever their specialization, many were good at it, some very good.[27]

Committed

Those who work for the humanitarian community are drawn by a genuine desire to alleviate suffering in the world, in the widest sense, and to make a real difference in their chosen area of concern. Their organizations are usually committed for the long haul, not a short six-month tour, which is the usual length of time a U.K. solider is deployed on an operation. While some individuals do move in and out, the organization itself may well be committed to a particular area or problem for years, working with local staff and local engineers. They usually have been in country for many years, developing an understanding of the problems inherent within the situation; they may not have all of the answers, but they at least understand the questions. Because they are in it for the long term, they know that they will have to run with any "solutions," so they work hard to get it right. Ian Loring, for example, is a U.K. civilian who had been a successful lawyer in London before deciding to give up the rat race and work for the Laurasi Foundation in Erseke, Southern Albania. He had been there since before the fall of the Hoxeth regime, had lived through the turmoil of the 1990s, and was building a community of faithful workers attempting to alleviate real suffering. He, like so many others, may not have worn any campaign medals, but he certainly deserved a few. Such people are worth listening to, and having identified key individuals, I used them unmercifully! Even hardened cynics of the international aid business can agree that "NGO staffs are well motivated. They rarely do significant harm; sometimes they do great good."[28]

Networked

Knowing each other's organizations well, and often having strong individual personal relationships, the humanitarian community is usually predisposed to cooperate with one another. Most of the key NGOs are used to working with the UN. Multinational and multilingual organizations such as MSF, World Vision, and OXFAM are truly worldwide, with well-established contacts, both between each other and into governments and civil structures. Given devolved responsibility from the home-based HQ, the representatives on the ground operate under mission command; they have the authority to make decisions, and do so, being accountable to their donors and fellow workers.[29]

Linked to the Media

Importantly, these agencies are good at working with, if not manipulating, the media. With a bias toward drama, crisis, and controversy, there is a natural alliance. The media often accept the NGO/UN perspective and quote it uncritically, allowing them to voice their concerns and criticisms. Together they can effectively mobilize public opinion. Whatever the rights and wrongs of individual NGOs, they, together with the media, have become searchlights, illuminating and drawing attention to particular causes and conflicts, and influencing both the participants and the outside world community. Between them they are often the catalyst for a military deployment in the first place.[30] The world is now so interdependent and so vulnerable to public opinion mobilized by these humanitarian "lobbies" that, even where professional instinct and advice argues against intervention, Western governments in particular will often succumb. Global audiences, particularly those in the rich, liberal democracies, demand action of some sort—and humanitarian action, as Alan Roberts, the British historian, has pointed out, is usually much easier to reach agreement on than wider political action. As Western foreign policy increasingly includes human rights issues, staying neutral seems not to be an option. In Dante's *Inferno,* there is a special place of torment reserved for those who have remained neutral in life. Their sin is considered to be so grave that they are not even allowed into hell, only its vestibule, separated from hell by the river Acheron.[31]

The Role of Women

Finally, I was struck by the number of women who work within the humanitarian agencies, often over 50 percent. Their drive and professionalism were impressive, and they brought a palpable touch of humanity to the situation, especially working with the refugees. It is remarkable how many well-established NGOs owe their early success to energetic, tough, and determined women; the same applies today. Their numbers were in stark contrast to our male-dominated army, and they were too often dismissed by arrogant officers—many senior—who tended to either brush their opinions aside, condescendingly attempt to ingratiate themselves, or were simply distracted![32]

WEAKNESSES

That all said, like any organization, the UN/NGOs are far from perfect. My admiration for much that I saw was tempered with several harsh realities.

Resources

NGOs often lack resources, and their lean structures are simply not able to cope with twenty-four-hour operations. They need to find their own accommodation, food, transportation, communications, etc., and, unlike the military, prefer not to operate from the "field" but from offices and apartments. Even relatively large organizations, like the UNHCR, have no equivalent of a brigade headquarters. The ability to establish and operate from a "Tac HQ" and maintain a "Main HQ" a considerable distance away is simply beyond them. Traveling light may have advantages, but to sustain operations in all conditions over protracted periods needs a structured command team and the resources to sustain them; there was little evidence of either.[33] Key among resources are people. Inevitably the quality varies, but many that I met were young and inexperienced, with little staying power or self-discipline. With relatively impressive salaries and allowances, they often portrayed a moral arrogance and cultural imperialism that alienated local agencies and angered many of my officers and soldiers.[34]

Responsiveness

Recognizing the advantages inherent in our position in Macedonia, I was nonetheless taken aback at the length of time the various agencies, including the UNHCR, took to arrive, establish, and become effective. The refugee crises had been building for some time and should hardly have been a surprise, yet even the key medical NGOs took over a week to establish themselves at Brazda, even with our not insignificant assistance. While some individuals arrived after the Easter weekend, they were initially focused on their own administration—finding vehicles, accommodation, etc.—and then, frustratingly, spent hours, even days, driving around in their 4x4s talking over mobile phones as they seemingly dispassionately observed our operation.[35]

In stark comparison, the Israeli Defence Force (IDF) Field Hospital announced itself on Tuesday night (April 6) and was up and running and open for business within forty-eight hours. Many lives were saved by KFOR's medical facilities and by the IDF; one cannot help but wonder how many IDPs/refugees die around the world waiting for NGOs to get organized. While recognizing Macedonian bureaucracy, I reluctantly join those who level criticism at the "1st XI" NGOs and the UNHCR for being caught out in the first place, and for their inadequate field office staffing levels.[36] There were too many "chiefs," usually referred to as "spokespersons," and not enough "Indians," i.e., workers to get on and make a difference; and those that did sometimes portrayed an almost disinterested, callous view of events. This phenomenon Walkup ascribes to the emotional coping strategies that aid workers have to adopt in order to maintain effectiveness (and sanity).

Figure 9.4 illustrates these defense mechanisms and shows how they link back into the organizational culture of the NGOs discussed earlier.

In hindsight it is now easy to recognize some of these defense mechanisms at play among the aid workers in Kosovo. A few junior staff worked flat out but could not maintain the pace for more than a few days—*overwork and burnout.* Others appeared aloof and uninterested in the suffering of the refugees and spent long, unexplained periods away from the camp—*detachment.* After the initial emergency phase, there was a disturbing period of minor tit-for-tat media confrontations between the military and the aid agencies—notably the UNHCR, who were countering the media portrayal of their failure to respond to the crisis rapidly enough and who were embarrassed that the military had been able to fill the void so effectively. This was perhaps *transference* at work, whereby aid workers tend to blame others—in this case the military, but sometimes even the refugees themselves—for their own failures. And finally comes the *reality distortion:* "when reassigning the blame no longer satisfies the ego, or when it is no longer possible to conceal their inadequacies, aid workers create false illusions of success to enable them to feel a sense

Figure 9.4
Humanitarian Organization Behavior (Walkup 1997)

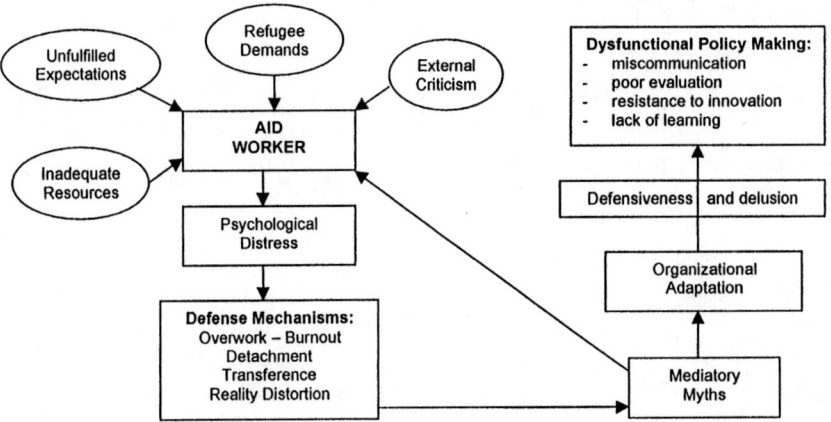

of self-worth and accomplishment in the midst of institutional inadequacies or failure."[37]

It would be unfair to complete this sensitive exposé of aid worker personality types without reflecting on the peculiarities of some military minds—because borderline dysfunctionality is hardly a malaise suffered exclusively by aid workers. Even today the army has its fair share of "misfits, missionaries, and mercenaries" and, despite some highly developed selection and training mechanisms, self- and group-delusion, blame transference, detachment from reality, overwork, burnout, and just plain stupidity are not uncommon occurrences during periods of intense operational stress. If the reader is in doubt on this score, I recommend a quick dip into Norman Dixon's *On Psychology of Military Incompetence*.[38]

Single Issue Focus

While bringing tremendous expertise and strengths to bear in their particular fields, several NGOs struck me as being very narrowly focused. A lack of understanding or acceptance of wider issues can (and did) come across as arrogance; indeed, in one or two cases as a dogmatic selfishness of their own aims/needs to the detriment of others. Not comfortable with pragmatism, there is a constant fear of losing their integrity. They are very cagey about being manipulated, by any side, don't want to be "used," and worry about their independence; they thus want their own space and freedom to operate—as they see fit. While lessons have been learnt during the 1990s, an agreed-upon code of conduct is still needed; one is being developed, but agreement will be far from easy.[39]

Rivalries

Notwithstanding their knowledge of each other, and willingness to network, there are many rivalries.[40] The NGOs in particular are dependent upon profile and income, and they can be fiercely independent and competitive. Running a large humanitarian NGO is big business, and most employ public relations men and women whose aim in life is to touch the heartstrings of the rich West. Appealing to the emotions of both governments and the public is a key element of maintaining profile and raising money, but to do so they must be seen and heard.[41] The NGOs can also be reluctant to share information with each other, sometimes not surprisingly. In the Korce region of Albania, the UNHCR asked for tenders from any agency wishing to run the camps we were building. While it might be unfair to call them business plans, they were not far short. This is a "competitive" process, with interested agencies bidding against each other, not to pay UNHCR from their funds but to receive significant sums of money from the UNHCR to fund their work; in doing so they inevitably tie themselves into UN/governmental policies. Sadly some agencies see disasters as "business opportunities" and put great effort into ensuring that their logo is both large and prominently displayed. The worst example of this in Brazda was the refusal by MSF to allow a Médecin du Monde doctor to operate from "their" compound. While surrounded by literally tens of thousands of refugees, I watched and listened in amazement as the argument raged between the two organizations, while flags/banners were being unfurled to ensure that the media carried particular images into homes and offices around the world. Such petty turf wars and mutual mistrust, linked to the spontaneity and creative nature of the individuals within these organizations, can lead to serious rivalries, indeed anarchy. MSF reluctantly decided, as an NGO, to withdraw from Rwanda; some members followed "orders," others didn't! As Hugo Slim has commented, "the only consistent factor in NGO approach to cooperation is a lack of consistency."[42]

Relationships with the Military

Many NGOs are intrinsically hostile to the military, and most "fidget" when the military are around. Their perception of the military is not an unfair caricature, given the range of military forces around the world, and most are prepared to recognize that some military are "better" than others, with U.K. forces generally held in high regard. Few of the individuals that I met were pacifists; most had no problems with the idea of "just force." Nonetheless the "blood-line" was real. While some were prepared to come to military-led meetings, they were instinctively suspicious, expecting them to be highly structured and for "orders" to be given;[43] at least initially, many steered clear or were reluctant participants. The survey of military attitudes about the NGOs conducted by Tomlinson (see "Survey of Military Attitudes Toward NGOs Following the Kosovo Campaign" in Appendix 3 at the back of this book) may have highlighted a significant degree of antagonism fueled, in part at least, by an ignorance of the roles, motivations, and modus operandi of the humanitarian community/agencies, but the reverse is certainly true. The NGO community is not only ignorant of the military but have ingrained suspicions—usually seeing the humanitarian world as their province, an area where only they have the necessary expertise to make a difference; they too often regard the military as amateurish and even dangerously incompetent. These mutual mistrusts and lack of respect have triggered a damaging downward spiral in the interagency relationships that, in turn, have served to reduce the potential effectiveness of the combined strengths (see fig. 9.5 and table 9.3).

A UNHCR reluctance to live and work permanently from my tactical headquarters, despite repeated offers in the early days, was, I suspect, linked to a fear of being too closely associated with the military. There was, throughout the humanitarian community, a noticeable determination not to be controlled, let alone commanded. The end result was that all too often, military resources were not put to best effect.[44]

Meetings

By the end of the first week in Macedonia, I was involved in interminable meetings with a large number of NGOs, both with and

Figure 9.5

The Downward Spiral (Hall 1990)

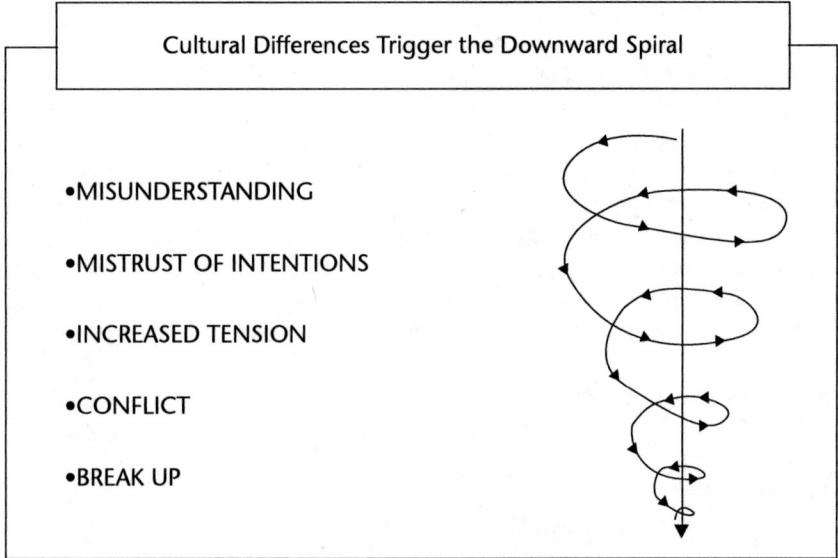

Cultural Differences Trigger the Downward Spiral

•MISUNDERSTANDING

•MISTRUST OF INTENTIONS

•INCREASED TENSION

•CONFLICT

•BREAK UP

Source: W. Hall, as presented to KLM Royal Dutch Airlines, 1990.

without the UNHCR. Any idea of punctuality was a naïve hope on my part, and none thought it in the least bit unusual to take mobile phone calls during a meeting, or to wander in and out at will. I attended many UN/NGO-led meetings, and they ran from a mixture of chaos and confusion through to well structured and useful—inevitably, personalities were the key. One of my Royal Engineer Majors commented that "the daily meetings were something to behold as every day we went over the same ground for the benefit of the new staff or for the simple reason that no one took notes or issued direction." By the middle of the second week in Macedonia, and early on in Albania, I had successfully reached a position where the chair was taken by the senior UNHCR representative, with me beside him and my HQ running the administration; it seemed to be a good compromise! It worked well as it asserted cooperation, rather than coordination (which smacks of control for the NGOs) or collaboration (even

Table 9.3   Reasons Why Some Agencies Will Not Work with the Military

- Loss of neutrality
- Loss of media profile—the military are more tele-visual than NGOs
- Military security paranoia hinders two-way transfer of information
- Loss of independence
- Increased security threat—some agencies believe that aligning themselves with the military may make them targets for factional violence in some areas
- Military are profligate with resources
- Military forces tend to arrive too late and leave too soon—they are therefore unreliable
- Military forces appear obsessed with self-protection and exit strategies
- Military forces are too political
- The humanitarian task usually becomes subordinate to the military mission
- Military forces have little or no understanding of aid work
- The military tend to be arrogant and have over-inflated views of their own humanitarian capabilities

worse); cooperation requires trust and respect—on both sides—and can certainly not be taken for granted.

WHERE NOW?

As noted at the beginning of this chapter, there has been a noticeable increase in the number of ferocious intra-state conflicts, often referred to as "complex emergencies"[45] over the last couple of decades. The troubling echoes of Bosnia and Rwanda are now imprinted on the psyche of the UN and the international community; just about every politician who spoke with me during my deployments showed that to be true. Kosovo, East Timor, and Sierra Leone are simply the latest examples of the world's desire to stop ethnic cleansing and avert, or at least minimize, the effects of such conflicts.

Future developments are far from clear, but if the emerging

consensus that state sovereignty is being redefined strengthens, then the results could be significant. Henry Shue, for example, argues that people have a "right not to become victims of genocide," and that the effective protection of this right involves both changes to the prevailing idea of the sovereign state and also the recognition that other states sometimes have a duty to intervene.[46] He is not alone. Kofi Annan and Tony Blair have spoken along similar lines. Kofi Annan, in his address to the UN General Assembly on September 20, 1999, spoke of humanitarian intervention in the twenty-first century. He pointed out that the idea of state sovereignty is being redefined by the forces of globalization; individual human rights are of increasing importance. Tony Blair has spoken in a similar vein. Unlike previous wars, which he argues were fought on grounds of realpolitik or national self-interest, Kosovo, he asserts, was "fought for a fundamental principle necessary for humanity's progress: that every human being regardless of race, religion, or birth, has an undeniable right to live free from persecution."[47] At the height of the conflict in 1999, he delivered a speech in Chicago in which he sketched out his thoughts on a world where dictators will not prosper nor ethnic crimes go unpunished. The Czech president, Vaclav Havel, has also argued that the "glory" of the nation state has passed, and that "human beings are more important than the state."[48] Many, particularly the young (and 40 percent of the world's population is under twenty), now argue that a universal, global respect for human rights will emerge, along with civic equality.

Those who oppose such a notion, arguing that it is both dangerous and unrealistic, point out that the doctrine of noninterference in other states' borders—enshrined in the UN charter—lies at the heart of national sovereignty. Henry Kissinger has warned that noninterference emerged "at the end of the devastating Thirty Years War, to inhibit a repetition of the depredations of the seventeenth century, during which perhaps 70 percent of the population of Central Europe perished in the name of competing versions of universal truth." Edward Luttwak, in his recent article on Kosovo in *Foreign Affairs*, has argued that

"Governments should resist the emotional impulse to intervene in other people's wars—not because they are indifferent to human suffering but precisely because they care about it and want to facilitate the advent of peace."[49] Nonetheless, there can be no doubt that the ending of the Cold War has given governments, particularly in the West, a freer reign to intervene and "the traditional strict doctrine that a human rights problem concerns none but the state where it takes place . . . is becoming an increasingly eccentric position."

Henry Kissinger, Edward Luttwak, and many others may, therefore, argue that such a doctrine could lead to "everlasting humanitarian war," but the reality is that the deployments of the 1990s are unlikely to suddenly cease as the impetus for ethical/humanitarian foreign policies gain strength, and deployments of choice will increasingly include operations driven by humanitarian instincts. Recent comments expressed in frustration at the ineffectiveness of UN operations in Sierra Leone are unlikely to bring about a retrenchment; indeed, the opposite may be true as increasingly the NGOs, the media, and the UN itself argue for more effective intervention. The British Spearhead Battalion Group deployment had a significant impact on the situation in Sierra Leone, in stark contrast to the much larger but inexperienced and ill-equipped UN forces; policy-makers will be increasingly caught between the desire, indeed, the imperative, to act, and a recognition that these deployments require strong combat power. In the context of Sierra Leone, "European officials, normally prompt in their praise of UN authority, voiced stinging criticism of Secretary-General Kofi Annan and his top peacekeeping staff for jeopardising the UN's prestige in an increasingly hopeless-looking operation;"[50] a military force need not be large, but it must be effective.

We must recognize this and learn the appropriate lessons from Kosovo and elsewhere. These lessons include improving the way we relate to one another, the essence of this chapter, while not losing sight of the fact that any operation that begins at a relatively low level has the potential to escalate and relationships will therefore not be fixed (see fig. 9.6).

AGRICOLA started as helping to implement a peace agreement; it involved humanitarian operations on the one hand, but also preparations for forced entry into Kosovo on the other. This latter option would have entailed serious combat power, and the military focus would inevitably have shifted if that option had been implemented. See table 9.4 for some "Guiding Principles."

Notwithstanding the crucial need to recognize the variable nature of military forces around the world (bullet 2, table 9.4), most professional military organizations welcome involvement in "humanitarian" deployments. Complex emergencies are demanding, and they provide excellent vehicles for maintaining the professionalism of our forces, a professionalism needed as much in the early stages of emergency aid provision, disaster relief, and humanitarian operations as in peacekeeping, peace enforcement, and war fighting.

British soldiers happen to be extremely good at this business and take great pride in making a difference.[51] They switch easily from one role to another, and psychologically had no difficulty with helping refugees one day and preparing to fight their way into Kosovo on another. Force protection issues were no barrier, with our soldiers striking an admirable balance as the situation dictated. The tasks were often grueling, but they responded will-

Figure 9.6

The Spectrum of Operations

Disaster Relief	Humanitarian Assistance	Peace Keeping	Nonessential Evacuation Operation	Peace Enforcement	War Fighting
(DR)	(HA)	(PK)	(NEO)	(PE)	(WF)

◄——— ——————————— ———►
LOW INTENSITY   HIGH INTENSITY

Note: Peace Support Operations (PSO) encompass PK to PE. Complex Emergencies encompass DR to PSO.

Table 9.4 Guiding Principles When Dealing with the Military

- Do not assume that military personnel have any training or experience in humanitarian matters—it is not their "core" business
- Recognize that there are many different military organizations around the world. Like NGOs/other agencies, not all are professional, and some may well be the cause of the problem you are embroiled in
- Seek out key military commanders, at all levels, who you can relate to personally—personalities matter
- Seek opportunities to inform the military of your organization's capabilities
- Send the right person to meetings with the military
- Do not be afraid to ask for military favors
- Do not be concerned about the military taking credit for your organization's accomplishments
- Invite the military leadership to visit your organization and learn about its activities
- Keep in mind what the military does best (logistics, trained manpower, and security)
- Position your organization to take over from the military when they leave
- Recognize that the military focus will shift as situations change—particularly if the security situation worsens

ingly, displaying their humanity alongside their professionalism in a way that was noted by many of the other participants.

As far as commanders are concerned, these operations provide, at all levels, sufficient uncertainty and friction to ensure that they are well tested. We need commanders who are comfortable with chaos, and the humanitarian community, never mind the situation itself, ensures that there is plenty of that! Nothing is ever easy on these deployments, and cool heads are needed to bring order out of the chaos. The Right Rev. Dinis Sengulane, CMG, the Bishop of Lebombo in Mozambique, commented during his talk to the RCDS on the crisis there that we "need people who are trained to deal with chaos and who can bring order and control."[52] The experiences gained within my brigade from AGRICOLA have resulted in better commanders, at all levels, and we emerged from the deployment a far more professional brigade than when we went in. (Read about the essentials of Operation AGRICOLA in Appendix 2 at the back of this book.)

DEVELOPMENT OF DOCTRINE: "JOINED UP" APPROACH

That all said, the doctrinal debate on how effective action can best be orchestrated and executed must be widened. U.K. military doctrine has developed well throughout the 1990s, and it is held in high regard. Nonetheless, there is work to be done, particularly in the area of working alongside the various humanitarian organizations and other governmental departments. A recent U.S. State Department report provides an "unusually frank" assessment of why past American action has been slow or ineffective: "it is a tale of poor coordination, missions being duplicated or falling through the cracks and confusion inside the Administration and the private humanitarian groups that sometimes cannot be sure with which agency to work."[53] It is tempting to argue that the United Kingdom's involvement over the last ten years has had a better track record, and there is some truth in that. However, the wave of press comment that followed the interdepartmental "debates" on the U.K.'s response to the floods in Mozambique rightly touched a nerve,[54] and my AGRICOLA experiences confirm that we, too, have much to learn.

While it is idle to suggest that it is easy to establish a single doctrine for complex emergencies, the realities of these deployments mean that all of the relevant agencies must enhance their links and work closer with each other, including the key donors.[55] Our collective and "joint" doctrine must reflect agreed principles, on everything from intelligence gathering and analysis, provision of the means, including funding, the roles of the military, and the links with and status of nonmilitary aid agencies and civilian contractors. There is a need for an integrated "campaign plan," covering the political, diplomatic, legal, economic, media, and humanitarian imperatives, alongside the military ones. While inevitably events on the ground will dictate and modify, and commanders will need to respond to these changes, such a campaign plan, prepared jointly by the key players using a framework set within an agreed doctrine, will both guide and educate, support and, where necessary, constrain.

The military role is to support, not supplant, the work of the humanitarians; we are there to serve, not to be served. Logistic, medical, and engineering support, encompassing the management of airheads and seaports, transportation, shelter, route protection, and the provision of a secure environment, are all key roles, and the Logistic and Engineer Brigades of the British Army, for example, are both equipped and structured to provide such support. Linked to ongoing work within the Civil-Affairs Group, these brigades, recently brought together under the umbrella of a divisional level "Support Command," are becoming the military focus for the development of an integrated training and exchange program, to educate and prepare like-minded people for future deployments.[56]

Conflict prevention, early warning, and early deployment of forces must, of course, be set alongside preventative diplomacy, disarmament, and peace-building measures, including focused aid. This broader definition of security policy seems some way off, but developing the doctrinal debate will bring it closer. The U.K.'s Joint Doctrine and Concepts Center (JDCC) at the RMCS, Shrivenham, is currently developing the principles, practice, and procedures that together will make up the doctrine from the U.K. military perspective for PSO and CIMIC issues. But the process must be, and is being, politically driven. While it is a truism to say that there is no such thing as purely military success in any conflict, this is particularly so in complex emergencies, where military involvement is simply a means to an end. Politics dictates the speed and nature of response, and determines priorities, and it is politicians who need to bring together the key players in a coordinated manner and allocate the resources as appropriate. The natural lead in the U.K. is DFID, which has responded so well in recent years and which is most ably led at the moment;

some structural change may be necessary to ensure an ability to plan ahead and, particularly, to maintain a close link with the PJHQ. One thing is clear; if we are to avoid the complete militarization of humanitarian assistance, which would be a grave mistake in my view, then a clear and widely understood doctrine is required quickly.[57]

CONCLUSION

Operation AGRICOLA, the U.K. deployment to Macedonia/Kosovo, was but one of a continuing series in which military commanders, at all levels, found themselves working closely with nonmilitary organizations. While the scale of humanitarian assistance provided may have been exceptional, and it was certainly unusual for the military to have to fill such an enormous vacuum and to take such a strong lead, military involvement in such complex emergencies is unlikely to end.

My perceptions will not be a surprise to most readers. But it seems to me that the important fact to recognize is simply that differences do exist, and no amount of wishful thinking will change them. We must learn to live with the realities. Through an understanding of the strengths, and an acceptance of the weaknesses, strong working relationships can be developed, and, indeed, friendships forged. In one sense, both sides of the "blood-line" divide are a mixture of "missionaries, mercenaries, and misfits," and both share very similar problems. Often, if not usually, put into and operating within a vacuum, with poor mandates and force structures, each can be humanitarian "fig leaves" covering neglect. The crowded theater of operations is made up of uneven actors, with poor and good quality players on both sides being asked to make hard moral choices. Often unable to take the decisive action needed, and being put into dangerous situations—self-sacrifice may be the ethic but it is not the objective—both sides are accountable to donors or governments who can be very wise after the event and who can be unfairly critical of decisions taken under enormous pressure. These similarities bind the players together. Both get it wrong now and then, but our joint aim must be to develop the natural synergies that exist in order to ensure that the achievements eclipse the failures.

This being so, there is work to be done. The military, in particular, need to appreciate the cultural and psychological makeup of the nonmilitary players; we need to better understand the ethos and psyche of the various organizations and agencies, and acknowledge the strengths that they bring to such deployments. We must put effort and resources into improving our capabilities and our relationships with the key players, NGO, UN, and governmental, encouraging and participating in a wide doctrinal debate to ensure better and closer cooperation. The future fate of many people, all around the globe, caught in the middle of inter-, and increasingly intra-state, violence will depend on this; and the stakes are too high to be left to the sometimes-inadequate efforts of well-intentioned individuals.

10

An Introduction to NGO Field Security

Randolph Martin

ALTHOUGH CLEAR DATA on the security of humanitarian aid workers are hard to come by, virtually anyone involved in the management and delivery of humanitarian assistance will attest to the deterioration of the security environment over the past ten to twenty years. Anecdotally, the evidence seems striking, from the appalling murders of ICRC staff in Chechnya and UNHCR staff in Timor and Guinea to the day-in and day-out challenges of fielding staff in dangerous environments. This chapter will explore some of the reasons why humanitarian assistance has become more perilous, but it will also offer a paradigm through which we might better understand security in the context of humanitarian assistance. Much of the thought in this chapter reflects the work of InterAction's Security Task Force, in which the author was a participant, and the subsequent work of Koenraad Van Brabant,[1] who also participated on the Task Force.

In a 1997 article,[2] Van Brabant explored some of the ways in which changes in the nature of war itself has lent itself to the deterioration of security for humanitarian aid workers. The following builds upon Van Brabant's thesis.

Increase in the Number and Duration of Conflicts

There has been a dramatic increase in the number of wars and conflicts in the post-communist era. Throughout the 1990s over fifty conflicts have been going on at any given time. Wholly one-third of these wars have lasted over twenty years.[3] "Chronic emergencies" as we have seen in Sudan, Burma, Afghanistan, and Angola can grind on for years if not decades, during which humanitarian aid—and those who deliver it—provides the only thin lifeline for tens of thousands of people. At the same time, new conflicts arise with alarming frequency. In response, many of the leading humanitarian NGOs have increased many-fold in size over the past decade, while at the same time there has been a proliferation of new NGOs involved in humanitarian assistance. These expansions have produced significantly increased numbers of aid workers exposed to dangerous security environments.

Absence of Rules of Conduct

The recent war between Eritrea and Ethiopia is a throwback to an earlier era of conflict. There were two nation-states very much concerned with the legitimacy of their respective purposes, fielding two professional national armies fighting over a relatively well-defined front line under observation by much of the world. However horrible war may be, this one presented a relatively high degree of structure and clarity around which humanitarian actors could function. But the Eritrean-Ethiopian conflict was an anachronism. Indeed, fewer than 10 percent of the wars in the 1990s were classic interstate conflicts of this sort.[4] Contemporary wars are more likely to be intra-state conflicts. These conflicts are less likely to draw international attention and scrutiny. Conflicts such as the civil wars in Liberia, Sierra Leone, and Angola, though touting some rhetoric as a rallying cry, are often fought by poorly disciplined militias who are fighting as much for their own sustenance as for any broader purpose or aim. The increasing use of child soldiers is both a symptom and a perpetuator of this phenomenon, as is the proliferation of small arms.

Impunity

Aid agencies are often perceived as "soft" targets that can be attacked or robbed with impunity due to their lack of communal or diplomatic links with the combatants. Often our work must be carried out in areas where there are no viable law enforcement agencies or justice system. This was typical of the conflicts in Liberia and Sierra Leone in the 1990s. Alternatively, institutions of justice may exist, but there may be insufficient resources or political will to pursue crimes against humanitarian actors. Finally, there are situations in which humanitarian actors may find themselves working under regimes where the justice and police systems are themselves corrupt, alien, or unaccountable.

Erosion of Neutrality

Civilian population displacement and casualties have increasingly become the purpose rather than a by-product of war. Civilian casualties of war have increased from 10 percent in the nineteenth century, to 50 percent in the Second World War, to anywhere between 75 percent and 90 percent in contemporary conflicts. Since 1980, the number of refugees has increased from 2.4 million to 14.4 million,[5] while internally displaced persons have increased from 22 million to 38 million.[6] In wars such as Sudan's—which has gone on for all but eleven of the last forty-five years—not only are the vast majority of casualties civilian, but the cause of death is more often than not war-induced famine and disease. Regardless of how humanitarians may perceive themselves, as civilian casualties and displacement have increasingly become the purpose of war, then those who come to the assistance of its victims have effectively become partisans in the conflict.

NGO Competition and Culture

In many ways, dangers to humanitarian aid workers arise out of the culture and nature of humanitarian organizations themselves. With the proliferation of NGOs responding to humanitarian crises, competition between agencies has increased. Aid workers are often under pressure to "get there first" and work closest to the lines of confrontation in order to increase their agency's media exposure and thus appeal to both public and private donors. NGOs are also under pressure to maximize the portion of their budgets going to direct services, forcing difficult compromises on managers contemplating the high costs of the hardware often required for good security. Moreover, the culture of NGO workers is too often ill disposed to the discipline necessary for proper security protocols. This both reflects and perpetuates the lack of development of professional standards and "best practices" in the field of security.

SAFETY VERSUS SECURITY

One often hears the terms "safety" and "security" used interchangeably. For our purposes here, the term "safety" relates to protection from illness and accidents, whereas "security" relates to protection from acts of violence and crime. Although the *security* of staff, assets, and programs necessarily requires the investment of considerable time and resources, it is important not to lose sight of the fact that the greatest risks to the well-being of humanitarian aid workers arises not from security threats, but from safety issues. *Safety threats such as vehicle accidents, malaria, water-borne disease, HIV, and other health threats continue to be by far the largest causes of casualties among relief workers.* Strategies for addressing safety issues are necessarily different from those that address security. Although our focus here in on *security*, it is important that aid workers and their employers are well aware of threats to their *safety* and prepared with means to limit vulnerability to these threats (see table 10.1).

INDIVIDUAL RESPONSIBILITY

While it is incumbent on aid organizations to develop strong security provisions for their staff, it is also imperative for individuals to understand and accept the unique personal responsibilities

Table 10.1

Threats to Safety	Threats to Security
• Vehicle and motorcycle accidents* • Malaria/tropical disease* • Sexually transmitted diseases • Accidents related to poor facilities and infrastructure	• Abduction • Angry mobs/riots • Death threats • Extortion • Arson • Rape/sexual assault • Car jacking • Assault • Robbery • Burglary • Sabotage • Disgruntled staff and employee malfeasance* • Checkpoints • Hostile authorities • Landmines • Open war/shelling/crossfire • Sniper fire • Terrorism

*Largest sources of casualties

incumbent on aid workers. Living and working in one's home country, a personal security incident is by and large an individual's own responsibility to deal with. In a humanitarian response environment, the behavior of an individual can impact dramatically on the security of the team and the effectiveness of the program. A single isolated security incident can precipitate the restriction or suspension of aid efforts by all humanitarian actors in the area. Persons contemplating involvement in humanitarian aid work must be willing to accept this responsibility and surrender some of the risk-taking behavior that we might undertake as individuals living and working under different circumstances.

THE IMPACT OF AGENCY MANDATE AND MISSION ON SECURITY

One often hears the complaint that NGOs do not effectively coordinate policy and operations on security. Surely there is much that can and should be done to facilitate communications between NGOs on security, but in fact, NGOs *should not* have the same thresholds of acceptable risk, evacuation plans, and security policies. An NGO's exposure to security threats is directly related to its mandate and mission (as well as other agency-specific vulnerabilities). As each NGO has its own individual purpose and identity and its own sectors of operation, each must define its security exposure and policies accordingly.

Defining *mandate* as the overall purpose of the organization, and *mission* as an organization's activities in a particular environment, one can easily imagine how mandate and mission might impact on security. For example, an organization whose *mandate* involves evangelism or overtly religious ideals will be at higher risk in some environments than a secular organization. It is interesting to note that local interests may be as threatened by the appearance of NGOs representing opposing sects of the same faith than they would be by an NGO associated with an entirely different faith. Religious organizations often mitigate the impact of their mandate by secularizing their activities in the field.

Human rights organizations face unique security threats stemming from different aspects of their mandate. In many, if not most, of their operating environments they are perceived by important elements in the society as hostile outside observers and meddlers. Furthermore, they often lack a formal operational platform or even legal status. Their strategies for coping often involve work through local actors, thus limiting the exposure of international workers or the profile of a formal presence. Largely for security reasons, human rights organizations are less likely to implement services projects, and non-human-rights organizations are very careful about how they manage their positions as witnesses to human rights violations.

"Solidarity" organizations are those whose purpose is to support a particular party or cause in a conflict. They will face different risks than organizations guided by the principles of impartiality or neutrality. Their partisanship may be expressed clearly in the agency mission statement or even name, or it may be evident only by the agency's presence on one side of a conflict, in which case the perception of solidarity may weigh more than the actuality. Solidarity groups have been actors in many of the more prominent conflicts of the last decade—Bosnia, Afghanistan, and Sudan, most notably.

Organizations whose mandates include development are by definition involved in institution development. They assist established institutions to become more effective. In times of civil conflict, the legitimacy of those institutions may be called into question by other groups in the society. To the extent that an NGO is associated with these institutions and policies, they too may become targets in such conflicts. Furthermore, although increasingly "development NGOs" are building or enhancing their ability to respond to humanitarian crises, many do not have the experience or capacity to deal with security issues that arise in crises, and are thus all the more vulnerable.

Organizations that respond only to emergencies have different vulnerabilities. They often do not have staff that speak local languages or understand the nuances of local culture and history. They often do not take the time to develop relationships with communities that can serve to protect and inform them. They bring a high profile and valuable assets into an environment where the local economy may have collapsed along with law and order.

Finally, organizations whose mandate focuses on refugees or internally displaced persons (IDPs) face their own set of vulnerabilities. Their efforts may target refugee or IDP communities while ignoring host communities that may be equally destitute. They may serve unpopular minority or foreign groups. With their ability to deliver services to a community, they may be perceived as competing with indigenous political groups for the hearts and minds of the refugee population.

It is very important for the managers and staff of humanitarian organizations to understand how the larger *mandate* of their organization will be perceived in the local context. Similarly, an organization's *mission* in a given country will impact on the security of staff. Education programs can challenge indigenous notions about who should be educated and what they should be taught. Projects aimed at improving the quality and quantity of clean water delivered to a community may undermine local entrepreneurs who make a living through the sale of water. Irrigation projects may inadvertently divert water from other communities sharing the same river or aquifer. Reproductive health programs upset traditional notions about birth control, gender roles, and other traditional practices and values in a community. Virtually any sector of activity can carry with it security threats, given the wrong environment. It is important to understand thoroughly the extent to which an agency's mission produces vulnerability in the local context.

Returning to the point that agencies *should not* have the same policies and procedures for security, the reasons should now be evident: the vulnerability of NGOs varies significantly with the overarching mandate and in-country mission of the organizations. Moreover, an organization whose *mission* in a given country is life saving or life sustaining has an ethical obligation to withstand higher levels of risk than an organization involved in, for example, economic development. Individuals considering humanitarian work should also accept the added responsibility that comes with live-saving or life-sustaining functions in humanitarian crises and be willing to work under more dangerous circumstances than other technicians and generalists.

The Security Triangle: Acceptance-Protection-Deterrence

One of the more curious scenes that one finds in complex humanitarian emergencies is the presence of fully armed and armored peacekeeping forces—replete with assault rifle, helmet, ballistic jacket, and armored vehicles—appearing side-by-side with jeans-and-a-T-shirt humanitarian aid workers. Who is more secure? Most of us who have been in this situation feel that the humanitarian aid worker is just as, if not more, secure than the soldier. How can that be? Unfortunately, security is often conceptualized in terms of military or police models that appear—albeit superficially—to emphasize equipment and tactics. Although there is much that we can learn from these models, NGO security is far more complex. Fancy communications gear, logistics capabilities, and compound security have their place, but are only a small part of what constitutes security for aid workers.

Effective security management for humanitarian organizations should embrace a locally developed security protocol that includes each of the three elements of the security triangle: acceptance, protection, and deterrence. The three elements need not be balanced, and in fact rarely do balance. Rather, deficiencies in one should be accommodated with strengths in another. A strong acceptance strategy with supportive protection and deterrence elements is perhaps ideal, though not always possible. Where local conditions limit the effectiveness of the acceptance strategies, it is necessary to build stronger protection and deterrence capabilities.

Acceptance, protection, and deterrence will be discussed in detail below, along with the personal and institutional characteristics that are necessary for each of the strategies.

Acceptance

In a word, "acceptance" means *softening the threat*. It means that the community supports our presence and activities, and out of that acceptance grows security. Lest "acceptance" appear too utopian, note that acceptance strategies include the security that may be provided by local law enforcement authorities (in situations where they are viable). Some of the elements of acceptance are:

- The community has a stake in the program and participates actively
- The community has been involved in the assessment and design of the program

- The community is involved in the evaluation of the program
- The agency's mission is transparent and broadly communicated
- The agency's activities are *impartial*
- The agency's staff and presence are culturally and politically sensitive
- The agency's program reflects local priorities and enhances local capacities and institutions
- The agency's professionalism
- The agency's time commitment—the longer the better
- The agency has developed good working relationships with local governmental authorities, including the police and military where appropriate
- The agency's programs reflect basic development concepts and a willingness to invest the time and effort to involve the community in every facet of project assessment, planning, implementation, and evaluation

Acceptance is the cornerstone of security for NGOs with a development mandate but is often challenged under the time frames and political circumstances of complex emergencies. In wartime relief operations, acceptance by the beneficiary community may seem to be grossly overshadowed by the hostility of one or more of the combatants. For example, the *acceptance* of humanitarian operations by Sarajevans was overshadowed by the hostility of the forces laying siege to Sarajevo, making it necessary for agencies there to build strong *protection* and *deterrence* strategies. However, it should be noted that some agencies mitigated their vulnerability in this situation by providing humanitarian services to both sides of the conflict, thus gaining "acceptance" by all parties and more access to the city under siege.

Acceptance strategies are also weakened when agencies must base themselves in a location removed from their service area. An agency's field office, its fleet of expensive vehicles, and noisy generator may be perceived as intrusive by the surrounding community if there is no tangible benefit coming out of it all. This problem is quite common and leaves the field office vulnerable to local resentment unless the organization can offer services locally, in some way educate the local population to the importance and relevance of the agency mission, or otherwise lower its profile.

In emergency operations the pressure to get programs moving may limit the ability of staff to involve the local community thoroughly. However, it is imperative that organizations not let their *mission* obscure this critical element in the security triangle and core element in quality programming: the community's involvement.

For an individual to be successful with acceptance strategies, he or she must have strong diplomatic skills, self-awareness, patience, and a willingness to devolve responsibility authority to local counterparts. Listening and communications skills and cross-cultural sensitivities are essential. The ability to converse in local languages is very helpful.

At an institutional level, organizations that are committed to community participation and development are at a real advantage, as are those who have developed guidelines and policies requiring thorough program evaluations involving local stakeholders. Recruiters for these organizations value character references as highly as technical qualifications. What should be clear is that an organization that emphasizes quality program design and implementation is by definition going to be strong in its acceptance strategies.

Protection

Simply stated, protection calls for strategies that "harden the target." It is the element that many people most readily associate with security, though it is by no means the most important element in the triangle. Elements of "protection" are presented under two headings: security equipment and standard operating procedures.

Security equipment refers to the materials and equipment needed to provide adequate security. The inventory of items should reflect an assessment of the local security environment and the agency's vulnerabilities therein. Not all environments require ballistic jackets! The following is a list of some of the types of equipment that might be called for:

- Communications equipment including high frequency (HF) radios (radios used in longer distance communications), very high frequency (VHF) radios ("hand-held" radios used in local and intermediate distances), satellite telephones ("sat phone"), beepers, "land-line" telephone, etc. There should be redundant forms of communication if reliability of any one form is questionable
- Reliable vehicles and maintenance facilities
- Perimeter security devices including walls, barbed wire, alarm systems
- Protective gear: ballistic jackets, helmets
- Use (or non-use) of the agency emblem (or other symbols)

Standard Operating Procedures (SOPs) are the institutional policies and procedures that enhance security. Some examples:

- Clear and equitable national staff personnel policies—including transparent salary scales and hiring, firing, promotion, disciplinary, and grievance procedures—that are communicated to staff and implemented consistently. *Incidents involving disgruntled staff are one of the largest causes of security infractions for NGOs*
- Clear financial policies and procedures. *Employee malfeasance— often the product of poor policies and procedures—is among the largest causes of security incidents for NGOs*
- Proper warehouse management policies and procedures *(also related to employee malfeasance)*
- Clear vehicle operations policies and strict discipline regarding vehicle operations
- Curfews and no-go zones where appropriate
- Development of and/or participation in a "warden system" or communications pyramid for conveying emergency messages
- Communications protocol, training, and disciplined radio usage
- Security orientation for incoming staff and routine security briefings for staff
- Ongoing security training related to personal security and local threats

- Convoy operations protocol
- Visitor screening protocol
- Clear and consistent discipline for infractions of security policy, including the inclusion of security compliance in routine performance reviews
- Coordination with other NGOs and UN agencies

Some elements of protection are important in all situations, even in stable settings where *acceptance* is the primary strategy. Good communications, sound policy structures, and interagency coordination are always the mark of quality operations. *Protection* strategies need to be enhanced when conditions deteriorate and *acceptance* strategies become less effective, but should never be viewed as an alternative to strong community support.

If good *acceptance* strategies imply good programming, good *protection* strategies imply good management. Poorly managed organizations—organizations without solid operating policies and procedures—are far more vulnerable to security problems. This is particularly true for core human resource and financial management capacities. However, the part of *protection* that emphasizes accoutrements associated with military operations—the radios, convoy operations, expensive vehicles, compound walls, and lighting—can undermine an agency's *acceptance* strategy by raising the agency's profile and creating resentments in the community. This must be carefully weighed in each environment.

To be strong in *protection* strategies, organizations must have a strong framework of institutionalized policies and procedures. They should have the technical and human resources to back up their operations in the field and the funding base to cover the equipment necessary.

Deterrence

Deterrence is *the ability to pose a credible counter-threat.* Most NGOs are neither large enough, nor appropriately suited to pose a credible counter-threat on our own. The focus of *deterrence* strategies is the relationships that we are able to build with larger regional or international institutions that in turn can effect our security. We will look at deterrence under two headings: diplomatic and physical.

DIPLOMATIC DETERRENCE

This is the product of an organization's relationships to larger international actors that can exert diplomatic or military pressure on our behalf, influencing local authorities and actors who either pose security threats themselves or are well placed to promote the security interests of the NGOs, but are not adequately doing so. Elements include:

- The quality of relationships with American and European diplomatic missions
- The quality of relationships with the United Nations
- The quality of participation in NGO coordinating bodies that are capable of presenting a unified front
- The ability to attract positive media coverage
- Memberships and affiliations in national or international organizations that can leverage influence

Diplomatic deterrence is most useful in situations where one or more of the parties to a conflict are concerned with their international credibility. Despite its appalling human rights record and ongoing war, the government in Sudan, for example, has been responsive to international pressures to provide humanitarian access. On the other hand, before its ouster, the Taliban government in Afghanistan was an example of a governing authority that showed little regard for international pressure, making a diplomatic deterrence strategy of little use in that setting.

Organizations that are strong in diplomatic deterrence are actively involved in the humanitarian community. They coordinate with other NGOs, join professional organizations, share information, and have healthy relationships in the diplomatic community. There are organizations that, because of their mandate, prefer to limit their affiliation with governments and/or the UN system, or for various reasons prefer to operate independently with little consultation or coordination with others. These organizations are more vulnerable in deterrence strategies and must be prepared to compensate with other strategies or accept a higher threshold of risk.

PHYSICAL DETERRENCE

This is perhaps the least common form of deterrent strategy, usually appearing in conjunction with peacekeeping missions when NGOs formally coordinate activities with international or United Nations military forces. We have witnessed this in Northern Iraq, Somalia, Bosnia, and Kosovo, to mention a few. In each case NGOs have worked closely with military actors who provided a physical security umbrella under which humanitarian organizations have been able to implement assistance programs. Needless to say, military deterrent strategies are less than ideal and should be pursued only when the other legs of the security triangle are clearly insufficient.

Also under the rubric of physical deterrence one finds the use of guard forces. The use of unarmed guards is common among NGOs. The use of armed guards and escorts is not as common and is the subject of much debate among NGOs. Some organizations embrace global policies against the use of armed protection. Others are more agnostic, making decisions on a case-by-case basis. There are clear dangers in using armed protection. It can have the effect of militarizing relief, effectively creating an arms race between humanitarian actors as those with the least protection struggle to limit their vulnerability by taking on their own armed protection. All too often, those offering the protection are partisans in the conflict and may attempt to manipulate aid delivery to suit their own political agenda. Assistance during Somalia's famine emergency in the 1990s presented many examples of these scenarios. Humanitarian organizations are poorly equipped to manage armed protection. On the other hand, there have been numerous instances where humanitarian access would have been greatly curtailed without armed protection, creating substantial human consequences.

DEVELOPING SECURITY POLICIES

Although it is important for organizations to have some global policies with regard to security, most of the planning for operational security must be done at a local level. After identifying the vulnerabilities inherent in the organization's mandate and mission in the local context and assessing the general threat environment, the organization should consider ways of reducing vulnerabilities under each of the strategies in the security triangle. Each leg of the triangle should be incorporated in a way that is appropriate to the local setting. In a relatively peaceful setting, *acceptance* strategies will dominate, although good communications and firm policy foundations of the *protection* leg and the diplomatic linkages of the *deterrence* leg should also be evident. As security threats increase, it is important to redouble efforts in the *acceptance* leg, but to build increasingly on the *protection* and *deterrence* strategies. Your local security protocol should be structured to accommodate changes in the security environment. It will be helpful to identify security phases through which a progressive program of security preparedness builds on all three legs of the triangle as security threats increase.   .

Also note that your protocol should reflect changes in the security environment in the various regions of your country of operations. For example, you may feel that you have a good *acceptance strategy* in the area of project implementation, however, you have virtually no *acceptance strategy* when traveling between your field headquarters and the field sites. Thus, you may strengthen your *protection strategy* through convoy operations and HF radio communications and your *deterrent strategy* by liaising with the United Nations, the U.S. Embassy, and an NGO coordinating group to pressure improvements in security from the host government or local authorities along the route.

The security triangle should also be helpful in telling you when it is no longer safe to operate. For example, if you are in a situation where you are assisting a locally persecuted beneficiary group (thus weakening your *acceptance strategies*) and where there is limited international presence (thus weakening your *deterrence strategies*), your program would be unacceptably reliant on your *protection* capacities. Similarly, if you are working with a locally persecuted group under a United Nations umbrella, but are ill-equipped with communications capacity, vehicles, or other protective devices (due to lack of resources or host government restrictions), the security situation may also be unacceptable.

THREAT, VULNERABILITY, AND RISK

Threat and risk are often treated as if they are interchangeable terms. They are not. Along with the "vulnerability" they can be useful in understanding security management.

Threat: Dangers inherent in the security environment
Vulnerability: The extent to which the organization is exposed to threats
Risk: The potential outcome of a security incident

Table 10.2, though not exhaustive, should help establish the distinction between these three concepts.

THREAT ASSESSMENT

NGO security plans are typically full of various procedures and precautions. Oddly, one of the elements most often left out is a description of the context and exactly what the threat is that is being planned for. The following provides a very simple framework for identifying the key threats in a security environment and prioritizing a response. It is often assumed that accurate threat assessments can only be carried out by "security experts." To the contrary, much of what is needed can be learned through a simple process of observation and consultation with other agencies, UN, embassy, and local contacts—not the least of which are national staff members, neighbors, and the local newspapers.

Table 10.2

Threats	Vulnerability	Risks
Abduction	Mandate	Staff casualties
Angry mobs/riots	Mission	Program closure
Death threats	Location	Lost/damaged assets
Extortion	Timing	Damaged reputation
Arson	Staff experience	Loss of donor support
Rape/sexual assault	Staff training	Inefficient operations
Car jacking	Staff orientation	
Assault	Community relations	
Robbery	Evacuation options	
Burglary	Transportation	
Sabotage	capacities	
Disgruntled staff and	Staff nationality	
employee	Staff gender	
malfeasance	Staff ethnicity	
Checkpoints	Affiliations/	
Hostile authorities	associations (UN,	
Landmines	U.S., etc.)	
Open war/shelling/	Perimeter site security	
crossfire	Staff stress/attitude	
Sniper fire	Quality of	
Terrorism	information	
	Coordination with	
	other agencies	
	Cultural sensitivity	

Threat assessments—and their companion, vulnerability assessments—should be ongoing, leading to adjustment in plans as changes are detected in the operating environment. Working from the above list of threats or from a list that is developed locally, threats can be placed in a matrix based upon the probability and consequence of each threat in a local environment (see fig. 10.1). "High probability" does not refer to the chance that an incident will happen on any given day. Rather, it refers to threats that are known to be typical of the local environment. "Consequence" refers to the consequence to the program or individuals involved.

This simple matrix should provide a basic profile of the secur-

Figure 10.1

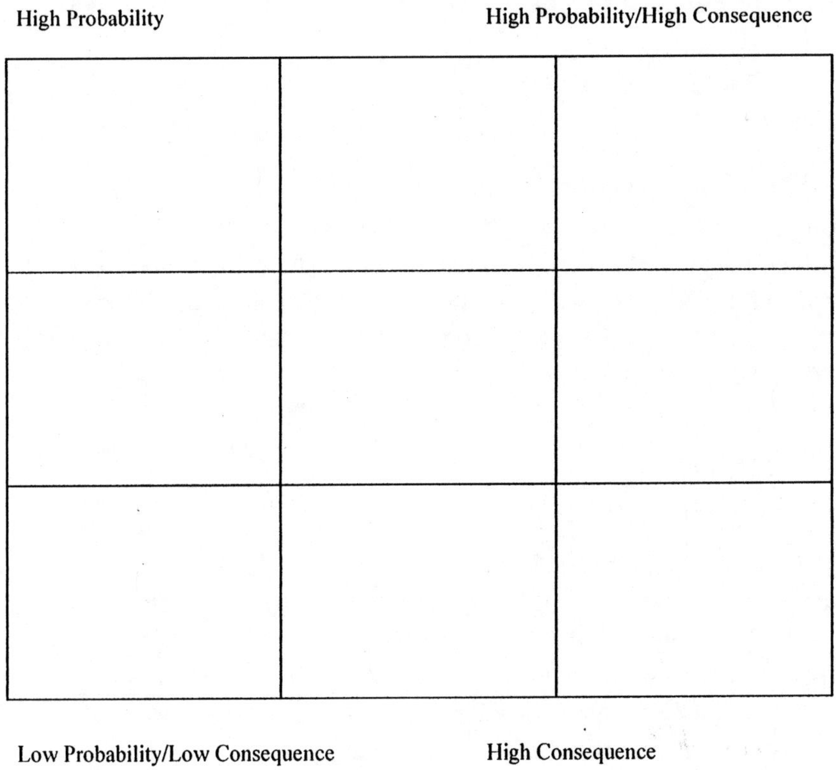

High Probability   High Probability/High Consequence

Low Probability/Low Consequence   High Consequence

ity environment from which one can begin to construct an appropriate security plan or evaluate a current plan. Obviously, threats that fall in the highest probability and consequence boxes will deserve the greatest focus of attention—and an assessment of vulnerability.

Vulnerability assessment is the frank and open assessment of an agency's weaknesses against the identified threats. How do the agency's mandate and mission make it vulnerable? How well trained are staff? How does the nationality, gender, or racial makeup of staff make staff vulnerable? How well does the agency relate to the community? How well managed is the agency—does it possess appropriate policies and procedures for operating in the local environment?

SYNTHESIS—BRINGING SECURITY CONCEPTS TOGETHER

Consider the following formula:

Threat × Vulnerability = Risk

This formula can be used to think through security problems and prepare an appropriate response. For example, if you have determined that landmines are a *threat* of high probability and consequence, how can you reduce *vulnerability* to that threat, thus reducing the risk to your staff? The Security Triangle can come into play:

Threat: Landmines
Vulnerability Reduction

Protection: Train staff in landmine detection, withdrawal, and first aid. Create "no-go" areas. Circulate landmine maps. Post pictures of common landmines. Participate in NGO security meetings and share information on landmine locations. Establish clear medical evacuation procedures and maintain complete emergency personnel files (blood type, allergies, prescriptions, contact information, etc.).

Acceptance: Local communities are typically very aware of where landmine dangers exist. Develop community contacts to learn where mines are—are there truck stops, farmers groups, etc., that can be routinely tapped for information about land mines?

Deterrence: Work through diplomatic channels to pressure parties not to set mines.

The following are some of the more outstanding threats that humanitarian agencies face, with some suggestions for reducing vulnerability and thus risk.

Open Conflict

Only programs providing critical life-saving service should consider operating in an environment where there is current or anticipated open conflict. Other programs overtaken by open conflict should seek immediate evacuation.

Acceptance response: Local communities can provide safe haven. It is very important that the agency's mission be transparent and supported by the community. From this relationship, NGOs may derive prior warning of military offensives as well as shelter in emergencies.

Protection response: Very strong protective capacities are imperative for operating in this type of environment. Specialized security technicians should be retained to develop capacity in communications, logistics, shelter, and operating protocols.

Deterrence response: Very strong deterrence relationships are also imperative to this type of operation. Operations should not be attempted outside of the umbrella of United Nations and/or multinational peacekeeping forces.

Terrorism

Terrorism is planned and targeted aggression against humanitarian agencies aimed at intimidation, extortion, or political ends.

Acceptance response: It is important that the agency mission be transparent and effectively communicated. Terrorist attacks often arise in environments where news and information regarding NGO activities are being distorted in order to discredit them. Community *participation* helps to counter this. However, terrorist threats also arise in situations where NGOs are perceived as aiding and abetting an opposition group. In this case, opportunities should be found for providing appropriate assistance impartially to all groups. Relationships should be built with local police authorities (where viable) for additional protection.

Protection response: Staff training in surveillance detection and techniques for avoiding routines. Training for guards and domestic staff on how to handle visitors, inquiries, packages, mail handling, etc.

Deterrence response: Strong relations in the diplomatic community should be used to pressure terrorist parties or local authorities that are in a position to provide protection.

Death Threats and Assassination

Threats of assassination need to be taken seriously. Staff who receive such threats should consider transfer out of post, or be prepared to take extraordinary precautions.

Acceptance response: Contacts within the community may be tapped to gain a better understanding of the threat and its credibility. Community representatives are sometimes able to influence the parties involved.

Protection response: Much of the burden will fall on the individual under threat to vary routes and times of travel, limit public exposure, and tolerate additional guards. If the threat arises from disgruntled staff, explore and address the reasons.

Deterrence response: Serious threats can be reviewed with United Nations and/or embassy representatives.

Car Jacking

Car jacking is an all-too-common criminal activity in many countries. Staff should be advised never to resist a car thief, but staff should also know strategies to avoid theft.

Acceptance response: Relationships with local police/military are important. Clearly, communities that have a stake in an agency's program are less likely to steal its property. Furthermore, local communities are sometimes able to recover stolen vehicles. However, car theft often happens outside of the community served by the agency's programs. Car jacking can sometimes be reduced by renting vehicles from the communities in and around those served. Rented vehicles are less likely to be stolen as local owners are more likely to exercise retribution on the thieves. This also provides support to local economies rather than foreign car manufacturers, and limits the cost of maintenance and loss. The downside is vehicle quality and the ability to control vehicle safety (often the owner becomes the driver).

Protection response: Vehicle protocols governing vehicle parking, routes taken, times of travel, and the use of convoys—coordinated with other agencies when possible—can greatly reduce vehicle theft. Locks, alarms, and engine shut-off mechanisms are also of some value. Comprehensive insurance should be obtained.

Deterrence response: The United Nations and embassies can sometimes influence the parties responsible or the local authorities capable of responding more effectively. Major governmental and UN donor organizations are often motivated to work with NGOs on these issues. Alternatively, if car jacking is endemic to an area served by many NGOs, the NGOs may jointly warn that services will be suspended if the car jacking continues.

Kidnapping

Kidnapping is a very serious security infraction. Agencies should have an institutional policy regarding negotiation or payments to kidnappers and be prepared for specialized assistance in managing this type of crime.

Acceptance response: Community relations may become valuable in garnering the release of a hostage.

Protection response: Kidnapping can sometimes be identified as a key threat in some security environments. When operating in these areas, it is important that staff orientation and training include advice on how to handle hostage situations.

Deterrence response: Diplomatic relations may be valuable in pressuring action in hostage situations.

Burglary, Robbery, and Other Criminal Threats

It is important for field staff to be aware of the primary criminal threats in the local environment, that is, the places and specified common activities (moneychangers, confidence rackets, pickpockets, etc.). In general, staff should be advised not to resist such crime if it happens, but rather to focus on preventing it from happening.

Acceptance response: Being accepted in a community can go a long way to providing protection from common crime and can often lead to recovery of stolen goods. Good relations with local police are also important.

Protection response: Thorough staff orientation, appropriate curfews and travel restrictions, and proper compound security are key elements.

Deterrence response: A well-trained and disciplined guard force is important. Diplomatic relations and/or relations with peacekeeping forces can be valuable, especially in failed-state situations.

Undisciplined Military, Road Blocks, etc.

This threat is a major concern in many countries of operation, particularly where we are assisting a persecuted group or operating across lines of confrontation. There are a number of precautions:

Acceptance response: In some situations it is possible to develop relations with local authorities who are able to exercise control. In many instances, civilian authorities involved in programs are able to make inroads with their military counterparts.

Protection response: Use of convoys, curfews, nonpayment policies are among the response strategies. It is very important to orient staff on how to behave under such threats, including methods of diffusing hostility.

Deterrence response: This is often a key response strategy. Large actors such as the United Nations, embassies, and/or NGO coordinating groups can exert sufficient pressure to curtail excesses.

Official Harassment

Official harassment is most typical in situations where an agency is assisting a refugee or IDP group persecuted by the host government, or where an agency is operating across lines of confrontation.

Acceptance response: Designing programs that benefit all needy population groups—not just refugees—can go a long way to improving official support. Strategies that work through local institutions to respond to refugee crises are another effective means of getting official support. Engaging various offices of government to take on our cause is also often helpful—that is, if implementing health programs that have involved the Ministry of Health, call upon the ministry to approach on your behalf the offices causing the problems with visas or customs clearances. The transparency of agency mission is also important here.

Protection response: Thorough orientation of staff who deal with local authorities is important. Staff need to be patient and diplomatic. They need to understand the agency's mandate and mission and be able to represent the agency in a mature and nonthreatening way. They need to know how to diffuse hostile innuendoes and threats.

Deterrence response: This is often a key response strategy. Large actors such as the United Nations, bilateral donors, embassies, and/or NGO coordinating groups can exert sufficient pressure to curtail excesses.

Stalking/Rape

These threats are greater in some areas than others. In situations where a pattern of criminal or genocidal rape has been a clear pattern, extra efforts need to be made to orient and protect staff.

Acceptance response: Community support is critical in the prevention of rape as well as in the identification of perpetrators—the latter contributes to limiting impunity.

Protection response: Incoming staff should be thoroughly oriented in situations where rape has been endemic. Dangerous areas should be identified. Varying routes and times of travel and traveling, jogging, or walking in groups are helpful strategies. "Buddy systems" are also helpful. The Orientation for Personal Security provides additional suggestions.

Deterrence response: Deterrent strategies are most important in situations where rape has been employed as an act of war as well as in follow-up to instances of rape.

MAINSTREAMING SECURITY:
INSTITUTIONALIZING SECURITY AT HEADQUARTERS

While it is essential that security planning and management take place in the field, there are clear and critical roles that must be played at a headquarters level. In the absence of central involvement, security measures tend to be episodic and uneven in an organization. Staff do not have a clear message about the priority that should be placed on security. Accordingly, it is imperative that senior management in an organization clearly and emphatically support the security functions of the organization. Yet it is equally important that security not be micro-managed from afar. The role of headquarters should be to establish overarching, global policies and to create structural frameworks on which security plans and preparations can be built in the field.

Global Policy

At a field level, security plans and policies may be lengthy and detailed. However, organizations need to spell out *global* policies in a concise statement emanating from headquarters. This policy document may be no longer than a few pages, but should encompass the organization's broad positions on key security issues:

Organizational mandate: What is the central mandate of the organization, and how might it impact on security? Fundamentally, does the organization embrace neutrality, or does it advocate the position of a particular social group or social issue—and in either case, how does this affect the security of the organization's staff and programs?

Threshold of risk: To what extent does the organization expect its employees to risk their lives to protect the mission and the property of the organization? This can be a challenging statement, but might be approached by stressing that the outcomes to be achieved should always outweigh the risks taken. An organization—or an individual—engaged in agricultural development should not be expected to sustain the same level of risk as one engaged in life-saving food distributions or health care.

Kidnapping and ransom: It would be unwise to state as a policy that your organization would consider paying ransom, and, indeed, payment of ransom by one organization leads to greater kidnapping threats to other organizations. If, on the other hand, your organization as a matter of principle refuses to consider ransom, it is important for your staff to understand this. A nonpayment of ransom policy may also have some deterrent effect in the field. There is more to this issue than a policy on ransom: what support is your organization willing to provide to the kidnapped and his or her family and for how long? Are you committed to post-incident psychosocial support for the individuals involved?

Bribery: There is enormous pressure on staff in some countries to pay bribes for any number of services from visas and customs clearances to safe passage at checkpoints. Paying bribes may smooth the way in the short term but, over time, greatly undermines the effectiveness and security of all NGOs. A clear statement from headquarters proscribing bribery is often welcomed by field staff.

Right to withdraw or remain: Does your staff have the right to leave their posts on security grounds without facing disciplinary or career difficulties? Does your organization reserve the right to order the departure of staff due to security reasons? In both cases, it is useful to state your organization's position.

Security is a disciplinary matter: The distinction between personal and professional conduct in the field can be quite gray. In insecure environments, the off-duty misbehavior of staff can put all staff, if not the agency's mission, in jeopardy. Global policy should set forth the agency's willingness to pursue disciplinary action on security grounds.

Evacuation: What is your policy toward evacuation of staff? Who decides when to evacuate? Who is evacuated and who pays? Are dependents of expatriate staff evacuated and at whose expense? Can they be evacuated independently (before) from staff? Does your organization have different categories of expatriate staff (third country nationals, expatriates hired locally on local contracts, dual nationals, etc.), and how are they regarded in an evacuation? What are your obligations to national staff in an evacuation? The latter can be a particularly difficult issue but is all the more important to spell out clearly.

Armed security: What is your organization's policy on the use of armed guards or armed escorts? There is considerable debate in the humanitarian community on this subject. There are a number of NGOs that categorically refuse to accept any form of armed protection. Others make decisions on a case-by-case basis. In either instance, it is important clarify the position of your organization.

Equal opportunity employment: It can be challenging to reconcile equal opportunity principles with security. The ethnicity, gender, race, politics, and religion of an individual may impact enormously on the security of that individual as well as the organization that places him or her in the field. At a minimum, your organization should be committed to clearly educating potential employees of the dangers they may face in a given field assignment. At a policy level, it may be useful to outline the conditions under which the organization may close positions based on gender or membership in social or ethnic groups.

Responsibility for security: Who is responsible for security decisions in the field and at headquarters? If you have dedicated security staff, are they advisory or are they authorized to "trump" program staff for security reasons?

Human Resource Management

Recruiting: Organizations that put maturity and character on par with technical competence in selecting staff are less likely to face security problems. Language and cultural skills are also important.

Orientation: All staff should receive a thorough orientation from headquarters *and* the field. From headquarters, incoming staff should be made well aware of the security environment that they are headed into (if this was not done during the hiring process). The organization's global security policies should be included in the staff hiring package. Not all organizations can afford to bring staff through headquarters for orientation—but regardless, new staff must be made aware of these basic issues and impressed upon with the organization's commitment to security. Personal security guidelines for travelers might also be issued from headquarters prior to the departure of newly hired staff.

Insurance: Does your organization adequately insure its staff? In addition to health and life insurance policies, do your policies include medical evacuation of staff? Do your policies adequately cover posttraumatic psychological recovery? Have you considered kidnapping and ransom insurance (these policies vary considerably, but the core purpose is to cover the costs of family support, salary, and benefits during captivity, cost of expert consultation, etc.)?

National staff personnel policies: Poor policies for national staff are the source of one of the greatest causes of security incidents for humanitarian organizations. In many organizations, national staff policy is left to the field staff to write. To what extent does your organization provide guidelines for the development of national staff personnel policies and monitor their implementation? National staff policies should have clear policies for hiring, promotion, and disciplinary action. Equitable salary scales and grievance procedures are important. Policies need to be transparent and made available to all employees.

Performance management: Security training, planning, and management indicators must be included in routine performance reviews of field managers.

Financial Management

Financial policies and procedures: As with human resource management, clear financial policies and procedures are a cornerstone of security. Checks and balances, cash transfer systems, and well-

governed procurement procedures are among the most important pieces to have in place. Warehouse management and asset
control are also very important. Policies and procedures are
worthless if not implemented. Monitoring and auditing should
be conducted annually.

Capitalization of assets: In high-risk environments, it is essential
to have good equipment in place. Vehicles, radio equipment, and
satellite phones are among the expensive items that are critical
to an effective protection strategy. Yet often organizations cannot
afford these items under short-term emergency funding from donors who are reluctant to fund asset procurement. Having the
policies in place to purchase and capitalize these assets and de-
preciate them over time—and over numerous grants and contracts—can be enormously helpful in addressing this situation.

Budgeting for security: There is a temptation in the aid industry
to identify needs, set up a proposal and budget, and let the donors decide what will happen. This should not be allowed to happen with security costs. Security line items and stand-alone
security budgets should be avoided whenever possible. Costs
should be built into program budgets: if the program is funded,
security will be included. Security orientation and training can
be built into staff benefits budgets; the cost of mobile radios included with vehicle budgets; the cost of perimeter security for
offices and housing absorbed in office and housing budgets, etc.

Fundraising and Advocacy

Fundraising: Are field staff unduly pressured to work in dangerous environments or to complete projects under time pressures
that are unrealistic given the security environment? Is there a
process for vetting fundraising strategies that involves field managers?

Advocacy: Do the public positions taken by your organization
jeopardize your staff in the field? How do you vet them? Are there
strategies for advocating positions that would be less detrimental
to your field programs?

Operational Support

Training: Field offices can and should be encouraged to plan and conduct security training. However, a headquarters-driven security training program carries with it a number of advantages: it signals the organization's prioritization of security; it creates a forum where organization-specific issues in security can be candidly discussed and through which organizational security polices and frameworks can be disseminated; it provides a conduit for field staff to communicate security concerns and issues to senior management; it creates a cadre of in-house expertise on security.

Most humanitarian organizations are not large enough to afford an in-house security training team, or even a dedicated security officer. This problem can be overcome by working either with other organizations to increase the economies of scale, or by contracting a specialized organization to conduct security training. In the latter instance, great caution should be exercised: there are dozens of security firms set up to provide advice to international businesses. The lessons are not necessarily transferable. Likewise, there are as many former-military consultants eager for security training contacts with NGOs. Alone, the military paradigm for security is inadequate for humanitarian organizations. It is important to find trainers who understand and are experienced with the unique nature of security in humanitarian contexts—the dynamic between acceptance, protection, and deterrence and the vulnerabilities that arise out of NGO missions, mandates, and culture. Even when such trainers can be found, it is important to work closely with them in designing a training agenda that fits the unique needs of your organization. The training agenda should reflect your organization's mission, mandate, and culture, and your organization's policies and procedures. The British NGO RedR (Registered Engineers for Disaster Relief) has developed specialized NGO security management courses based on the work of InterAction's Security Task Force and the ODI Good Practice Review. RedR also works with NGOs to develop customized training.

There are other challenges to security training programs organized from headquarters. There is a tendency to focus on training expatriate staff. In many, if not most, NGOs, the vast majority of employees are national staff. They are often the ones who face the most danger, who are left behind in evacuations, and who stay the longest with the organization, yet they are the most frequently overlooked for training. One strategy for ensuring that national staff are reached is to set up your training program with a training of trainers strategy through which centrally trained security trainers (who themselves may be national staff) return to their field sites and conduct dissemination training with staff in the field.

Another challenge to headquarters-driven security training programs is to make them relevant to the unique and varied threat environments in which field staff live and work. Landmine training, for example, may be of utmost importance for staff in one country program, but of little or no priority in another setting where hostage taking is a more common threat. There are a few approaches that can help a headquarters-initiated security training program remain relevant. One approach would be to regionalize training, focusing on groups of countries that have common threat environments. Another approach would be to work with other NGOs on a joint security training program in a particular country or region. Finally, the training of trainer approach mentioned above can be ideally suited to address this problem: centrally trained security trainers can be given the tools and curriculum to present training modules relevant to their working environment.

Guidelines for security planning: Although security planning must happen in the field, field offices need guidance for the planning process and the final product. Guidelines from headquarters ensure that all the elements of an effective security plan are addressed and in a logical and accessible order. They provide for institutional uniformity in the structure and general appearance of security plans, making them easier to use and evaluate. Finally, they allow the organization to create a common language and concepts that are applied throughout the organization.

Minimum standards for security: Senior managers in humanitarian organizations should create a framework for establishing minimum operating standards security at the field office level. Exactly what those standards are is going to depend upon the mission and mandate of the organization as well as on the level of threat. The following are some example standards linked to five levels of security threat. These are offered only by way of example and may vary substantially by organization and field location. The importance of the example is in the structure— which could be required from an agency headquarters—upon which a field office could fill in the details. The standards from the lower levels are carried upwards whenever possible.

Level 1 Conditions

Functioning public services (including police, communications). No outward signs of significant social disruption or instability. Crime is within normal limits and a functioning system of justice is in place.

The following minimum standards should be maintained:

- The community is involved in program design, implementation, and evaluation
- Program management has strong relations with community leaders and institutions
- All staff receive orientation (including security) upon arrival and are given a map locating hospitals, clinics, embassies, police stations, NGO offices, and/or other "safe havens"
- Emergency personnel files on all staff include blood type, emergency contact numbers, notation of allergies or other heath conditions, copies of prescriptions, copies of passports, and other pertinent personal information
- All staff must carry agency ID cards
- All staff issued with key contact information cards—telephone numbers of the agency's field and HQ, embassy, police, etc.
- All field offices must have a *reliable* local and international phone

link. Where reliable phone service is unavailable, a satphone should be requisitioned and all staff instructed in its operation
- Vehicle operations policy is in place including mandatory provisions (seat belt usage, maximum speed limits, after dark regulations, etc.)
- Local staff policy is in place that includes a functioning employee grievance policy
- Comprehensive financial policies and procedures in place
- All offices and houses have first aid kits and fire extinguishers
- Field representative has cultivated strong working relationships with relevant embassies and UN agencies

Level 2 Conditions

One or more of the following conditions prevail:

- High crime, ineffective police and/or justice systems
- Local animosities/hostilities toward NGOs and/or foreigners
- Significant political upheaval, coup, local demonstrations
- Martial law
- Hyperinflation, economic deterioration

The following minimum standards should be maintained:

- Redundant communications capacity established by acquisition of radios, cell phones, and/or satellite phones
- Calling tree/pyramid established within the organization and/or in conjunction with other organizations to facilitate communication of security notices. The system should be tested
- An evacuation plan is developed and introduced to staff (see below)
- Expatriate staff are encouraged to know their neighbors
- "Buddy system" or other system of notification established and maintained
- Trained guards provided on a full-time or part-time basis as appropriate to homes, offices, and/or program sites
- Security should be coordinated with other NGOs, IOs, and/or embassies. If no coordinating group exists, take the initiative
- Vehicles:
—Are never left unattended

—Are never stopped in traffic less than a full car's length behind other vehicles allowing room for maneuver or escape
—Are never operated with less than a half tank of fuel
—Vary routes and times of travel
—Vary vehicles used where possible
—Weigh pros and cons of marking vehicles with the organization's logo

- Staff and dependents should routinely notify someone trusted when they are going out, where they are going, and when they expect to return
- Maintain minimum cash reserve for each expatriate staff and dependent, plus additional funds adequate to pay current obligations to national staff, etc.
- Staff encouraged to keep up with news by radio, newspapers, talking with locals, etc.
- Develop national staff policy for heightened security environment. Consider more frequent salary payments, developing family security guidelines, and other means of enhancing the security of national staff and their families

Level 3 Conditions

One or more of the following conditions prevail:

- Widespread lawlessness, weakened central authority and justice systems
- Incidents of local rioting or looting reported
- Terrorist activities or other violence targeted at NGOs or foreign presence
- Fighting within twenty kilometers of offices or housing
- Markets closed or grossly limited

The following minimum standards should be maintained:

- Reduction or suspension of programs that are not directly life saving or life sustaining
- Dependents of expatriates evacuated and visitors prohibited
- Twenty-four-hour radio dispatcher, daily radio checks
- Test calling tree system weekly
- Travel outside of town in convoy of two or more vehicles only

- Consider curfews or travel limitations
- Vehicles should be kept *fully* fueled (full fuel tanks are *less* explosive than partially filled) and should be parked headed out
- Staff and dependents required to travel, shop, etc., in groups of two or more
- Public exposure should be limited
- Staff should maintain personal "ready packs" including copy of passport and current visa, cash, two changes of clothes, prescription/critical medications, basic toiletries, and other essentials
- All staff housing should maintain water and food stocks sufficient for one week minimum
- Staff should be briefed on security developments on a routine basis—weekly or biweekly—including a review of incidents and response protocol
- All travel should be planned and monitored including time of departure, estimated time of arrival, and persons traveling. A board for this purpose is helpful
- Establish security communications and coordination with other NGOs and UN agencies
- Create security circulars for national staff and their families to share information and provide advice for enhanced family security
- Prepare a summary of critical institutional documents that would be taken in the event of an evacuation. Consider evacuating or destroying local staff personnel files if local staff could face persecution under a new regime
- Establish and maintain routine *scheduled* communications headquarters

Level 4 Conditions

One or more of the following conditions prevail:

- Incoming artillery, bombardment, or fighting in the area of operations
- Widespread looting or rioting
- Economic collapse
- Cessation of most public services

The following minimum standards should be maintained:

- Suspension or reduction of program activities
- All expatriate staff restricted to designated safe areas
- Staff on leave are prohibited from returning. Leave schedule for other staff moved forward where appropriate
- Nonessential staff evacuated
- Constant radio monitoring by all staff under the oversight of a dispatcher. Radio checks daily or more frequent. Staff should check in and out of each location with the radio dispatcher keeping record of staff whereabouts
- Revise general evacuation plans and prepare for closure of office and/or local administration of IRC interests

Level 5 Conditions

One or more of the following conditions prevail:

- Immediate and demonstrated threats to the organization or humanitarian activities in general
- Open warfare or imminent warfare in the immediate vicinity of staff housing and offices
- Civil unrest to such a magnitude as to pose an immediate threat to staff and operations

The following minimum standards should be maintained:

- Suspend all program activities
- Weigh pros and cons of evacuation versus hibernation response
- Maintain daily contact with headquarters, embassy, United Nations, and other agencies concerned with security until evacuation can be implemented
- All expatriate staff restricted to designated safe areas and *prepared for* immediate evacuation

EVACUATION PLANNING

Organizations working in volatile security environments should prepare well in advance for various evacuation contingencies. The contingencies would include various routes, partial evacuations, and evacuations that will be permanent versus those that may only be temporary. Evacuation plans should be revised during periods of heightened threat. Although elements of the plan should remain confidential, concerned staff should be aware of the key elements. Most evacuations are partial and temporary. A common shortfall of evacuation plans is that they focus on getting people—usually expatriate staff—out, but overlook what is to be done with the staff, assets, and programs that remain behind. Evacuation plans should include:

- Delegation of authority (to local or expatriate staff or other institutions)
- Disposition of bank accounts and assets
- Identification of sensitive files—especially personnel and financial—and plans for their safekeeping, removal, or destruction
- Routes, means of transport, meeting points, etc.
- Destination of departing staff—establishment of remote administration
- Coordination with other agencies
- Communications systems and equipment
- Policy toward national staff
- Payment of remaining staff, debts, etc.
- Plan for dealing with contracts, rental agreements, retainers, etc.
- Cash, travel documents, tickets, etc., for departing staff
- Personal items which can be taken in an evacuation

SUMMARY AND CONCLUSION

The security of aid workers is a growing concern for humanitarian organizations, underscored by tragic events and their consequences on individuals, organizations, and their humanitarian mission. Given the nature and frequency of modern crises, this trend can only be expected to continue. Military and police models for addressing security are, alone, insufficient to meet the needs of humanitarian organizations working in complex security environments. Similarly, corporate security models miss the mark. Although there is much to be learned from these models, humanitarian NGOs must look beyond protective equipment and procedures. The quality of our programs—measured in community involvement in design, implementation, and evaluation—is every bit as important as convoy operations and radio gear. Likewise, good management practices, including transparent human resource policies and solid accounting, are also essential. Finally, the relationships that organizations form in the diplomatic community at home and abroad are critical to working in insecure environments. These strategies make up the acceptance-protection-deterrence triangle that is at the heart of effective NGO security.

Managing field security requires a working balance between field-driven planning and management built upon structures and global policies set forth from agency headquarters. At the headquarters level, security involves policy commitments from senior management as well as operational capacities from the program, finance, and human resource sectors. An organization's commitment to security at this broad level sends an important message to field managers and staff about the priority of security. With priorities and structure set at a global level, field management must be expected to conduct training and planning processes, and given the freedom and support to manage security incidents.

Individuals must also take responsibility for not only their personal security, but also for their role in the security of the humanitarian mission. There is really no distinction between professional and private life in crisis settings. It is incumbent upon all who enter the profession to realize that security is among the many unique challenges of humanitarian assistance.

Part 4

One of the first tasks for a humanitarian worker entering a complex emergency operation is to begin planning an exit. This is not a cold decision, reflecting a lack of compassion. Rather, it is the essential discipline that marks a true professional. The goal of international assistance is not merely to offer immediate succor; a comprehensive approach must consider, as early as possible, how to encourage that always-difficult transition from desperation and utter dependence to self-management and ultimate freedom. The move from war to peace may take many paths. Phases of rehabilitation, reconciliation, and sustainable development are integral parts of an emergency relief operation.

11

Resolutions, Mandates, Aims, Missions, and Exit Strategies

Larry Hollingworth

"The Secretariat must tell the Security Council what it needs to know, not what it wants to hear, when formulating or changing mission mandates."

Lakhdar Brahimi

"No exit without a strategy."

Security Council Press Release 6951

GENERAL CONSIDERATIONS

SINCE THE EARLY 1990s, in times of crisis the two questions most feared by both military and humanitarian planners formulating a response are "What is the mandate?" and "What is the exit strategy?" They are closely linked. "What are you going to do?" and "When will you know that you have done it?" They are sometimes asked before any action takes place, more often they are asked just as the momentum of the plan begins to roll. Once asked, they refuse to go away. They are never easy questions to answer. The exit strategy is especially difficult if the mandate proves to be unclear or vague or fluid.

In the UN system whenever there is a crisis in the world, the Security Council meets to decide how the United Nations should respond. There are no hard and fast guidelines; it can be a considered response taken after an assessment mission, a response to passionate pleas of national representatives; it can be in response to pictures on the TV, a response to public opinion, a response to political influence or to a single horrific act.

If it decides to act, the UN Security Council will issue a resolution that will call upon member nations to respond to the crisis. This resolution will mandate,[1] give power to, will give an aim and a mission to the members of those nations, agencies, and individuals that respond and act on behalf of the United Nations.

Resolutions

Resolutions are written and drawn up by delegates from member states, usually from those states serving on the Security Council. They are adopted by the Security Council at a meeting on a given date. They are numbered, and the year is placed after the resolution number in brackets. Resolutions consist of short paragraphs, each beginning with a key word. The Security Council "Reaffirming," "Supporting," "Demanding," "Condemning," "Recommending," "Calls," "Encourages," "Decides" something. Member states are obliged to accept and carry out the decisions of the council.

Peacekeeping resolutions may be issued under chapter 6 of the UN Charter: Pacific Settlement of Disputes. "Where a wide range of advisory possibilities and mediation methods are posed, all designed to settle interstate disputes without resorting to military force."[2] Also under chapter 7 of the UN Charter: Action with Respect to Threats to the Peace, Breaches of the Peace, and Acts of Aggression. "Calls for severing diplomatic relations, disrupting economic ties, boycotts, and then if those methods fail, describes how and in what circumstances the Security Council may authorize the use of military force."[3]

Mandates

Lakhdar Brahimi, former Foreign Minister for Algeria and Chairman of the UN Committee on Afghanistan, wrote in his report that "mandates should be clear, credible, and achievable."[4] The first and cardinal point is that a mandate must be achievable. It must be "doable." The mandate is not a wish list, it is not a first guess; it is a directive written to produce a result.

The second and equally important point is that the task must be matched with the resources needed to carry it out. The mandate must be credible. Inadequate manpower, materiel, or funding will defeat it:

> Mandates must be matched by the necessary resources. Focus on keeping costs down are cheaper in the short-run but more costly later if missions failed to achieve their objectives. The council must have staying power to ensure that the international community's investments in peace were not lost because of a short-sighted political expediency. The conditions for sustained development must be created.[5] (Canada)

The mandate must be clear: it empowers, it has the force of law. It must be written in the clearest of language that can be understood by those who are to carry out the task and those who are to receive its consequences. The mandate is the initial route map. It should, as a minimum, indicate, in outline, the beginning, the middle, and the end of the journey: the "what" is to be done, the "how" it is to be done, and the "by when" it is to be done.

Aims

The mandate is the big picture defined in a minimum of words. To transform it from words to deeds, each of the participating groups including the political, the military, and the humanitarian agencies will carry out an assessment of their role in the crisis. This assessment will define the aims from which they will produce a plan of action.

Missions

The plan will have an overall single mission statement, and each task within the plan will have its own mission. Each mission has the same three criteria as the mandate. The mission must be achievable, credible, and clear. To maintain an even clearer focus, the mission can be further fine-tuned by a statement of its intent and purpose. "Go to that village" is a mission. But what happens when you arrive? What do you do there? Do you stay forever? Hand things over to someone else? "Go to that village, set up a clinic, and then come back" is a much clearer mission.

EXIT STRATEGY

No exit without a strategy. We shouldn't talk about getting out but getting it right. (Namibia)

A major reason why an exit strategy succeeds is that the local population take ownership of the peace process.[6] (Germany)

The "exit strategy," the endgame, the "when do we leave" is the most difficult, the most moveable, and the most emotive part of the equation. How is the finishing post recognized? What has to be achieved before the journey is over? "Is it a passage of time or the occurrence of events?"[7] Are political, social, or cultural features more important than temporal or financial?

Furthermore the exit strategy is vulnerable to changes caused by new resolutions that may amplify or modify the mandate. The aims and ambitions of the actors and the rate of progress can cause the mission to creep in size, shape, and speed and alter the exit strategy. Fulfilling the mission invariably depends on acquiring objectives and overcoming limitations. Recognizing quantifiable, plausible, and reliable assessors of progress in a volatile post-conflict environment is as much an art as a science.

Exit strategies should not be confused with exit deadlines. Exit strategies must be directed to specific objectives and not based on arbitrary deadlines. (United States)

An exit strategy is not an escape route. (Egypt)

There is a distinction between end state and end state exit strategy. An exit strategy for the military components of the mission based on an end date and disconnected from the overall objectives of the peace operation reduces the chances for success. (Norway)

Any exit strategy should be based on the notion of local ownership. (Denmark)

Objectives

Before exiting, a peacekeeping mission must ensure its objectives have been attained and the causes of the conflict have disappeared. A stable political, economic, and social climate needs to be established to prevent a reoccurrence of conflict.[8](China)

What are the objectives to be achieved before the actors can safely leave or, more importantly, leave the recipients of their support in safety? The establishment of political, security, economic, and social conditions for a lasting peace are the ultimate goal.

The first requirement is for a dialogue between the adversaries that will lead to a signed peace agreement or, at least, to one of the interim measures, a truce or cease-fire, which may initially be local, then regional, then countrywide.

Simultaneous action to restore water and power supplies, to repair roads, to clear war detritus, and to reopen clinics, hospitals, and schools is vital. The establishment of law and order is of the highest priority if citizens are to feel safe and the displaced and the refugees are encouraged to return.

A withdrawal from occupied territories and the disarmament, demobilization, and reintegration of combatants is essential. The release of prisoners of war and other detainees should be accompanied by the return of displaced persons, then refugees, then the reuniting of families and the rehabilitation of victims, and the wounded, sick, traumatized, and handicapped.

The introduction of a plan for the material, economic, social, and democratic reconstruction is vital, to be accompanied by the implantation of free and fair elections, the healing of collective wounds through truth and reconciliation, and the reintegration into the regional and international community.

The implementation of a program for each of these objectives takes us a step closer to leaving and is part of the exit strategy. Each is a quantifiable event, and each must be realistic in its scope. International and national political will is essential to achieve the objectives, but both can wane with the passage of time.

The international community, especially donor states, will be faced with differing views of when to exit. Will it be when the state is where it was before the crisis, where it could be if there had been no crisis, or where it would like itself to be? The precrisis level of the socioeconomic development of the country is a firm guide to the level to be achieved post-crisis.

An important consideration is to assess how the exit strategy end state affects the neighboring states. Throughout the rebuilding, the international community needs to be able to monitor the situation to prevent the recurrence of the conflict. We should note that donor enthusiasm for an exit strategy may not be shared by recipient state. Frankly, there are states that like the aid that goes with the problem and are reluctant to see the international community leave.

Notwithstanding all of these objectives and caveats, the United Nations has managed to enter into and to exit from more than thirty-nine operations in twenty-seven countries. Let us look at some of the successes and failures.

CYPRUS

Cyprus is an island no more than 120 miles from west to east and fifty miles from north to south, with a population of 726,000.

Security Council resolution 186 (1964) established UNFICYP with a mandate to prevent a recurrence of fighting between the Greek Cypriot and the Turkish Cypriot communities and to contribute to the maintenance and restoration of law and order and a return to normal conditions. The Security Council has subsequently adopted a number of resolutions expanding the mandate to include supervising a de facto cease-fire, and maintaining a buffer zone between the lines of the Cyprus National Guard and of the Turkish and Turkish Cypriot forces.

The mandate is clear and credible, and if there were political agreement from both sides, it is achievable. The mandate has now run for more than three decades, at a cost of approximately $42 million per year. It is hard to believe that the adoption of a more robust pressurized exit strategy could not have achieved an earlier solution.

SOMALIA

In the case of Somalia, key actors made many errors of judgment. The decision to walk away completely without leaving behind any kind of presence to help improve the situation is a blot on the United Nations's conscience. Somalia almost killed peacekeeping operations.[9] (Singapore)

In April 1992, the UN Security Council approved Resolution 751 establishing the United Nations Operation in Somalia (UNOSOM). The initial mandate was to monitor the cease-fire in Mogadishu and to escort deliveries of humanitarian supplies. President George Bush ordered U.S. forces to initiate Operation "Provide Relief" in support of this mandate. It is worth observing how the mandate was translated into a military task.

The mission was "to provide military assistance in support of emergency humanitarian relief in Kenya and Somalia." The objectives were the following:

- To deploy a humanitarian assistance survey team to assess relief requirements
- To activate a joint task force to conduct an emergency airlift of food and supplies into Somalia and northern Kenya
- To provide daily relief sorties into Somalia

Security Council Resolution 775 August (1992) strengthened the initial mandate to enable it to protect humanitarian convoys throughout Somalia. Despite this, the security situation deteriorated, and on December 3, the Security Council issued Resolution 794 (1992) that welcomed a U.S. offer to help create a secure environment for the delivery of humanitarian aid. The resolution, under chapter 7 of the Charter, authorized the use of "all necessary means."

"Operation Provide Relief" ended and "Operation Restore Hope" began, under which the United States would assume the unified command of a multinational coalition to be known as the Unified Task Force (UNITAF). The UN mandate implied two important missions:

- To provide humanitarian assistance to the Somali people
- To restore order in southern Somalia

From December 9, 1992, until May 4, 1993, UNITAF deployed more than thirty-eight thousand troops from twenty-one coalition nations. UNITAF had a positive impact on the security situation and on the effective delivery of humanitarian assistance, but a secure environment was not established. Furthermore, there was no deployment of UNITAF or UNISOM to the northeast and northwest or along the Kenya-Somalia border.

On March 26, 1993, the Security Council established UNOSOM II. This was under chapter 7 enforcement provisions. The mission was to establish a secure environment for humanitarian relief operations throughout Somalia. It implied disarming the Somali clans, rehabilitating political institutions, and the building of a secure environment. This was an ambitious mandate, and it threatened the power base of clan warlords.

In the mandate the Secretary-General included an outline "exit strategy." The operation was to be conducted in four phases; the latter two included the reduction of the force and the redeployment of the force.

On June 5, 1993, twenty-four Pakistani soldiers were killed, and the United Nations issued Security Council Resolution 837, which called for the immediate apprehension of those responsible. This quickly led to U.S. forces being used in a highly personalized manhunt for Mohammed Aideed. A major engagement occurred on October 3, in which eighteen Americans were killed and seventy-five wounded. Shortly thereafter President Clinton announced a phased withdrawal of American troops that would end by March 31, 1994.

The mandate was extended in time, but the mission was altered and the force downsized by subsequent resolutions. With these major reductions, UNOSOM II was not able to provide protection even within Mogadishu. Agencies were advised to evacuate international staff, and the withdrawal of UNOSOM II was complete by March 28, 1995.

UNOSOM I and "Provide Relief" provided few entry or exit questions, but the criterion for success was clear: "provide food supplies."

The UNITAF mandate was based on better security and more food distribution. It was clear and credible but not achievable. The exit strategy became simple: handover to UNOSOM II. This event was clearly identified but not clearly reached. Although the handover was not complete, U.S. forces were withdrawn on schedule. The lack of an effective transition clearly complicated conditions.

In the aftermath of the June 5 ambush, the United States played a prominent role in drafting UN Security Council Resolution 837, which constituted de facto changes in the mission. Its terms were rapidly translated into a manhunt for Mohammed Aideed. The deepening involvement of the U.S. forces in combat operations during UNOSOM II has been criticized as mission creep.

It is easy to dismiss the efforts of UNOSOM as a failure and to cite a lack of political will on behalf of the international community to continue as the cause. The earlier mandates failed, the later succeeded through modification. The exit strategy achieved was not that initially envisaged. It was not all bad. The DPKO end-of-mission report credits it with "a cease-fire, first in Mogadishu and then nationally." And "it did put in place fifty-two (out of ninety-two) district councils and eight (out of eighteen) regional councils." But it saves its major praise for "the humanitarian field. Millions of Somalis benefited from these activities and at a minimum an estimated quarter of a million lives were saved."

UNOSOM I cost $42,931,700; UNOSOM II cost $1,643,485,500.

The poorest countries cannot emerge from conflict without generous aid. There can be no exit strategy without an assessment establishing whether the conditions are right for the termination of the mission. (Namibia)

Will the country be allowed to plunge into chaos if we withdraw?[10] (Ukraine)

RWANDA

The United Nations Assistance Mission in Rwanda (UNAMIR) was established by Security Council Resolution 872 of October 19, 1993, to help implement the Arusha Peace Agreement. The mandate was the following:

- To assist in ensuring the security of the capital of Kigali
- To monitor the cease-fire agreement, including the establishment of an expanded demilitarized zone and demobilization procedures
- To monitor the security situation
- To assist with mine clearance
- To assist in the coordination of humanitarian assistance activities

The mandate was clear; the latter three missions were achievable, one and two were credible and achievable given sufficient resources. The mandate was appropriate to the circumstances at the time of drafting. But implementing it got off to a slow and ominous start. The UN requested 2,548 troops, but initially only Belgium and Bangladesh answered the call, each with four hundred. It was to take five months to achieve the target figure.

General Romeo Dallaire, the UNAMIR commander, has written that:

In the midst of the complexity and confusion (of the political situation), international indifference to the crisis combined with the UN's chronic limitation to raise, equip, and sustain military forces produced disastrous results. Half battalions from Belgium and Bangladesh created an inefficient command, control, and support system with few troops available for operations. The Ghanaians were deployed ahead of time because of the urgent need for troops on the ground and with the grudging acceptance that their equipment would follow later. They were in theatre for over two months before any substantial equipment arrived. The Bangladesh half battalion could transport neither their own infantry companies nor the attached Tunisian company to conduct their operations. Only five of the eight Bangladesh armored personnel carriers out of twenty originally promised could be counted on at any given time. There were no spare parts, manuals, or mechanics to maintain these essential vehicles nor had the crews ever fired their main weapon. The UN military observers were employed throughout the country in the monitoring tasks with next to no communications capability.[11]

On April 6, 1994, the assassination of President Habyarimana triggered an escalation of violence. The Security Council on April 21 responded with an adjusted resolution 912 (1994). The adjusted mandate included the following:

- To act as an intermediary between the warring Rwandese parties in an attempt to secure their agreement to a cease-fire
- To assist in the resumption of humanitarian relief operations to the extent feasible
- To monitor developments in Rwanda, including the safety and security of civilians who sought refuge with UNAMIR

This was a tall order for a commander who wrote: "In my opinion, no individual state would have permitted its troops and its operations to be put into such a predicament, one that would surely lead to disaster in the face of altercations or violence between belligerents."

It was an impossible order for a commander who had his strength cut from 2,500 to 450 as a reaction to the brutal murder of ten Belgian paratroopers assigned to guard the prime minister. This outrage caused panic in some capitals and concern in others.

Amazingly, a multinational force of fifteen hundred troops from France, Italy, and Belgium, supported by U.S. Marines on standby in Burundi, evacuated from Kigali expatriate civilians and a few Rwandans,

> and then left in the face of the unfolding tragedy with the full knowledge of the danger confronting the emasculated UN force. UNAMIR was abandoned by all including most of our civilian staff (by order) and we were left to fend for ourselves for weeks. That we were left in this state, with neither mandate nor supplies, with only survival rations that were rotten and inedible is a description of inexcusable apathy by the sovereign states that made up the UN.[12]

It was two months into the genocide before the Security Council expanded the mandate under Resolution 918 (1994) dated May 17. UNAMIR was now to contribute to the security and protection of refugees and civilians at risk through the establishment and maintenance of secure humanitarian areas and the provision of security for relief operations. Thankfully this was only "to the degree possible." The mandate was made more credible by authorizing the size of the force to grow to fifty-five hundred personnel. Five months later the general was still waiting for the reinforcements to arrive, despite the fact that nineteen countries had offered a total of thirty-one thousand soldiers as part of the standby forces agreement.

There was little enthusiasm to send troops to Rwanda. Further resolutions concerned the return of refugees and support for the International Tribunal.

The international community expended $2 billion, of which the U.S. provided $750 million, which equaled the entire budget of the USAID African Development Fund for Sub-Saharan Africa over the same period. The cost of a force of fifty-five hundred for three months at the earliest and most crucial time would have been $700 million.

The best that can be said for the earlier UNAMIR mandates is that they were clear. For milestones to an end strategy to have included genocide is a stain on the history of the United Nations and a blot on the conscience of the international community.

Somalia and Rwanda were examples of cases in which peace operations had been terminated for political motives. Cases when the Security Council decided to end a peacekeeping mission or reduce its military component only to have those situations remain unstable or descend again into violence or chaos.[13] (Egypt)

BOSNIA HERZEGOVINA

The Security Council should leave in draft form resolutions authorizing missions with sizeable troop levels until such time as the Secretary-General has firm commitments of troops and other critical mission support elements, including peace building elements, from member states. (Lakhdar Brahimi)

On April 16, 1993, the Security Council, acting under chapter 7 of the UN Charter, adopted Resolution 819, in which it declared Srebrenica "a safe area" that should be free from any armed attack or hostile act. It demanded the immediate withdrawal of Bosnian Serb paramilitary units from areas surrounding Srebrenica and the cessation of armed attacks against the town. It requested the Secretary-General to take steps to increase the presence of the United Nations Protection Force (UNPRO-FOR) in Srebrenica and to arrange for the safe transfer of the ill and wounded. Moreover, it demanded the unimpeded delivery of humanitarian assistance to all parts of Bosnia Herzegovina and in particular to the civilian population of Srebrenica. It also condemned the deliberate actions of the Bosnian Serb party in its campaign of "ethnic cleansing," and members of the council decided to send a mission to see the conditions for themselves.

The resolution did not involve itself in the definition of a safe area or how it differed from a safe haven. Britain, France, and Spain were pragmatic proponents of "safe area" and opposed the creating of a "safe haven." The difference is that safe havens do not depend on the consent of the warring parties and can be enforced, while safe areas are based on consent.

The mandate could have been clearer. Was it credible? The experience of the previous year would have indicated that it was highly unlikely that there would be unimpeded delivery of aid.

Was it achievable? Not without a drastic change of heart by the Serbs or an equally severe change of tactics by UNPROFOR.

Did the mandate create expectations that Srebrenica would be safe and that the UN would protect it? The answer surely must be yes.

The next Security Council Resolution, 824 (1993) issued on May 6, had the benefit of the report from the mission sent in by Resolution 819. It declared Sarajevo, Tuzla, Zepa, Gorazde, and Bihac also to be "safe areas" and added the same demands as in 819.

If Resolution 819 looked doubtful, Resolution 824 looked distinctly "not doable."

But on June 4, Resolution 836 (1993) came to the rescue. Acting under chapter 7 of the UN Charter, the mandate of UNPROFOR was expanded to enable it to protect the safe areas. It could deter attacks against them. It could promote the withdrawal of military or paramilitary units. It could occupy key points, and, acting in self-defense, UNPROFOR could take necessary measures including the use of force, in reply to bombardments against the safe areas or to armed incursion into them or in the event of deliberate obstruction to the freedom of movement of UNPROFOR or of protected humanitarian convoys.

But the sting came in the tail of the resolution. Member states acting nationally or through regional arrangements might take all necessary measures through the use of air power in and around the safe areas to support UNPROFOR.

There was no way that UNPROFOR could carry out the mandate of Resolution 836 within its shape and size. Therefore the council wisely asked the Secretary-General to report on the requirements to implement it.

After ten days' deliberation the Secretary-General gave his report. It spoke of light options and heavy options. The light option needed seventy-six hundred troops based in the six enclaves "to deter aggression;" the heavy option was thirty-four thousand, which would "oppose any aggression." Four days later, Resolution 844 (1993) authorized a reinforcement with the lower number. It was accepted that this would provide a basic level of deterrence and assumed the consent of the parties. Fortunately the resolution reaffirmed the use of airpower to support the force in the safe areas.

But it had already become painfully clear from the debate on light and heavy options that finding the seventy-six hundred was not going to be easy. Nation after nation refused to provide, prevaricated, or pleaded other commitments both within Bosnia and without Bosnia. Only the Dutch agreed, and to provide only 1,170 troops. It was to take until March 3, 1994, to get 570 of them into Srebrenica.

This was another mandate with only clarity as its strongpoint.

The people in the surrounding areas of Srebrenica believed in the mandate and came into the safe area for protection. They were heartened to hear on May 9, 1994, the Secretary-General state "the intention of a safe area is primarily to protect people," but their enthusiasm waned when he continued "and not to defend territory. The UNPROFOR protection of these areas is not intended to make it a party to the conflict."

The exit strategy from Srebrenica was concluded swiftly and tragically. At least eleven thousand men died because the resources did not match the task.

The Security Council issued an average of twelve resolutions per year from 1992 through 1996 on Bosnia alone.

Changing mandates reflect the situation for good or evil. (Shashi Tharoor, UN Secretariat)

EAST TIMOR

East Timor has been on the United Nations books since 1960 when it was added to the list of nonself-governing territories. In 1975 and 1976, it was the subject of two resolutions as a result of its occupation by Indonesia. From 1982 there were regular talks with Indonesia and Portugal aimed at resolving the status of the territory. In June 1998 Indonesia proposed a limited autonomy for East Timor within Indonesia. The United Nations was entrusted with organizing and conducting a "popular consultation" to ascertain whether the East Timorese people accepted or rejected a special autonomy within the Republic of Indonesia.

The Security Council established the United Nations Mission in East Timor (UNAMET) on June 11, 1999. The mandate was "to organize and conduct a popular consultation." It was clear and credible, but was it achievable? The election registered 451,000 from a population of 800,000. The vote took place, and 78 percent voted for a move toward independence. The mandate was clearly and credibly achievable. But the results sparked off a wave of violence in which many East Timorese were killed and almost 500,000 were displaced from their homes.

The Security Council undertook strenuous negotiations with the Indonesian government to stop the violence. This resulted in Security Council Resolution 1264 (1999) authorizing a multinational force, the International Force in East Timor (INTERFET) with the mandate to pursue the following:

- To restore peace and security in East Timor
- To protect and support UNAMET in carrying out its tasks
- To facilitate humanitarian assistance operations

This small, professional military force cautiously pursued its mandate.

On October 22, the Security Council issued Resolution 1272 (1999), which established the United Nations Transitional Administration in East Timor (UNTAET) with the comprehensive mandate for the following:

- To provide security and maintain law and order throughout the territory of East Timor
- To establish an effective administration
- To assist in the development of civil and social services
- To ensure the coordination and delivery of humanitarian assistance, rehabilitation, and development assistance
- To support capacity building the self-government
- To assist in the establishment of conditions for sustainable development

The exit strategy of INTERFET was also clearly defined. It was to hand over its operations to UNAMET on February 28, 2000.

The mandate of UNTAET was extended to May 20, 2002, a date that proved to be generous. UNTAET achieved its mandate ahead of schedule. Strong leadership and excellent administration played a large part in this success, but the presence of political will, enthusiastic and benevolent international support, and no violent opposition were the outstanding and rare features that brought the mandate to a satisfactory exit.

East Timor has the pleasure of governing itself, but it is a long way away from economic independence. Furthermore it does and always will lie in the shadow of a teeming, turbulent nation.

> Economically the short-term impact of the UN's exit could mean the loss of a significant source of demand and income. In cases where the United Nations has a major impact on the national economy the council must give weight to these economic factors when considering the exit strategy. (Australia)

> We should not be in a hurry to exit as often the existence of a peacekeeping operation is seen as an important symbol of international presence. (Egypt)

EXIT STRATEGY

Whenever there is a crisis and the UN responds, it is worth connecting to www.UN.org/welcome/documents/resolutions to see how it intends to reply. Work out for yourself the mandate and the exit strategy, and sit back and wait and see how it works out.

> In most cases the best the peacekeepers can do is to maintain the status quo. (Pakistan)

12

The Transition from Conflict to Peace

Richard Ryscavage, S.J.

HUMANITARIAN ASSISTANCE workers may find themselves hopelessly confused by the range of problems facing a society struggling to move from war to peace. These problems can be approached from many directions: the shift from emergency relief into longer-range development assistance; the religious, cultural, and psychosocial models for dealing with trauma, recovery, and reconciliation; conflict management and conflict resolution methods; the place of civil society organizations; the challenges of refugee repatriation and internally displaced people; the role of international peacekeepers and outside military forces; the connection between peace, democracy, and development.

This chapter will survey the various approaches and try to organize them into levels and "lenses" that, depending on where the humanitarian actor is in the process, he or she may find a helpful starting point for analysis and action.

CONFLICT TO PEACE: SOME BASIC QUESTIONS

Most humanitarian actors make the basic assumption that peace is good and war is bad. By all means, at certain levels a peaceful world seems preferable to a planet torn by violence. Yet too much emphasis on peace for its own sake can block the paths to peace. Many people, not just rich people, profit immensely from war. Economies on a wartime footing can be much more productive than peacetime economies. So simply from the socioeconomic perspective, a quick transition from war to peace may not be in the best interests of a society. It is always useful to stand back from a violent conflict and do a cost-benefit analysis. Who benefits from this war? Who bears the most costs?[1]

More importantly, the process of moving from war to peace is almost never a straight line. The process has a more cyclical nature characterized by one step forward and two steps back. Large-scale violent conflict might end, but smaller sporadic outbursts of violence can continue for many years. A fragile peace agreement can quickly break down, and an even more violent stage of conflict erupt. So in general it is not very useful to view the transition from war to peace as a continuum. In some senses peace begins to emerge in the midst of violence, and violence can emerge even when peace seems rather secure. This is the reason Johan Galtung and other peace theorists have argued for years that peace building must begin before the conflict ends.[2]

How one builds peace in the midst of violence can be addressed only by looking at the various actors or potential actors: military, guerrillas, governments, UN, local nongovernmental organizations, international nongovernmental organizations. Peace-building actions must be tailored to the nature of the specific actor. For example, the military is not trained for nation building and strengthening democracy. Similarly a humanitarian NGO should not be expected to provide security or disarm warring parties.

From the perspective of most UN member states and most nongovernmental humanitarian actors, the transition from violent conflict to social peace requires international assistance designed to strengthen local socioeconomic and cultural development. It does this by helping societies recover from war and limiting future violence.

This mission seems more straightforward than it actually is. The approach rests on the assumption that socioeconomic and cultural development is good. Many ecologists would challenge that assumption. "Sustainable development" can damage the local small market economy and make people more, not less, vulnerable.[3] The policy also presumes some rather long-term commitments and relationships with the international community.

Most international politicians and military people are hesitant to lock themselves into a long-range development for peace strategy. Overall, though, the current consensus seems to be that the transition from violent conflict to peace must be addressed through a development perspective.

RELIEF TO DEVELOPMENT MODEL

In the classic vocabulary of humanitarian assistance there are three phases: relief, rehabilitation, and development. These three phases often involve different goals, skills, agendas, and ways of operating. Yet there is much controversy over the actual boundaries between the three phases. Conflict resolution and peace strengthening can be aspects of all phases, but the limits of each phase must be respected if the peace activity is to have any chance of success.

Relief

Relief usually means the earliest operational phase of assistance. Sometimes the term is qualified by saying "emergency relief." Although the development phase is characterized by considerable governmental controls and the involvement of multilateral organizations, the relief phase is dominated by private international and local voluntary organizations. A high-profile crisis can generate millions of dollars in government and private donations for immediate relief. Hundreds—even thousands—of NGOs will try to jockey for a piece of the relief money.[4] This relief aid may not often fit well with the longer-range development needs of a country.

By the end of the twentieth century, governments and private donors had shifted most of their humanitarian assistance away from development into relief aid.[5] Not only were the emergency needs in places like Rwanda and the Balkans enormous, but also they were well publicized and required fewer long-term budgetary commitments.

It was in the context of postgenocide Rwanda and the war in the Balkans that the term "complex emergency" arose. It is a useful term because it highlights the fact that certain humanitarian disasters are multidimensional. In essence it refers to civil war, manmade disasters, political chaos, and power struggles that accompany and cause a humanitarian crisis. Because the need for emergency food or water exists in the middle of violent conflict and complicated political and military maneuvering, the road out of that emergency stage will be equally complex.[6]

Rehabilitation

Rehabilitation is a kind midwife stage between relief and development activities. It has a very important role to play in peace building. Rehabilitation usually means activities that restore basic services (water, electricity, schools, and health clinics), rebuilding houses and roads, and restoring some agricultural production and normal economic life.[7]

In many situations the most important rehabilitation activity will be the process of demilitarization, including de-mining. To strengthen a budding peace and to proceed with social and economic reconstruction, it is essential to neutralize weapons stocks, disarm the irregular forces, and find jobs for the demobilized army youth. For medical, agricultural, and social reasons, de-mining becomes an urgent need. It has been shown that mine clearance is an activity that tends to foster national reconciliation by involving formerly hostile parties in the mutually beneficial task of identifying and clearing mines. De-mining is an example of how building peace can be integrated into social reconstruction during the period of rehabilitation.[8]

It is within the rehabilitation phase that human rights and legal issues of land ownership and justice can also begin to be addressed more systematically. This is particularly important where there is a problem of large-scale refugee repatriation or a situation where citizens have been displaced by war and now want to go home. If the "right of return" is not faced squarely, the fragile structures of peace will be threatened. Sometimes coming home means rebuilding houses; more often it involves complicated legal, ethnic, and political issues, especially if people have been gone for a long period. One point is very clear: a refugee camp, by its nature, is not a place for social reconstruction and development. One way or another, refugees and displaced people need to settle permanently somewhere before lasting peace can be established.

Development

Most economists define development as economic growth, improved living standards, and the creation of wealth. Through a wider lens, development means anything that improves the society. That wider perspective would include promotion of democracy, human rights, protection of the environment, and social justice.[9]

Full-blown development stage has traditionally involved multilateral institutions such as the World Bank, International Monetary Fund, and the United Nations Development Program. Development, which emphasizes material assistance, building infrastructures, and sustaining bureaucracies, tends to reinforce and strengthen the role of the state as the chief agent for development. But if the state is corrupt and poorly managed, development can be turned to the political and personal advantage of the leadership. Certain forms of development that stress money, infrastructure, and state regulation may not contribute at all to the reconciliation of groups previously at war. Within the development stage, more direct attention is needed on psychological, cultural, and even spiritual determinants of violence. Attention to behavior that disrupts peace and the continual reinforcement of confidence and trust building measures will be equally important. Even years after a war has ended, if peace building does not continue, a new social cycle of violence can form, undermining everything that has been achieved.

The relief-rehabilitation-development continuum is a way of organizing our thinking about social problems. In reality the pure continuum does not exist.[10] In some cases these "phased" activities can be taking place at the same time in the same country. One section of the country—less touched by war—might be ready for some prime large-scale development programs while another section is still without clean water or enough food. Within the rehabilitation phase are activities that might be considered both relief and development.

The most important point for a humanitarian actor to consider is that the introduction of humanitarian assistance, no matter what phase, can have a direct long-term impact on the achievement of peace. Humanitarian assistance is never really neutral. It always has political, social, economic, and cultural consequences. Peace-strengthening approaches can be consciously built into any humanitarian assistance action—even at the very earliest emergency phase. But peace-building measures must never be introduced uncritically.

APPROACHES TO PEACE

Over the past thirty years the academic fields of peace research and conflict resolution studies have grown enormously. Diplomats, politicians, and humanitarian actors have been using methods derived from this research to facilitate the transition from violent conflict to peace.[11]

One can roughly divide the research into two approaches. One approach concentrates on the social psychological aspects of overcoming conflict. Emphasis is placed on the attitudes and perceptions of the parties to the conflict. Changing perceptions—usually through small group work—characterizes the methodology. Theoretically the participants then feed the changed perceptions back into the political and decision-making process. The other approach tends to concentrate on the operational environment. Changing structures can change behavior. By shifting the way we give assistance, peace can be strengthened.[12]

If evaluated carefully, both approaches can suggest ways of building peace during a period of transition. Churches, for example, have been active in convening small groups of people from opposing sides in order to foster reconciliation and reduce misperceptions. Sometimes referred to as "Track II" diplomacy, nongovernmental organizations have become involved in creating problem-solving "workshops" that bring together community leaders from various parties to a conflict. The long-term benefits and cultural relevance of these "workshops" are not yet clear. In the wrong hands they can also be heavily manipulative.[13]

Using a more structural approach, some humanitarian relief workers have been able to change the food distribution system in such a way that the more marginalized and least powerful members of a community are helped. The assumption often is that by "empowering" certain people, a more just social order can be promoted and, therefore, a stronger base on which to build peace. But there is also the inherent danger of "social engineering" by outsiders who do not understand the culture and who can inadvertently create tensions and promote violence.

THE ROLE OF CIVIL SOCIETY AND THE MILITARY

"Civil Society" is a term rarely used before 1990. But with the collapse of communism, the weakening of state governments, and the phenomenal growth of nonstate actors and nongovernmental organizations, the term has taken on a new salience in the field of social and political development, including peace building. Most simply, civil society refers to the social "space" that lies between relationships derived from family obligations and relationships derived from obligations to the state. Civil society is the mediating structures between the family and the state. Like the term "nongovernmental organization," civil society is so broad a concept that it can mean anything from organized crime groups and labor unions to church congregations and women's social clubs. Everything that is not family and not state can fit into the category of civil society.[14]

Many observers believe that the hopes for peace in a society or region rest less with governments and more with members of civil society. The approaches to conflict resolution described in the following section are all based on the importance of activating civil society in the search for peace.[15]

The military has become an increasingly important actor in large complex humanitarian emergencies. Typically the political-diplomatic actors concentrate on prevention and peace settlements; the NGOs and the UN humanitarian agencies focus on delivering humanitarian assistance; and the military are charged with providing security and logistical support. Such a neat division of labor has often been more muddled.

Military presence and mandates can radically differ from place to place. The classic UN peacekeepers—as they still exist in places like Cyprus—are there to separate the conflicting parties, at the request of the parties. But even as early as 1960 in the Congo, the UN peacekeepers took up a more aggressive role in deterring the succession of Katanga. The peacekeepers became peacemakers. But the humiliations suffered by the UN peacekeeping force in Bosnia in the 1990s, where eventually NATO military had to step in, showed the confusion that exists around the use of UN military troops for purposes of peace.

Yet it is hard to see how the use of some kind of military force can be avoided in complex violent situations. Even in the transition from war into peace, some form of military presence is often essential for maintaining security, monitoring cease-fires, clearing mines, and reopening bridges, roads, and airports.

For the humanitarian worker there is a continual problem of how to relate to the military in such a transitional situation. Humanitarian agencies have a very different organizational culture

from the military. The potential for bad communications between them is high. There is a long and distinguished history
of military involvement in humanitarian issues. Coordination is
perhaps the most challenging aspect of the relationship between
the military and humanitarian work. The military are used to a
highly disciplined centralized operation; the NGOs often cannot
speak with one voice or require a participatory decision-making
process that is cumbersome. Efforts at peace building can be sty-
mied by this asymmetry unless conscious steps are taken to bridge
the divide.[16] Regular communication and information sharing
are critical. Although the military cannot be expected to take
on major "nation-building" tasks, it can provide some important
peace supports. Ideally, transitional rehabilitation activities
should be planned with the military and within a long-term development context that includes strengthening local civil society
groups that can contribute most to the peace.[17]

SPIRITUAL TRANSFORMATIONS AND RECONCILIATION

Any serious social transition from war to peace must involve psychological, cultural, and spiritual transformation. In the secular
realm of social psychology there is considerable literature in the
West on recovery from social trauma.[18] Much less attention has
been paid to the religious, cultural, and spiritual dimensions of
the transition from war to peace. How, for example, does a deep-
seated "culture of violence" become a "civilization of love"? Is
such a transformation ever possible?[19] Cultures do change. Indeed, some would say that they are in the constant process of
change. But to what extent should the promotion of cultural
change be integrated into the plans and programs for transitional peace building?

International humanitarian workers might feel uncomfortable
even discussing these questions because someone outside the
specific culture can never answer the questions. Yet sometimes it
takes an outsider who has some "emotional distance" from the

conflicts who can initiate a dialogue on reconciliation and for-giveness. Unfortunately most international humanitarian actors, even if they work for a faith-based organization, are rarely pre-pared to enter into this arena of peace building. Reconciliation is a profound multidimensional process that does not lend itself to easy analysis because often it involves very personal transfor-mations. Sometimes in a postconflict situation the move toward reconciliation seems much too rushed and premature. Reconcili-ation does not replace the need for justice. Earlier I mentioned the workshops sponsored by churches that try to move a commu-nity toward the goal of reconciliation. But there is very little eval-uative research on how successful these attempts have been.

Peace Building through Democracy

The thesis that democracies do not wage war against other de-mocracies has been receiving increased academic attention. It is sometimes referred to as the "democratic peace proposition." The causal link between democracy and peace may not be direct, but if the proposition is basically valid, then it would follow that the promotion of democracy should be a constituative element of peace building in a transitional society. What this practically would mean is the promotion of participatory institutions and processes both within the state governmental structure as well as in civil society. External intervention, however, rarely succeeds in establishing a democratic culture. The impetus and the work must come from the society itself. Building the institutional struc-tures for democracy may take decades. It is not something that can be imposed.[20] But humanitarian assistance in the transitional stage can in small incremental ways try to introduce some partici-patory decision-making at the local level. International NGOs, for example, by establishing full-fledged partnerships with indig-enous local NGOs can begin to support and spread participative institutions in a society.[21]

Conclusion

There is an endless supply of specific proposals for how best to anchor peace in a postwar society. Many projects, from "self-esteem" classes in Bosnia to "computer connectivity" sessions for children, have been suggested or tried. Sometimes, however, the success of a specific project or approach diverts us from the fact that most large-scale efforts at international peace building over the past thirty years have been miserable failures. The United States has spent probably in the range of a trillion dollars trying to establish secure environments and peaceful transitions to democracy in places like prewar Vietnam, Lebanon, Somalia, Bosnia, Kosovo, and Haiti.[22] The government acted in partnership with hundreds of NGOs working on specific aspects of the transition. Although certain efforts may have contributed on a micro-level to peace building, the overall effort never succeeded in any of these countries. What conclusion must we draw from these experiences?

Some major research argues that the transition to peace and the democratization of a country is almost entirely the product of domestic internal factors. Other analysts suggest that proactive forms of humanitarian and military intervention do not in any way prevent the recurrence of conflict in a postwar society.[23]

It would appear that externally engineered, even highly vigorous peace-building programs are not enough to transform a country into a peaceful democratic, economically healthy society. Other conditions must be present. The people must truly want such social change and the culture must be ripe to receive it. As Harrington and Huntington put it in their recent book, *Culture Matters:* "The core values of a society are what finally shape human progress. Those values can change and be changed, but that type of change comes slowly, and, though heavily influenced by international developments, the change must finally come from within the culture itself."[24]

We must face the challenges of humanitarian assistance in the transition from war to peace with a stronger sense of realism and a bigger dose of cultural humility.

SELECTED WEB SITES

The United Nations Office for the Coordination of Humanitarian Affairs: *http://www.reliefweb.int/ocha_ol/index.html* or *http://www.un.org/ha*
Food and Agriculture Organization: *http://www.fao.org*
United Nations Development Programme: *http://www.undp.org*
United Nations High Commissioner for Human Rights: *http://www.unhchr.ch*
United Nations High Commissioner for Refugees: *http://www.unhcr.ch*
United Nations Children's Fund: *http://www.unicef.org*
United Nations Relief and Works Agency for Palestine Refugees in the Near East: *http://www.unrwa.org* and *http://www.un.org/unrwa*
UNAIDS: *http://www.unaids.org*
World Food Programme: *http://www.wfp.org*
World Health Organization: *http://www.who.org*
International Organization for Migration: *http://www.iom.ch* and *http://www.iom.int*
International Monetary Fund: *http://www.imf.org*
World Bank: *http://www.worldbank.org*

REGIONAL ORGANIZATIONS

The European Community Humanitarian Office: *http://europa.eu.int/comm/echo/en/present/manda_en.html*

Bilateral Organizations

The [British] Department for International Development: *http:// www.dfid.gov.uk*

Canadian International Development Agency: *http://www. acdicida.gc.ca*

Centers for Disease Control and Prevention: *http://www.cdc.gov*

Japan International Cooperation Agency: *http://www.jica.go.jp/ Index.html*

United States Agency for International Development: *http:// www.info.usaid.gov*

Red Cross and Red Crescent Movement

International Committee of the Red Cross (ICRC): *http://www. icrc.org*

International Federation of Red Cross and Red Crescent Societies: *http://www.ifrc.org*

Nongovernmental Organizations (NGOs)

Amnesty International: *http://www.amnesty.org*

Catholic Relief Services: *http://www.catholicrelief.org*

Center for International Health and Cooperation: *http://www. cihc.org*

Doctors Without Borders: *http://www.dwb.org*

Human Rights Watch: *http://www.hrw.org*

InterAction: *http://www.interaction.org*

International Diploma in Humanitarian Assistance: *http://www. idha.ch*

International Rescue Committee (IRC): *http://www.reliefnet.org/ rnet/irc.html*

Médecins sans frontières: http://www.msf.org

Oxfam: *http://www.oxfam.org*
World Vision: *http://www.worldvision.org*

INTERNATIONAL COURTS

The International Court of Justice: *http://www.icj-cij.org*
International Criminal Tribunal for the Former Yugoslavia: *http://www.un.org/icty*
International Criminal Tribunal for Rwanda: *http://www.ictr.org*

CHAPTER NOTES AND REFERENCES

NOTES TO CHAPTER ONE

EARLY WARNING SYSTEMS: FROM SURVEILLANCE
TO RISK ASSESSMENT TO ACTION

Ted R. Gurr and Barbara Harff

1. This chapter incorporates materials from T. R. Gurr and Barbara Harff, *Early Warning of Communal Conflict and Genocide: Linking Empirical Research to International Responses* (Tokyo: Monograph Series on Governance and Conflict Resolution, GCR 05, United Nations University Press, 1996), and from Barbara Harff, "Assessing Risks of Genocide and Political Mass Murder: Estimating and Applying a Structural Model," pre-publication paper, April 2002.

2. A normative and policy argument about the connection between early warning and action is made by Barbara Harff, "Rescuing Endangered Peoples: Missed Opportunities," *Social Research* 62 (spring 1995): 23–40.

3. In his introduction to Kevin M. Cahill, ed., *A Framework for Survival: Health, Human Rights, and Humanitarian Assistance in Conflicts and Disasters* (New York: Basic Books for the Council on Foreign Relations, 1993), p. 7.

4. This information is compiled from T. R. Gurr, Monty G. Marshall, and Deepa Khosla, *Peace and Conflict 2001: A Global Survey of Armed Conflicts, Self-determination Movements, and Democracy* (College Park, MD: Integrated Network of Societal Conflict Research, Center for International Development and Conflict Management, December 2000), pp. 24–28. Current information from INSCR global surveys of armed conflicts, state failures, and democratic regimes are reported on its Web site at *http://www.bsos.umd.edu/cidcm/inscr.*

5. This paragraph summarizes evidence developed by the Minorities at Risk (MAR) Project, directed by the first author and based at the University of Maryland's CIDCM. The project compiles systematic information about 275 politically active ethnic groups' cultural and reli-

gious traits; where they live, their status and inequalities; their past and present involvement in conflict; and many other variables. For other findings of the study see Gurr, *Peoples versus States* and the project's Web site at *http://www.bsos.umd.edu/cidcm/inscr/mar.*

6. United Nations, *An Agenda for Peace: Preventive Diplomacy, Peacemaking and Peace-Keeping. Report of the Secretary-General Pursuant to the Statement Adopted by the Summit Meeting of the Security Council on 31 January 1992.* New York: UN General Assembly/Security Council document A/47/277, June 17, 1992.

7. For descriptions of these and several other early warning systems, written by officials who have managed them, see John L. Davies and T. R. Gurr, eds., chapters 15–19 in *Preventive Measures: Building Risk Assessment and Crisis Early Warning Systems* (Lanham, MD: Rowman & Littlefield, 1998).

8. An example of the Conflict Prevention Center's work is Heinz Vetschera and Andrea Amutek-Riemer, "Early Warning: The Case of Yugoslavia," paper presented at the World Congress of the International Political Science Association, August 1994. Max van der Stoel describes the OSCE's preventive activities in "The Role of the OSCE High Commissioner in Conflict Prevention," in *Herding Cats: Multiparty Mediation in a Complex World,* ed. Chester A. Crocker, Fen Osler Hampson, and Pamela Aall (Washington, D.C.: United States Institute of Peace Press, 1999).

9. The concept of early warning was first widely used during the cold war by U.S. military and intelligence analysts who sought to anticipate East-West flashpoints. An account of empirical early warning research during this era is Edward Laurence, "Events Data and Policy Analysis: Improving the Potential for Applying Academic Research to Foreign and Defense Policy Problems," *Policy Sciences* 23 (1990): 111–32.

10. See "List of Open Access Early Warning Projects," in Davies and Gurr, *Preventive Measures,* pp. 268–80, for sketches and access information on fifty-five public, private, and academic projects on early warning, risk assessment, and preventive action projects that were active in the late 1990s. For recent and more detailed summaries of seven major initiatives, including several of those described below, see Maureen O'Neil and Necla Tschirgi, "The Role of Research and Policy Analysis," in Fen Osler Hampson and David M. Malone, eds., *From Reaction to*

Conflict Prevention: Opportunities for the UN System (Boulder: Lynne Rienner, 2002), pp. 282–92.

11. An example of the Center's country-specific reports and comparative assessments is Barnett R. Rubin, ed., *Cases and Strategies for Preventive Action: Preventive Action Reports,* vol. 2 (New York: Century Foundation Press, 1998).

12. The ICG has prepared several hundred such reports, with varying degrees of detail, accessible on the ICG Web site at *http://www.crisis web.org.*

13. European Center for Conflict Prevention, *Prevention and Management of Violent Conflicts: An International Directory, 1998 Edition* (Utrecht: European Center for Conflict Prevention, 1999). The first in the regional series is *Conflict Prevention in Africa* (Utrecht: European Center for Conflict Prevention, 1999).

14. For recent reviews of the modalities of preventive diplomacy, see Hampson and Malone, chapters 6–11 of *From Reaction to Conflict Prevention;* and contributions to Chester A. Crocker, Fen Osler Hampson, and Pamela Aall, eds., *Turbulent Peace: The Challenges of Managing International Conflict* (Washington, D.C.: United States Institute of Peace Press, 2001).

15. Juergen Dedring, "Early Warning and Preventive Diplomacy," paper presented to the International Peace Research Association meetings, Kyoto, Japan, July 1992.

16. The region later became the focus of a U.S. government effort at systematic early warning. In 1995, the Clinton Administration established the inter-agency Greater Horn of Africa Initiative, aimed at conflict prevention and food security. One of its tasks was to put in place an electronic early warning system to connect governments in the Horn, donor countries, international organizations, and NGOs. This task was the focus of intensive efforts by a working group in the Department of State called RADARS (Reporting, Analysis, Decision-making and Response System).

17. See Steven L. Burg, "Nationalism and Civic Identity: Ethnic Models for Macedonia and Kosovo," chapter 2 in Rubin, *Cases and Strategies for Preventive Action.*

18. This was a short-term success only, since in 1997 the country was devastated by civil war. For other examples of preventive diplomacy by the OAU, see the chapter by Salim Ahmed Salim in Kevin M. Cahill,

ed., *Preventive Diplomacy: Stopping Wars Before They Start* (New York: Routledge, 2000).

19. A study of successful preventive diplomacy in the Baltic states is reported in Bruce W. Jentleson, ed., *Opportunities Missed, Opportunities Seized: Preventive Diplomacy in the Post-Cold War World* (Lanham, MD: Rowman & Littlefield, 2000).

20. Lincoln P. Bloomfield and Amelia Leiss identify five phases: dispute, pre-hostilities conflict, hostilities, cessation of hostilities, and settlement, in *Controlling Small Wars: A Strategy for the 1970s* (New York: Knopf, 1969). The first author has used a more precise set of phases to analyze the management of ethnic wars: conventional mobilization, militant mobilization, low-level hostilities, high-level hostilities, talk-fight, cessation of open hostilities, post-hostilities, and settlement; see T. R. Gurr and Deepa Khosla, "Domestic and Transnational Strategies for Managing Separatist Conflicts: Four Asian Cases," pp. 240–90 in Hayward Alker, T. R. Gurr, and Kumar Rupesinghe, eds., *Journeys Through Conflict: Narratives and Lessons* (Lanham, MD: Rowman & Littlefield, 2001).

21. No models of social phenomena generate perfect predictions. Economists' models of national economic performance yield forecasts with a substantial range of indeterminacy. Pollsters' forecasts of electoral outcomes have error margins that make it difficult to predict reliably the winners in close elections. Results of the State Failure Project (see "The State Failure Project: Early Warning Research for U.S. Foreign Policy Planning," pp. 27–38 in Davies and Gurr, *Preventive Measures*) suggest that early warning research using macro-indicators can correctly classify at best 75 percent to 80 percent of state failures versus nonfailures.

22. "False negatives," or crises that are not anticipated, usually are thought to be the most serious challenges for early warning. On the other hand, a system that identifies too many "false positives" may prompt efforts at conflict prevention that are diffused too widely rather than focused on the highest-risk situations.

23. Akira Onishi, "The FUGI Model as a Global Early Warning System for Refugees," chapter 12 in Davies and Gurr, *Preventive Measures;* Susanne Schmeidl, "Exploring the Causes of Forced Migration: A Pooled Time-Series Analysis, 1971–1990," *Social Science Quarterly* 78, no. 2 (1997): 284–308.

24. T. R. Gurr and Will H. Moore, "Ethnopolitical Rebellion: A

Cross-Sectional Analysis of the 1980s with Risk Assessments for the 1990s," *American Journal of Political Science* 41 (October 1997): 1079–1103.

25. The design and rationale for the project are described by Daniel C. Esty, Jack A. Goldstone, T. R. Gurr, Barbara Harff, Pamela T. Surko, Alan N. Unger, and Robert S. Chen, "The State Failure Project: Early Warning Research for U.S. Foreign Policy Planning," pp. 27–38 in Davies and Gurr, *Preventive Measures*. Findings are reported in Daniel C. Esty, Jack A. Goldstone, T. R. Gurr, Barbara Harff, Marc Levy, Geoffrey D. Dabelko, Pamela T. Surko, and Alan N. Unger, "State Failure Task Force Report: Phase II Findings," *Environmental Change & Security Project Report*, the Woodrow Wilson Center, Issue 5 (summer 1999), pp. 49–72. The most recent report is available (as of June 2002) at *http://www.bsos.umd.edu/cidcm/inscr/statefail.*

26. See Alexander L. George, "Case Studies and Theory Development: The Method of Structured, Focused Comparison," in Paul Gordon Lauren, ed., *Diplomatic History: New Approaches* (New York: Free Press, 1979). Barbara Harff reports a comparative empirical study of the causes and accelerators of genocide in Rwanda and Burundi in chapter 3 of Gurr and Harff, *Early Warning of Communal Conflict and Genocide.*

27. Most of this research is for U.S. government use only. A published analysis is Harff, "Could Humanitarian Crises Have Been Anticipated in Burundi, Rwanda, and Zaire? A Comparative Study of Anticipatory Indicators," in Alker, Gurr, and Rupesinghe, *Journeys Through Conflict.*

28. The Serbian case was a politicide aimed at eliminating—by terror killings and ethnic cleansing—most Kosovar Albanians; it was checked by NATO intervention. A list and thumbnail description of all thirty-five cases can be found at the State Failure Web site at *http://www.bsos.umd.edu/cidcm/inscr/statefail.*

29. The theoretical argument sketched here was first developed by Barbara Harff, "The Etiology of Genocide," in *The Age of Genocide,* ed. Michael N. Dobkowski and Isador Wallimann (Wesport, CT: Greenwood Press, 1987), pp. 41–59.

30. Helen Fein, "Accounting for Genocide after 1945: Theories and Some Findings," *International Journal on Group Rights* 1 (1993): 79–106.

31. The coding and indicators used in the Polity study are described in Keith Jaggers and T. R. Gurr, "Tracking Democracy's Third Wave

with the Polity III Data," *Journal of Peace Research* 32 (November 1995): 469–82. The Polity data have been revised and updated through 2001 under the direction of Monty G. Marshall and are posted at *http://www. bsos.umd.edu/cidcm.inscr.*

REFERENCES TO CHAPTER TWO
INITIAL RESPONSE TO COMPLEX EMERGENCIES
AND NATURAL DISASTERS
Ed Tsui

Dabelstein, N. 2001. "Aid Response to Afghanistan: Lessons from Previous Evaluations." DAC Working Party on Aid Evaluation to DAC Senior Level Meeting.

IASC. 1994. "TOR of the Humanitarian Coordinator." Inter-Agency Standing Committee Policy Paper.

———. 1994. "Working Paper on the Definition of Complex Emergencies." Inter-Agency Standing Committee Policy Paper.

OCHA. 2002. *OCHA Orientation Handbook.* New York: United Nations Publications.

———. 2002. *Symposium on Best Practices in Humanitarian Information Exchange: Final Report.* New York: OCHA Advocacy, External Relations and Information Management Branch.

Porter, T. *An External Review of the CAP.* New York: OCHA Policy Development and Studies Branch, Evaluation Studies Unit.

Tsui, E. 2000. *Strengthening OCHA: Report of the Change Manager.* New York: OCHA.

Van Brabant, K. 1999. *Opening the Black Box: An Outline of a Framework to Understand, Promote and Evaluate Humanitarian Coordination.* London: Overseas Development Institute.

Wahlstrom, M. 2001. *UNDAC Review 2001: A Review of the United Nations Disaster Assessment and Coordination Team.* New York: OCHA Policy Development and Studies Branch, Evaluation Studies Unit.

Wahlstrom, M., and D. Harland. 2001. *The Role of OCHA in Emergency United Nations Operations Following the Earthquake in Gujarat, India, January 26, 2001: A Lessons Learned Study.* New York: OCHA Policy Development and Studies Branch, Evaluation Studies Unit.

Wahlstrom, M., and C. Hurford. 2001. *OCHA and the Timor Crisis, 1999:*

An Independent Study for OCHA. New York: OCHA Policy Development and Studies Branch, Evaluation Studies Unit.

Wiles, P., and N. Reindorp. 2001. *Humanitarian Coordination: Lessons from Recent Experience.* London: Overseas Development Institute.

NOTES TO CHAPTER THREE
EVIDENCE-BASED HEALTH ASSESSMENT PROCESS
IN COMPLEX EMERGENCIES
Frederick M. Burkle, Jr., M.D.

The author wishes to thank W. Courland Robinson, B.A., Research Associate and Resident Demographer, and Elizabeth Rowley, MPH, Research Asociate, both of Johns Hopkins University School of Public Health, for their insightful review and evaluation of this chapter.

1. S. W. A. Gunn, *Multilingual Dictionary of Disaster Medicine and International Relief* (Dordrecht: Kluwer, 1990), 7.

2. A. Zwi and A. Uglade, "Political Violence in the Third World: A Public Health Issue," *Health Policy and Planning* 6, no. 3 (1991): 203–17.

3. M. J. Toole and R. J. Waldman, "The Public Health Aspects of Complex Emergencies and Refugee Situations," *Annual Review of Public Health* 18 (1997): 283–312.

4. M. J. Toole, "The Role of Rapid Assessment," in *Humanitarian Crises: The Medical and Public Health Response*, eds. J. Leaning, S. M. Briggs, and L. C. Chen (Cambridge, Mass.: Harvard University Press, 1999), 15–39.

5. R. A. Margolis, R. R. Franklin, W. F. Bertrand, and T. A. Sellers, "Rapid Post-disaster Community Needs Assessment: A Case Study of Guatemala after the Civil Strife of 1979–1983," *Disasters* 13 (1987): 287–99.

6. Margolis, Franklin, Bertrand, and Sellers, " Post-disaster Community Needs Assessment," 287–99.

7. Toole, "Rapid Assessment," in *Humanitarian Crises, Public Health Response*, 15–39.

8. R. J. Brennan and F. M. Burkle, "Disaster Assessment for the Public Health Sector II: Risk Assessment and Rapid Health Assessment," in *Disaster Preparedness in Schools of Public Health: A Curriculum for a New Century*, ed. L. Landesman (Washington, D.C.: Association of

Schools of Public Health, and Atlanta: Centers for Disease Control and Prevention, 2000), 1–20.

9. Centers for Disease Control and Prevention, "Famine-Affected, Refugee and Displaced Populations: Recommendations for Public Health Issues, *Morbidity & Mortality Weekly Report (MMWR)* 41 (1992): 1–76.

10. M. J. Toole and R. J. Waldman, "Prevention of Excess Mortality in Refugee and Displaced Populations in Developing Countries," *Journal of the American Medical Association* 263 (1990): 3296–3302.

11. F. Davidoff, "In the Teeth of the Evidence: The Curious Case of Evidence-Based Medicine," *Mt. Sinai Journal of Medicine* 66 (1999): 75–83.

12. J. C. Desendos, D. Michel, F. Tholly, et al, "Mortality Trends among Refugees in Honduras, 1984–1987," *International Journal of Epidemiology* 19, no. 2 (1990): 367–73.

13. F. M. Burkle, K. A. W. McGrady, S. L. Newett, et al, "Complex, Humanitarian Emergencies: III. Measures of Effectiveness," *Disaster Medicine* 10, no. 1 (1995): 48–56.

14. World Health Organization, *Rapid Health Assessment Protocols for Emergencies* (Geneva: World Health Organization, 1999).

15. Sphere Project, *Humanitarian Charter and Minimum Standards in Disaster Response.* (Oxford: Oxfam Publishing, 2000).

16. Sphere Project, *Minimum Standards.*

17. C. J. Elias, B. H. Alexander, and T. Soky, "Infectious Disease Control in a Long-Term Refugee Camp: The Role of Epidemiologic Surveillance and Investigation," *American Journal of Public Health* 80, no. 7 (1990): 824–28.

18. Toole and Waldman, "Public Health Aspects," 283–312.

19. D. Guha-Sapir, "Rapid Assessment of Health Needs in Mass Emergencies: Review of Current Concepts and Methods," *World Health Statistical Quarterly* 44 (1991): 171–81.

20. P. A. Hakewill and A. Moren, "Monitoring and Evaluation of Relief Programs," *Tropical Doctor* 21, suppl. 1 (1991): 24–38.

21. Hakewill and Moren, "Monitoring and Evaluation," 24–38.

22. UN High Commissioner for Refugees, *Handbook for Emergencies,* 2nd ed. (Geneva: UN High Commissioner for Refugees, 2002), 40–46.

23. Toole and Waldman, "Prevention of Excess Mortality," 3296–3302.

24. WHO, *Health Assessment Protocols.*

25. Sphere Project, *Minimum Standards.*

26. Hakewill and Moren, "Monitoring and Evaluation," 24–38.

27. Ibid.

28. UNHCR, *Handbook for Emergencies,* 40–46.

29. A. P. Davis, "Targeting the Vulnerable in Emergency Situations: Who Is Vulnerable?" *Lancet* 348 (Sept. 28, 1996): 868–71.

30. UNHCR, *Handbook for Emergencies,* 40–46.

31. *Public Health Guide for Emergencies* (Baltimore: Johns Hopkins School of Hygiene and Public Health; and Geneva: International Federation of Red Cross and Red Crescent Societies, 2000).

32. F. M. Burkle, "Lessons Learnt and Future Expectations of Complex Emergencies," *British Medical Journal* 319 (1999): 422–26.

33. The Relief and Rehabilitation Network, "Counting and Identification of Beneficiary Populations: Registration and Its Alternatives" (London: Relief and Rehabilitation Network, ODI), review found at *http://www.ennonline.net/fex/03/rs6.html.*

34. Davidoff, "Teeth of the Evidence," 75–83.

35. *Public Health Guide for Emergencies.*

36. Toole and Waldman, "Public Health Aspects," 283–312.

37. Toole and Waldman, "Prevention of Excess Mortality," 3296–3302.

38. Toole and Waldman, "Public Health Aspects."

39. Ibid.

40. Desendos, Michel, Tholly, et al, "Mortality Trends among Refugees," 367–73.

41. Guha-Sapir, "Assessment of Health Needs," 171–81.

42. Hakewill and Moren, "Monitoring and Evaluation," 24–38.

43. J. M. Last, *A Dictionary of Epidemiology,* 4th ed. (Oxford: Oxford University Press, 2001), 186.

44. A. T. Bang and R. A. Bang, "Diagnosis of Causes of Childhood Deaths in Developing Countries by Verbal Autopsy: Suggested Criteria. The SEARCH Team," *Bulletin of the World Health Organization* 70, no. 4 (1992): 499–507.

45. D. Chandramohan, G. H. Maude, L. C. Rodrigues, and R. J. Hayes, "Verbal Autopsies for Adult Deaths: Issues in Their Development and Validation," *International Journal of Epidemiology* 23, no. 2 (1994): 213–27.

46. Chandramohan, Maude, Rodrigues, and Hayes, "Verbal Autopsies for Adult Deaths," 213–27.

47. Davidoff, "Teeth of the Evidence," 75–83.

48. Hakewill and Moren, "Monitoring and Evaluation," 24–38.

49. Davis, "Who Is Vulnerable?" 868–71.

50. M. Anker, "Epidemiological and Statistical Methods for Rapid Assessment: Introduction," *World Health Statistics Quarterly* 44, no. 3 (1991): 94–97.

51. P. T. Glaziou and E. M. Mackerras, "Vitamin A Supplementation in Infectious Diseases: A Meta-analysis," *British Medical Journal* 306 (1993): 366–70.

52. Organization for Economic Cooperation and Development, *Evaluation and Aid Effectiveness: Guidance for Evaluating Humanitarian Assistance in Complex Emergencies* (London: Development Assistance Committee/Overseas Development Institute, 1999), 13–14.

53. J. Cosgrave, "Refugee Density and Dependence: Practical Implications of Camp Size," *Disasters* 20, no. 3 (1996): 261–70.

54. WHO, *Health Assessment Protocols.*

55. Sphere Project, *Minimum Standards.*

56. Hakewill and Moren, "Monitoring and Evaluation," 24–38.

57. Davis, "Who Is Vulnerable?" 868–71.

58. *Public Health Guide for Emergencies.*

59. L. Roberts, *Mortality in Eastern Democratic Republic of Congo: Results from Eleven Mortality Surveys,* Final draft, May 2001 (New York: Health Unit, International Rescue Committee, 2001).

60. Davis, "Who Is Vulnerable?" 868–71.

61. Ibid.

62. B. T. Burkholder and M. J. Toole, "Evolution of Complex Emergencies," *Lancet* 346 (1995): 1012–15.

63. R. J. Brennan and B. T. Burkholder, Centers for Disease Control and Prevention, unpublished data (1997).

64. P. B. Spiegel and P. Salama, "War and Mortality in Kosovo, 1998–99: An Epidemiological Testimony," *Lancet* 357 (2000): 2204–9.

65. L. P. Boss, M. J. Toole, and R. Yip, "Assessments of Mortality, Morbidity, and Nutritional Status in Somalia during the 1991–1992 Famine," *Journal of the American Medical Association* 272, no. 5 (1994): 371–76.

66. OECD, *Evaluation and Aid Effectiveness,* 13–14.

67. Burkle, McGrady, Newett, et al, "Measures of Effectiveness," 48–56.

68. Burkle, McGrady, Newett, et al, "Measures of Effectiveness."

69. Ibid.

70. UNHCR, *Handbook for Emergencies*, 40–46.

71. WHO, *Health Assessment Protocols*.

72. I. Pluute, *Essentials for Emergencies* (Geneva: World Health Organization, Emergency and Humanitarian Action Division, 2002), 5.

73. Médecins sans frontières, *Refugee Health: An Approach to Emergency Situations* (London: Macmillan, 1997), 43–54.

74. MSF, *Approach to Emergency Situations*, 43–54.

75. F. M. Burkle, "Complex Emergencies and Military Capabilities," in *From Civil Strife to Civil Society: Civil and Military Responsibilities in Disrupted States*, ed. W. S. Maley (Tokyo and New York: United Nations University Press, 2002), 68–80.

76. Boss, Toole, and Yip, "Mortality, Morbidity, and Nutritional Status in Somalia," 371–76.

77. M. B. Gregg, *Field Epidemiology* (Oxford: Oxford University Press, 1996).

78. Boss, Toole, and Yip, "Mortality, Morbidity, and Nutritional Status in Somalia," 371–76.

79. Ibid.

80. Gregg, *Field Epidemiology*.

81. F. M. Burkle, "Characteristics of Complex Emergencies That Affect Epidemiology," Lecture for Combined Humanitarian Assistance and Response Training (CHART) course, Center of Excellence in Disaster Management and Humanitarian Assistance, Honolulu, 1997.

82. S. Hansch, "The Demography of Vulnerability: Somalia in the 1990s," unpublished paper presented at the National Academy of Sciences Workshop on Mortality Patterns in Complex Emergencies, National Research Council, Washington, D.C., November 18, 1999.

83. V. Brown, G. Jacquier, D. Coulombier, et al, "Rapid Assessment of Population Size by Area Sampling in Disaster Situations," *Disasters* 25, no. 2 (2001): 164–71.

84. W. C. Robinson, M. K. Lee, and G. M. Burnham, "Mortality in North Korean Migrant Households: A Retrospective Study," *Lancet* 354 (1999): 291–95.

85. Burkle, "Emergencies That Affect Epidemiology."

86. P. Spiegel, F. M. Burkle, C. C. Dey, and P. Salama, "Developing Public Health Indicators in Complex Emergency Response," *Disaster Medicine* 16, no. 4 (2001): 281–85.

87. Hakewill and Moren, "Monitoring and Evaluation," 24–38.

88. Burkle, "Military Capabilities," *From Civil Strife to Civil Society*, 68–80.

REFERENCES TO CHAPTER FOUR
INITIAL RESPONSE TO COMPLEX EMERGENCIES
AND NATURAL DISASTERS
Tom Arnold

Niall Roche, Manager, Health Support Unit, generously helped with this chapter.

General

Fitzpatrick, Martin, and Andreas Kappos. *Environmental Health Services in Thailand.* Bangkok: Desire, 1999.

Water

Adams, John. *Managing Water Supply and Sanitation in Emergencies.* Oxford: Oxfam, 1999.
Sphere Project. *The Sphere Project: The Humanitarian Charter and Minimum Standards in Disaster Response.* Oxford: Oxfam, 2000.
World Health Organization. *Drinking Water Guidelines.* Vol.1, 1993.

Excreta

Cairncross, S., and R. Feachem. *Environmental Health Engineering in the Tropics: An Introductory Text.* 2nd ed. Chichester: John Wiley and Sons.
DFID. *Guidance Manual on Water Supply and Sanitation Programs.* Loughborough: WELL, 1998.
World Health Organization. *Global Water Supply and Sanitation Assessment: 2000 Report.* Geneva: WHO, 2000.
WHO Commission on Health and Environment. *Our Planet, Our Health.* Geneva: WHO, 1992.
Winblad, Uno, and Wen Kilama. *Sanitation Without Water.* London: Macmillan Press, 1992.

Waste Management

Davis, Jan, and Robert Lambert. *Engineering in Emergencies: A Practical Guide for Relief Workers.* London: RedR/Intermediate Technology, 1995.

Vector Control

Lacarin, Christophe, and Bob Reed. *Emergency Vector Control Using Chemicals.* Loughborough: Water, Engineering and Development Centre, 1999.

Hygiene Education

Downie, R. S., F. Fyfe, and A. Tannahill. *Health Promotion: Models and Values.* Oxford: Oxford University Press, 1990.

Hubley, John. *Communicating Health: An Action Guide to Health Education and Health Promotion.* London: TALC and Macmillan, 1993.

Naidoo, Jennie, and Jane Wills. *Health Promotion: Foundations for Practice.* Bailliere: Tindall, 1994.

Tones, K., S. Tilford, and Y. Robinson. *Health Education Effectiveness and Efficiency.* London: Chapman and Hall, 1990.

NOTES TO CHAPTER FIVE
INTERNAL DISPLACEMENT: A CHALLENGE OF PEACE,
SECURITY, AND NATION BUILDING
Francis M. Deng

1. For a detailed overview of the crisis, see Roberta Cohen and Francis M. Deng, *Masses In Flight: The Global Crisis of Internal Displacement* (The Brookings Institution, 1998), 40–46 (herein after *Masses in Flight*); and *The Forsaken People: Case Studies of the Internally Displaced,* ed. Roberta Cohen and Francis M. Deng (The Brookings Institution, 1998), 139–74 (herein after *The Forsaken People*).

2. The working definition describes internally displaced people as "persons who have been forced to flee their homes suddenly or unexpectedly in large numbers, as a result of armed conflict, internal strife,

systematic violations of human rights, or natural or man-made disasters, and who are within the territory of their own country," *Analytical Report of the Secretary-General on Internally Displaced Persons,* UN Doc. E/CN.4/1992/23 (1992). For a preliminary discussion of definitional issues on the basis of this definition, see *Report of the Representative of the Secretary-General on Internally Displaced Persons,* UN ESCOR, 51st Sess., Agenda Item 11(d) ¶ 116–27, UN Doc. E/CN.4/1995/50 (1995). Further points for consideration and the rationale for refining the working definition appear in Cohen and Deng, *Masses In Flight, supra* note 1, 10.

3. Versions of this paper appear in 5 Wash. U. J. L. & Pol'y (2001), 141–55.

4. For some of the writings of the authors on this issue, see Francis M. Deng et al, *Sovereignty as Responsibility: Conflict Management in Africa* (The Brookings Institution, 1990); "Sovereignty and Humanitarian Responsibility: A Challenge for NGOs in Africa and the Sudan," in *Vigilance and Vengeance,* ed. Robert I. Rotberg, The World Peace Foundation (The Brookings Institution, 1996); "Reconciling Sovereignty with Responsibility: A Basis for Humanitarian Action" in *Africa, A World Politics,* ed. John Harberou and Donald Rothchild (Boulder Colorado: Westview, 1995); and *The Responsibility to Protect: Report of the International Commission on Intervention and State Sovereignty,* 2000.

5. Cohen and Deng, *Masses in Flight, supra* note 1, 10.

6. Roberta Cohen, "Protecting Internally Displaced Women and Children" in *Rights Have No Borders: Worldwide Internal Displacement* (Global IDP Survey of the Norwegian Refugee Council, 1998), 63–74.

7. Resolution 1992173 of the Commission on Human Rights.

8. UN ESCOR, 49th Sess., Annex, Agenda Item 11(a), at 1, UN Doc. E/CN.4/1993/35 (1993).

9. *Masses in Flight, supra* note 1, 275–80. See also reports on the countries discussed in this chapter.

10. *Annual Report of the Secretary-General to the General Assembly,* UN Doc. 5G/5M17136 GA/9596 (1999).

11. Francis Deng, *Compilation and Analysis: Report of the Representative of the Secretary-General,* UN Doc. E/CN.4/1996/52/add. 2 (1996) (submitted pursuant to the Committee on Human Rights resolution 1995/57).

12. See *Report of the Representative of the Secretary-General on Legal Aspects Relating to the Protection Against Arbitrary Displacement,* UN ESCOR, 54th Sess., Agenda Item 9(d), UN Doc. E/CN.4/1998/53/add. 1 (1998);

Report of the Representative of the Secretary-General on the Guiding Principles on Internal Displacement, UN Commissioner of Human Rights, 54th Sess., Agenda Item 9(d), UN Doc. E/CN.4/1998/53/add. 2 (1998).

13. *Report of the Representative of the Secretary-General on the Guiding Principles on Internal Displacement, supra* note 11.

14. *Strengthening of the Coordination of Emergency Humanitarian Assistance of the United Nations*, UN Doc. A/53/139-E/1998/67 (1998).

15. *Report of the Secretary-General to the Security Council on the Protection of Civilians in Armed Conflict*, UN Doc. S/1999/957 (1999).

16. UN Security Council, 4091st *mtg.*, UN Doc. SC/RES/1286 (2000).

17. See G. A. Res. 167, UN GAOR, 54th Sess., UN Doc. A/RE5/54/167 (2000); Commissioner of Human Rights Res. 47, UN Doc. E/CN.4/RES/1999/47 (1999).

18. Susan Forbes Martin, *The Handbook for Applying the Guiding Principles on Internal Displacement* (The Brookings Project on Internal Displacement and the Office for the Coordination of Humanitarian Affairs [OCHA], 2000), available at *http://www.reliefweb.int/ocha_ol/pub/IDP principles.PDF.*

19. *Manual on Field Practice in Internal Displacement*, Inter-Agency Standing Committee Policy Paper Series No. 1, Office for the Coordination of Humanitarian Affairs (OCHA), 1994, available at *http://www. reliefweb.int/ocha_ol/pub/IDPManual.pdf.*

20. *Guiding Principles on Internal Displacement: Annotations* (Washington, D.C.: The American Society of International Law and the Brookings Project on Internal Displacement, 2000).

21. The Brookings Project on Internal Displacement, *Report of the International Colloquy on the Guiding Principles on Internal Displacement* (The Brookings Institution, 2000).

22. Secretary-General Kofi Annan, *Renewing the United Nations: A Programme for Reform*, UN Doc. A/51/950 (1997).

23. The Inter-Agency Standing Committee, *Protection of Internally Displaced Persons*, at *http://www.idpproject.org.pdf_files/protectionpolicypaper.*

24. The Inter-Agency Standing Committee, "Supplementary Guide to Humanitarian/Resident Coordinators on their Responsibilities in Relation to Internally Displaced Persons," *http://www.idpproject.org. pdf_files/suppguidance.pdf.*

25. See OSCE, *Supplementary Human Dimension Meeting: Migration and Internal Displacement*, Final Report, Vienna, September 25, 2000.

26. UN Doc. E/CN.4/2002/95 (2002), para. 46.

27. Countries visited: Angola, Armenia, Azerbaijan, Burundi (twice), Colombia (twice), East Timor, El Salvador, Georgia, Indonesia, Mozambique, Peru, Russian Federation, Rwanda, Somalia, Sri Lanka, Sudan (twice), Tajikistan, and the former Yugoslavia. Reports of these missions are available at *www.unhchr.ch/*.

28. *Masses in Flight, supra* note 1; *The Forsaken People, supra* note 2.

Notes to Chapter Six
Protection Strategies in Humanitarian Interventions
Gerald R. Martone

1. United Nations High Commissioner for Refugees, *Protecting Refugees: A Field Guide for NGOs* (Geneva: Atar SA, 1999).

2. Disaster Policy Department, International Federation of Red Cross and Red Crescent Movements and Nongovernmental Organizations in Disaster Relief, Geneva, 1994.

3. Sphere Project, *Humanitarian Charter and Minimum Standards in Disaster Response* (Geneva: International Federation of the Red Cross, 1998).

4. F. M. Deng, "Don't Overlook Colombia's Humanitarian Crisis," *Christian Science Monitor* (October 6, 1999): 75.

5. M Frohardt, D. Paul, and L. Minear, *Protecting Human Rights: Challenges to Humanitarian Organizations* (Providence, RI: Thomas J. Watson Institute, 1999).

6. P. Perrin, *War and Public Health* (Geneva: International Committee of the Red Cross, 1996).

7. M. Ignatieff, *The Warrior's Honor* (New York: Henry Holt and Co., 1997).

Glossary of Terms to Chapter Seven
Issues of Power and Gender in Complex Emergencies
Judy A. Benjamin

Complex humanitarian emergencies: The term was first applied to the Great Lakes crisis and the Rwandan genocide, which involved hundreds of NGO and UN agencies working together to deliver aid in an unstable environment.

Disaster: A calamitous event resulting in loss of life, great human suffering and distress, and large-scale material damage.

Equality: The equal access by women and men to opportunities and resources. Upholding the rights of women and men without discrimination.

Gender: Gender refers to socially and culturally constructed perceptions of differences between men and women; a social construction often contrasted with "sex," which refers to biological differences between males and females.

Gender-Based Violence: Violence committed against women as women; violence particular to women such as rape, sexual assault, female circumcision, dowry burning, etc.; violence against women for failing to conform to restrictive social norms.

Internally Displaced Persons (IDPs): People who leave their homes but do not cross country boundaries to escape persecution or fear of persecution based on race, religion, nationality, membership of a particular social group or political opinion.

Refugee: A person who has fled from his/her country to escape persecution or fear of persecution based on race, religion, nationality, membership of a particular social group or political opinion.

Special Rapporteur on Violence Against Women: Official appointed by the Commission on Human Rights in 1994 to investigate and make reports on cases of violence against women worldwide.

Vulnerability: Susceptible to physical injury and/or attack.

NOTES TO CHAPTER SEVEN
ISSUES OF POWER AND GENDER IN COMPLEX EMERGENCIES
Judy A. Benjamin

1. The term "camp" may refer to sites of temporary shelter for either refugees or internally displaced persons. Shelters may be tents or constructed in local materials.

2. UNHCR report, *On Sexual Violence and Exploitation in West Africa,*

Note for Implementing and Operational Partners by UNHCR and Save the Children U.K., April 26, 2002.

3. Caroline Moser, *Gender Planning and Development: Theory, Practice and Training* (New York: Routledge, 1993).

4. In this chapter the terms "refugee women" and "displaced women" are interchangeable for the most part.

5. Universal Declaration of Human Rights (UDHR), General Assembly, A/RES/17 A (III), December 10, 1948.

6. The Convention on the Elimination of All Forms of Discrimination against Women (CEDAW), A/RES/34/180, December 18, 1979.

7. The Convention against Torture and Other Cruel, Inhuman or Degrading Treatment or Punishment (Torture Convention), General Assembly, A/RES/39/46, December 10, 1984.

8. See Michael Roe, "Displaced Women in Settings of Continuing Armed Conflict," in *Refugee Women and Their Mental Health: Shattered Societies, Shattered Lives, Women and Therapy* 13, nos. 1 and 2 (1992).

9. These examples are drawn from actual cases documented by the Women's Commission for Refugee Women and Children during field assessment missions by the author to Guinea, Sierra Leone, and Pakistan.

10. For references and additional reading, see the References section for this chapter, below.

11. Women's Commission for Refugee Women and Children, *Refugee Women in the Former Yugoslavia*, 1995.

12. The Committee on the Elimination of Discrimination Against Women was established to monitor compliance with the Women's Convention. The Committee is composed of twenty-three experts in the fields covered by the Convention. Experts are elected by the State Parties to the Convention for four years.

13. Source: *From Response to Solutions: Strengthening the Protection of Refugees through Economic, Social and Cultural Rights*, a discussion paper, WARIPNET and the Lawyers Committee for Human Rights, presented in Geneva at EXCOM, October 2000.

References to Chapter Seven
Issues of Power and Gender in Complex Emergencies
Judy A. Benjamin

Benjamin, Judy A. "Afghanistan: Women Survivors of War under the Taliban." In *War's Offensive on Women.* Edited by Julie A. Mertus. Bloomfield: Kumarian Press, 2000.

Benjamin, Judy A. "Issues of Power and Empowerment in Refugee Studies: Rwandan Women's Adaptive Behavior at Benaco Refugee Camp." *REFUGE* 17, no. 4 (October 1998).

Benjamin, Judy A. *Post-Taliban Afghanistan: Changed Prospects for Women? A Study on the Situation of Women and Girls in Afghanistan.* UN Coordinator's Office, Afghanistan, February 2002.

Cohen, Roberts. *Refugee and Internally Displaced Women: A Development Perspective.* The Brookings Institution/Refugee Policy Group Project on Internal Displacement, November 1995.

Davies, Wendy, ed. *Rights Have No Borders: Worldwide Internal Displacement.* Norwegian Refugee Council/Global IDP Survey, 1998.

Gunn, S. W. A. "The Language of Disasters: A Brief Terminology of Disaster Management and Humanitarian Action." In *Basics of International Humanitarian Missions.* Edited by Kevin M. Cahill, M.D. New York: Fordham University Press, 2003.

Harrell-Bond, Barbara. *Imposing Aid: Emergency Assistance to Refugees.* Oxford: Oxford University Press, 1996.

Kleine-Ahlbrandt, Stephanie. *The Protection Gap in the International Protection of Internally Displaced Persons: The Case of Rwanda.* University of Geneva: University Institute of International Higher Education, 1996.

Kunder, James. *The Needs of Internally Displaced Women and Children: Principles and Considerations.* UNICEF, February 1998.

Machel, Graça. *Report by the Expert of the UN Secretary-General on the Impact of Armed Conflict on Children.* UN Document A/51/306. 26, August 1996.

Maran, Rita, ed. *The Human Rights of Women: A Reference Guide to Official United Nations Documents.* http://www.umn.edu/humanrts/instree/women/engl-wmn.html.

Martin, Susan Forbes. *Refugee Women.* Oxford: Zed Books, 1992.

Mertus, Julie A., with Judy A. Benjamin. *War's Offensive on Women: The Humanitarian Challenge in Bosnia, Kosovo, and Afghanistan.* Bloomfield: Kumarian Press, 2000.

Physicians for Human Rights Report. *Women's Health and Human Rights in Afghanistan: A Population-Based Assessment.* Boston: PHR, 2001. http://www.phrusa.org.

Pickup, Francine, with Suzanne Williams and Caroline Sweetman. *Ending Violence against Women: A Challenge for Development and Humanitarian Work.* Oxford: Oxfam.

Reid, Elizabeth. "A Future, If One Is Still Alive: Challenge of the HIV

Epidemic." In *Hard Choices: Moral Dilemmas in Humanitarian Intervention.* Edited by Jonathan Moore. Boston: Rowman & Littlefield, 1998.

Roe, Michael D. "Displaced Women in Settings of Continuing Armed Conflict." *Women and Therapy: A Feminist Quarterly* 13, nos. 1–2 (1992).

Schuler, Margaret, and Dorothy Thomas, eds. *Women's Human Rights Step by Step: A Practical Guide to Using International Human Rights Law and Mechanisms to Defend Women's Human Rights.* Washington, D.C.: Women, Law & Development International and Human Rights Watch, 1997.

Sphere Document—see *Humanitarian Charter and Minimum Standards in Disaster Response.*

The Sphere Project. *Humanitarian Charter and Minimum Standards in Disaster Response. http://www.sphereproject.org.*

Turshen, Meredeth, and Clotilde Twagiramariya, eds. *What Women Do in Wartime: Gender and Conflict in Africa.* London: Zed Books, 1998.

UN Division for the Advancement of Women. *Report of the Expert Group Meeting on Gender-Based Persecution.* ECM/GBP/Report, 1997.

UNHCR. *A Framework for People-Oriented Planning in Refugee Situations Taking Account of Women, Men and Children.* UNHCR, 1992.

UNHCR. *Guidelines on the Protection of Refugee Women.* UNHCR, 1991.

UNHCR. *How to Guide Reproductive Health in Refugee Situations: A Community-Based Response on Sexual Violence against Women.* Ngara, Tanzania, January 1997.

UNHCR. *Sexual Violence against Refugees: Guidelines on Prevention and Response.* UNHCR, 1995.

UNOCHA. *Guiding Principles on Internal Displacement.* New York: UN, 2001.

WARPPNET and Lawyers Committee for Human Rights. *From Response to Solutions: Strengthening the Protection of Refugees through Economic, Social and Cultural Rights.* A discussion paper on the economic, social and cultural rights of refugees in West Africa. Presented during the 51st meeting of the Executive Committee of the High Commissioner's Program. Geneva, October 2000.

Women's Commission for Refugee Women and Children. *Internal Displacement in Kosovo: The Impact on Women and Children.* WCRWC 1998. *www.womenscommission.org.*

World Food Program. *Gender Mainstreaming in WFP: An Integrated Assessment.* WFP/EB.2/98/9, April 17, 1998.

NOTES TO CHAPTER EIGHT
CLINICAL ASPECTS OF MALNUTRITION
Kevin M. Cahill, M.D.

1. Kevin M. Cahill, *Famine* (New York: Orbis Press, 1982).
2. Kevin M. Cahill, *Health on the Horn of Africa* (London: Spottiswoode Ballantine, 1969).
3. Kevin M. Cahill, *Somalia: A Perspective* (Albany, NY: State University of New York Press, 1980).
4. K. Cahill and H. Gilles, *Tropical Medicine: A Clinical Text* (New York: CIHC, 2000).

NOTES TO CHAPTER NINE
MILITARY/NGO INTERACTION
Major General Timothy Cross

1. The International Committee of the Red Cross (ICRC) is an international organization whose mandate is to "help victims of war and internal violence, and to promote compliance with International Humanitarian Law."
2. From 1991 to 1994, seventy-nine out of eighty-two significant conflicts were intra-state. See David J. Whalley, "Improving UN Developmental Co-ordination within Peace Missions," *International Peacekeeping* 3 (summer 1996): 107.
3. See Edward Moxon-Browne, *A Future for Peacekeeping* (London: Macmillan, 1998), 199–200; and Sam Huntingdon, "Clash of Civilisations?" *Foreign Affairs* (summer 1993): 22–49.
4. Figures from Vladimir Goryayev, Department of Political Affairs at the UN Secretariat, during discussions at Stanford University, May 26–27, 2000.
5. The list is a long one. According to the *International Herald Tribune* 6 (June 2000), "Asian and Pacific countries are watching with concern as ethnic rivalries and violence blossom in an arc stretching

through Sri Lanka, Indonesia, the Philippines, Papua New Guinea, the Solomon Islands, and Fiji. . . . There is widespread concern that a successful insurgency would encourage other rebels who want to overthrow democratic governments."

6. See G. J. Speth, "Why the UN Is Essential to Successful Development Co-operation (and Vice Versa)," *UNDP* 17 (January 1996): 4.

7. From conversations prior to the Taormina conference, April 13–16, 2000.

8. This need is widely recognized in nonmilitary literature—see for example, Moxon-Browne, *A Future for Peacekeeping,* 16—but much less so in military journals.

9. Particularly Hugo Slim, "The Stretcher and the Drum: Civil-Military Relations in Peace Support Operations," *International Peacekeeping* 3, no. 2 (1996): 123–40; and Hugo Slim in John MacKinlay, ed., *A Guide to Peace Support Operations,* section 6, produced by the Thomas J. Watson Jr. Institute for International Studies, Brown University, July 1996.

10. Slim, "Stretcher and Drum," 124.

11. Slim, *A Guide to Peace Support Operations,* 93. Weiss's definition is a "nonprofit, voluntary, formal, nonviolent, nonpolitical organization whose objective is to promote development and social change." See Thomas G. Weiss, *Military-Civilian Interactions: Intervening in Humanitarian Crisis* (Lanham, MD: Rowman & Littlefield, 1999). The introduction and chapter 1 give a forceful and excellent overview of all of the humanitarian actors, including the military, with the following chapters detailing case studies.

12. OXFAM U.K. has a budget of around £124 million, employs 1,500 staff in the U.K. and 200 expatriate and 3,000 local staff abroad. CARE has an annual budget of around U.S.$350 million.

13. The end of the Vietnam War, 1968, and the African Civil Wars of the 1960s seem to have been the triggers for an exponential growth in nonviolent NGO intervention.

14. See Major S. R. Skeates, *Operating in a Complex Environment: How Can the British Military Improve Interagency Cooperation in Peace Support Operations?* Cranfield University (RMCS) MBA Course no. 12, July 1998; Commodore Tim Laurence, *Humanitarian Assistance and Peacekeeping: An Uneasy Alliance?* RUSI Whitehall Paper Series, no. 48; and *Economist* article (January 29, 2000): 25–28.

15. The nature of the UN is summarized in any number of refer-

ences; see, for example, "The MOD's Peace Support Operations" *JWP* (March 2001): 1–3; 1–8.

16. See Graham Hancock, *The Lords of Poverty* (London: Macmillan, 1989), which details the power, prestige, and corruption of the international aid business as he sees it; and M. Maren, *The Road to Hell: The Ravaging Effects of Foreign Aid* (New York: The Free Press, 1997). Also articles by Graham Boynton, *Daily Telegraph*, 8 May 2000, p. 18; and by Simon Jenkins, *The Times*, 10 May 2000, p. 20, which are indicative of a growing questioning of the effectiveness of Western aid intervention. Even those deeply committed to aid recognize the dangers. See William Shawcross, *Deliver Us From Evil: Warlords and Peacekeepers in a World of Endless Conflict* (London: Bloomsbury Publishing, 2000), particularly pages 4, 5, 33, 121, and 131. I met with William in Macedonia and discussed these issues; his book offers a reality check for those who clamor for "something to be done."

17. See Major R. K. Tomlinson, MBE, BSc (Hons), "Reversing the Downward Spiral: Exploring Cultural Dissonance Between the Military and NGOs on Humanitarian Operations," Royal Engineers (RE) Defense Logistics Management (MSc Dissertation, Cranfield University, Royal Military College of Science, July 2000).

18. Larry Minnear et al, "NATO and Humanitarian Action in the Kosovo Crisis," Occasional Paper, no. 36, Humanitarian and War Project, January 2000.

19. Thomas Weiss, "Learning From Military Civilian Interactions on Peace Operations," *International Peacekeeping* (1999): 113–25. The UNHCR also recognizes that there are likely to be difficulties when working with the military, and has produced a handbook for their field staff that states: "With respect to the military-civil disparity, experience indicates that many failures of cooperation and misunderstandings have resulted from the neglect to consider the diverging perspectives of the military and civilian actors" a *UNHCR Handbook for the Military on Humanitarian Operations, Journal of Humanitarian Assistance*, February 4, 1996. Perhaps this final comment from Mark Bowden in *Black Hawk Down* (Bantam Press, 1999), 33, on the so-called "humanitarian mission" to Somalia in 1993 sums up the sheer breadth of cultural divide that can develop between the soldier and the humanitarian. "If you wanted the starving masses in Somalia to eat then you had to outmuscle men like Aidid, for whom starvation worked. You could send in your bleeding heart do-gooders, you could hold hands and pray and sing

songs and invoke the great gods CNN and BBC, but the only way to finally open the roads to the big-eyed babies was to show up with more guns. And in this real world nobody had more or better guns than America."

20. To quote from an NGO representative at the Stanford University conference, "Some are there for Aid, others for Peace."

21. Power is a chapter in its own right. The best military commanders can balance their "legitimate" power—granted through their formal authority/position—and "coercive" power—the ability to punish— with "expert," "reverent," and "reward" power; the motto of the Royal Military Academy, Sandhurst, through which all regular British Army officers are commissioned, is: "Serve to Lead," and most try to live up to that.

22. For an interesting perspective of the military (albeit U.S. military), see the USAID *Field Operations Guide (FOG) for Disaster Assessment and Relief*, VI-35. Also Scott Peterson, *Me against my Brother: At War in Somalia, Sudan and Rwanda* (New York: Routledge, 2000). This includes a classic portrait of an army in its pomp, "ignorant, arrogant, and ripe for the humiliation it suffered"—the U.S. in Somalia.

23. These are my observations. See also Slim in *A Guide to Peace Support Operations*, 106–11; and the results of the survey conducted by Major R. K. Tomlinson for his Defense Logistics Course, MSc, March 25, 2000, some comments of which are included in these endnotes.

24. In discussions with MSF, this "bottom line" is usually drawn where their aid contributes to a rotten process, for example, where it is being turned against the refugees/people it is intended to help; where this is so they will pull out rather than be used. That said, it is rare for these agencies to do so.

25. For a wider analysis of the doctrine and principles of the NGOs, see, for example, ICRC, *The Fundamental Principles of the Red Cross and Red Crescent Movements*, 2d ed. (Geneva: ICRC, 1996). Their seven fundamental principles are "humanity, impartiality, neutrality, independence, voluntary service, unity, and universality," 1–2.

26. The human rights component of UNTAC worked hard under a New Zealander from UNHCR, Dennis McNamara; I worked with Dennis in Macedonia/Kosovo where he was the UN Deputy Special Representative for Humanitarian Affairs. Shawcross remarks that "they had an uphill job in trying to temper the brutal authoritarianism of the Phnom Penh authorities and no luck at all with the Khmer Rouge . . .

They were extraordinarily brave . . . A human rights campaigner in the provinces was truly alone in facing the wrath of either the Khmer Rouge or the secret police and army of the Phnom Penh regime" (see Shawcross, 57).

27. Comment by a U.K. Royal Engineers (RE) major: "Without doubt the most impressive crew we worked with was 'Mission Ost (East),' in Dersnik Camp in Albania, who were quite excellent. Their attitude, the way they worked and their practical ability were all first class . . . (they) put the job first without promoting their own image." See Tomlinson.

28. See Hancock, *The Lords of Poverty*, page 1 of the introduction.

29. OXFAM, for example, has 30,000 volunteer workers and 500,000 committed donors who provide both legitimacy and accountability.

30. This said, the media, and the NGOs, might sometimes do well to reflect on history. A *Punch* cartoon entitled the "Dogs of War" appeared in the edition dated June 17, 1876. It shows a man restraining four snarling dogs whose collars bear the names Bosnia, Montenegro, Serbia, and Herzegovina. A second man peering anxiously at them over a fence says: "Take care, my man! It might be awkward if you were to let 'em loose!" See Laurence, *Humanitarian Assistance and Peacekeeping*, 71.

31. See Shawcross, 32–33.

32. For an analysis of the proportion of females currently deployed, and a rationale for more, see Moxon-Browne, *A Future for Peacekeeping*, 195. One less than politically correct view offered by a British officer responding to the survey conducted by Major R. K. Tomlinson for his MSc thesis was: "The hundreds of people I worked with are but distant memories now, except the 1.8m tall Dutch girl with red hair who was stunning. She had the longest legs in the Western world and had a fantastic bum—but I can't remember her name!"

33. Comment by a U.K. Royal Signals major: "It is easy to be over-critical of the UNHCR effort. I think two things come to mind: firstly, the team working in Macedonia had dedicated people. They worked very hard, particularly during the first days when the flood of refugees started crossing the border. They worked day and night to provide the necessary support. However, and this is my main observation, they lacked the numbers and the structure to be effective on their own." See Tomlinson.

34. The UN and governmental aid agencies can be particularly guilty

here. One MSF worker I met had left the UN, for whom she had worked as a twenty-four-year old earning $6,000 a month, tax free, because her fellow "workers" were apathetic, disorganized, and arrogant. Comment by an RLC captain: "It's very personality driven with regard to the different aid agencies—some were very proactive, others were a disgrace. The general impression was very poor and they all seemed incredibly money-orientated." See Tomlinson.

35. Comment by an RE major: "They need to organize themselves for prompt response, not the gradual incremental response that they deem suitable and which ultimately threatens lives. Also, the workers should consider spending a longer day at the crisis and not disappearing to their comfortable hotel rooms. Few were about after normal working hours"; and by an RE lieutenant: "Most organizations functioned in a satisfactory manner once set up. Their complete inability to react, organize themselves, and make decisions rapidly was astounding." See Tomlinson.

36. The House of Commons International Development Report on the Kosovo Crisis, Third Report, printed May 11, 1999, is particularly harsh on the UNHCR, to the extent that it raises the suggestion that in future emergency situations, the UN office for the Coordination of Humanitarian Affairs (OCHA) might more appropriately take the lead in the coordination of humanitarian activities (paragraphs 12, 14–16, 18). To balance their criticisms of the UNHCR they (rightly) praise WFP and DFID for their response (paragraphs 9 and 73). In my view, UNHCR should remain the tactical (i.e., field) level focus; OCHA, which was originally the Department for Humanitarian Affairs (established by the UN in 1992 and renamed in 1997), was relieved of its operational responsibilities to concentrate on policy, advocacy, and coordination. That said, the UNHCR needs to learn lessons from Kosovo. They have initiated a number of studies, including an independent evaluation, and produced a series of relatively hard-hitting reports; they now need to be actioned. See UNHCR EPAU/2000/001, February 2000, and the *ICVA Newsletter* 2, no. 1 (February 18, 2000).

37. Mark Walkup, "Policy Dysfunction in Humanitarian Organizations: The Role of Coping Strategies, Institutions, and Organizational Culture," *Journal of Refugee Studies* 10, no. 1 (1997): 47.

38. See Tomlinson and Norman Dixon, *On Psychology of Military Importance* (Jonathon Cape Ltd., 1976).

39. The Sphere Project—see *http://www.ifre./org/pubs/sphere/ sphrdocl.htm.*

40. Comment from an RLC captain on the urgent need to provide additional rail lift capacity to move refugees and aid into Kosovo: "a number of agencies had the funding . . . the reason it didn't happen was due to the debate over who would be the lead agency, and the unwillingness of each agency to pool resources"; and by a RE lance corporal: "From what I gathered during Brazda, the top management of several aid organizations were to busy having bun fights as to who is the best organization instead of spending there *[sic]* time saving people." See Tomlinson.

41. See *The Economist* (January 29, 2000): 26. Also, comment from a QARANC (Nursing) captain: "The main agency I had contact with was the Red Cross Society. Their agenda was quite obviously a high publicity, low effort attempt." See Tomlinson.

42. See Slim, "Stretcher and Drum," 123–40; and The Hague Occasional Paper, no. 36, 115.

43. See USAID *FOG*, VI-36.

44. An enormous number of articles have been written on the subject of the linkages between "Humanitarians" and the Military in Kosovo—most expressing concern and "demanding" that alternatives to military involvement be sought—see, for example, *ICVA Newsletter* 2, no. 1 (February 18, 2000): 17–22. The output from the Hague Conference, Occasional Paper, no. 36, accurately reflects some pretty strong debate—see, for example, pages 15, 17, and 59.

45. See Laurence, *Humanitarian Assistance and Peacekeeping*, 3, 28; and Moxon-Browne, *A Future for Peacekeeping*, 192.

46. See Henry Shue, "Conditional Sovereignty," in *Res Publica* 8, no.1 (1999). Henry attended the Conference at Stanford University where we debated these, and many other issues.

47. Shawcross, 325.

48. Shawcross, 349.

49. Shawcross, 373.

50. *The International Herald Tribune* (London), Tuesday, 16 May 2000.

51. Comment by an RAMC corporal: ". . . the work we did in Kosovo was a great boost for the troops on the ground . . . it made us feel we were achieving something . . . treating 11,500 in thirteen days . . . the training and experience that will come from it will be invaluable." See Tomlinson.

52. See also the *Daily Telegraph,* 4 March 2000, p. 19.

53. See Editorial, *International Herald Tribune,* 6 June 2000.

54. See Editorial, *The Guardian,* 1 March 2000; Editorial and article p. 1, *The Times,* 4 March 2000; *Sunday Times,* 5 March 2000, p. 8; *Sunday Telegraph,* 5 March 2000, pp. 3, 4; *Independent,* Sunday, 5 March 2000, p. 13; *The Times,* 6 March 2000, p. 5; *The Guardian,* 7 March 2000, p. 5.

55. Ideally, the aim is to "integrate into one coherent approach different tools and forms of action—developmental, humanitarian, political, and military—so that they reinforce each other," see Whalley, "Improving UN Developmental Co-ordination within Peace Missions," 109; and The Hague Occasional Paper, no. 36, 113.

56. For an exhaustive, accurate, and achievable series of policy recommendations, see Skeates, *Operating in a Complex Environment,* RMCS MBA paper, 97, 98. I see little to fault his assessments, which follow logically from his summary and conclusions (93–96), except to add the need for an additional "Support Command" focus.

57. See also Lieutenant Colonel P. R. Wilkinson, *Sharpening the Weapons of Peace: The Development of a Common Military Doctrine for PSO,* BAR no. 118, June 1998, 3–7; and General Sir Michael Rose and General Sir David Ramsbottam, in J. Whitman and D. Pocock, eds., *After Rwanda: The Co-ordination of UN Assistance* (Basingstoke: MacMillan Press, 1996).

REFERENCES TO CHAPTER NINE
MILITARY/NGO INTERACTION
Major General Timothy Cross

Books

Hancock, Graham. *Lords of Poverty: The Power, Prestige and Corruption of the International Aid Business.* London: Macmillan, 1989.

Laurence, Tim, Commodore. *Humanitarian Assistance and Peacekeeping: An Uneasy Alliance?* Royal United Services Institute for Defense Studies, Whitehall Papers Series, No. 48.

Mackinlay, John, ed. *A Guide to Peace Support Operations.* Thomas J. Watson Jr. Institute for International Studies, Brown University, 1996.

Minear, van Baarda, Sommers. *NATO and Humanitarian Action in the Kosovo Crisis.* Thomas J. Watson Jr. Institute for International Studies and the Humanitarian Law Consultancy, Occasion Paper no. 36, February 2000.

Mitchell, John V., ed. *Companies in a World of Conflict: NGOs, Sanctions and Corporate Responsibility.* Papers from a workshop in Oslo by the Royal Institute of International Affairs, April 1997, London: Earthscan Publications, 1998.

Moxon-Browne, Edward, ed. *A Future for Peacekeeping?* London: Macmillan, 1998.

Pugh, Michael, Frank Cass, et al., eds. *The UN, Peace and Force.* London, 1997.

Ratner, Steven R. *The New UN Peacekeeping: Building Peace in Lands of Conflict After the Cold War.* London: Macmillan Press, 1997.

Rodley, N., ed. *To Loose the Bonds of Wickedness: International Intervention in Defense of Human Rights.* Brassey's 1992.

Rose, Michael, General Sir, and General Sir David Ramsbottom. In *After Rwanda: The Co-ordination of UN Assistance,* edited by J. Whitman and D. Pocock. Basingstoke: Macmillan Press, 1996.

Shawcross, William, *Deliver Us From Evil: Warlords and Peacekeepers in a World of Endless Conflict.* London: Bloomsbury Publishing, 2000.

U.K. MOD Publications:

Peace Support Operations. JWP 3–01, HMSO, September 1997.

AFM Vol.5, Pam.1: Peacekeeping Operations. HMSO, 1998.

AFM Vol. 5, OOTW Part 2: Wider Peacekeeping. HMSO, 1995.

USAID. *Field Operations Guide (FOG) for Disaster Assessment and Relief.* Ver. 3. U.S. Government Printing Office (ISBN 0–16–049721–3).

Weiss, Thomas G. *Military-Civilian Interactions: Intervening in Humanitarian Crisis.* Lanham, MD: Rowman & Littlefield, 1999.

Dissertations/Thesis

Bricknell, M. C. M., Dr. *Developing the Role of the Defense Medical Services in Operations Other Than War.* October 1998.

Skeates, S. R., Major. *Operating in a Complex Environment: How Can the British Military Improve Interagency Co-operation in Peace Support Operations?* Cranfield University (RMCS), no. 12 MBA course, July 1998.

Tomlinson, R. K., Major. *Inter-Agency Co-operation for the Provision of Effective Engineering and Logistical Support to Complex Humanitarian Emergencies.* Cranfield University (RMCS), no. 2, MSc Defense Logistics Management Course, July 2000.

Wade, M. W. E., Lt Col. *Twenty-First Century NATO: Matching Words with Deeds.* University of Cambridge, MPhil, July 15, 1999.

Articles and Reports

Bond, Michael Shaw. "Special Report: The Backlash against NGOs." *Prospect* (April 2000): 52–55.

House of Commons Session 1998–99. International Development Committee Third Report. *Kosovo: The Humanitarian Crisis.* May 11, 1999.

International Agency (Humanitarian) Steering Committee note on the *Guiding and Operating Principles for the Use of Military and Civil Defense Assets in Support of Humanitarian Operations.* 1995.

The International Council of Voluntary Agencies (ICVA) Meeting Report on the *UNHCR's Independent Evaluation on Kosovo.* Geneva, November 11–12, 1999.

The International Council of Voluntary Agencies (ICVA) Newsletter 1, no. 5 (August 11, 1999).

The International Council of Voluntary Agencies (ICVA) Newsletter 2, no. 1 (February 18, 2000).

Luttwak, Edward. "Kofi's Rule: Humanitarian Intervention and Neocolonialism." *The National Interest* (winter 1999/2000).

Medact Seminar. "Learning from Kosovo: The Future of Humanitarian Intervention." *The Royal Society of Medicine* (December 15, 1999).

Morris, Nicholas. *Humanitarian Aid and Neutrality.* An article provided by the author, originally published in French from the proceedings of a symposium held June 16–17, 1995.

———. *Humanitarianism and International Security.* A presentation to All Souls College, Oxford, October 29, 1999.

———. Speaking notes from a DFID/University of Essex Conference, provided by the author, February 12, 1998.

———. "UNHCR and Kosovo: A Personal View from Within the UNHCR." *Forced Migration Review* (August 1999).

Roberts, Adam. "NATO's 'Humanitarian War' over Kosovo." *Survival* 41, no. 3 (autumn 1999): 102–23.

———. "Willing the End but Not the Means." *The World Today* (May 1999): 8–12.

Rose, Michael, General Sir. "Are We Creating a Universal Culture of Violence?" *RUSI Journal* (April/May 1999).

Shue, Henry. "Conditional Sovereignty," *Res Publica* 8, no. 1 (1999).

"Sins of the Secular Missionaries." *The Economist* (January 29, 2000): 25–28.

Slim, Hugo. "The Stretcher and the Drum: Civil-Military Relations in Peace Support Operations." *International Peacekeeping* 3, no. 2 (1996).

Speech by the Foreign Secretary, Chatham House, January 28, 2000.

Spence, Jack. "A New International Order: Lessons of Kosovo." An abbreviated version of a talk given at the South African Institute of International Affairs, May 25, 1999.

Speth, G. J. "Why the UN Is Essential to Successful Development Cooperation (and Vice-Versa)," *UNDP*, New York (January 17, 1996).

Suhrke, Barutciski, Sandison, Garlock. *The Kosovo Refugee Crisis: An Independent Evaluation of UNHCR's Emergency Preparedness and Response*. EAPU/2000/001 (Pre-Publication Edition), February 2000.

Terry, Fiona. *Reconstituting Whose Social Order? NGOs in Disrupted States*. Paper presented at a Conference in Canberra, Australia, July 6–7, 1999.

UNHCR Standing Committee (14th Meeting). Report on *The Security, and Civilian and Humanitarian Character of Refugee Camps and Settlements*. EC/49/SC.INF.2, January 14, 1999.

UNHCR Standing Committee (17th Meeting). Report on *Strengthening UNHCR's Emergency Preparedness and Response Capacity*. EC/50/SC/INF.1, March 1, 2000.

Unknown Author. "Civil-Military Co-operation: Observations from Bosnia." *The Naval Review* 88, no. 1 (January 2000).

UN Press Release. Secretary General [Kofi Annan] Presents His Annual Report to the General Assembly, September 20, 1999.

Weiss, T. G. "Operational Relations between the UN System and NGOs: Recent Experience and Future Research." Address to "NGOs in Aid Conference," Bergen, Norway, November 3–5, 1997.

Whalley, David, Jr. "Improving UN Developmental Coordination within Peace Missions." *International Peacekeeping* 3 (summer 1996).

Wilkinson, P. R., Lt Col. "Sharpening the Weapons of Peace: The Development of a Common Military Doctrine for PSO." *BAR*, no. 118 (June 1998): 3–7.

Conferences

I attended two conferences during the research for this chapter:
"The Interaction of NATO-related Military Forces with Humanitarian

Actors During the Kosovo Crisis." The Netherlands Ministry of Foreign Affairs, The Hague, November 15–16, 1999.
The 3rd David Hamburg Symposium on Conflict Prevention. "Ethics and Civil Wars." Stanford University, May 26–27, 2000.

NOTES TO CHAPTER TEN
AN INTRODUCTION TO NGO FIELD SECURITY
Randolph Martin

1. Koenraad Van Brabant, *Good Practice Review # 8: Operational Security Management in Violent Environments* (London: Overseas Development Institute, 2000), is a comprehensive book on the subject, and recommended reading for NGO managers.
2. Koenraad Van Brabant, *Cool Ground for Aid Providers* (London: Overseas Development Institute, 1997).
3. Dan Smith, *The State of the World Atlas* (London: Penguin Books, 1999), 59.
4. Ibid.
5. UNHCR, *State of the World's Refugees* (New York: Oxford University Press, 1995), 26.
6. Smith, *State of the World Atlas.*

NOTES TO CHAPTER ELEVEN
RESOLUTIONS, MANDATES, AIMS, MISSIONS,
AND EXIT STRATEGIES
Larry Hollingworth

1. Mandate . . . [MF & L; *mandat,* fr. L *mandatum,* . . . pp. of *mandare* to entrust, enjoin, prob. irreg. fr. *manus* hand + *-dere* to put . . .] (1501) 1: an authoritative command . . .; 2: an authorization to act given to a representative (*Merriam Webster's Collegiate Dictionary,* 10th ed.).
2. Erskine Childers, ed., *Challenges to the United Nations* (London: CIIR, 1994).
3. Ibid.
4. Lakhdar Brahimi, *Report of the Panel on United Nations Peace Operations* (New York: United Nations, 2000).

5. Delegate to the UN debate "No Exit without Strategy."
6. Delegate to the UN debate "No Exit without Strategy."
7. Kevin C. M. Benson and Christopher B. Thrash, "Declaring Victory: Planning Exit Strategies for Peace Operations," *Parameters* (U.S. Army War College) (autumn 1996): 69–80.
8. Delegate to the UN debate "No Exit without Strategy."
9. Delegate to the UN debate "No Exit without strategy."
10. Delegate to the UN debate "No Exit without strategy."
11. General Romeo Dallaire, "The End of Innocence," in *Hard Choices: Moral Dilemmas in Humanitarian Intervention,* ed. Jonathan Moore (Oxford: Rowan, Littlefield & Lanham, 1998).
12. Ibid.
13. Delegate to the UN debate "No Exit without Strategy."

REFERENCES TO CHAPTER ELEVEN
RESOLUTIONS, MANDATES, AIMS, MISSIONS,
AND EXIT STRATEGIES
Larry Hollingworth

Allard, Colonel Kenneth. *Somalia Operations.* National Defense University: Institute for National Strategic Studies, 1995.

Brahimi, Lakhdar. *Report of the Panel on United Nations Peace Operations.* UN Document A/55/305–5/2000/809, 8/23/2000. New York: United Nations, 2000.

Childers, Erskine, ed. *Challenges to the United Nations.* London: CIIR, 1994.

Honig, Jan Willem, and Norbert Both. *Srebrenica: Record of a War Crime.* New York: Penguin, 1996.

Keane, Fergal. *Season of Blood: A Rwandan Journey.* New York: Penguin, 1997.

Owen, Lord David. *Balkan Odyssey.* New York: Harcourt Trade Publishers, 1997.

Strednansky, Susan. *Balancing the Trinity: The Fine Art of Conflict Termination.* Air University Press, 1996.

United Nations. *Basic Facts about the United Nations.* New York: United Nations, 1998.

NOTES TO CHAPTER TWELVE
THE TRANSITION FROM CONFLICT TO PEACE
Richard Ryscavage, S.J.

1. P. Weiss-Fagen, "The Challenge of Rebuilding War-Torn Societies: A Bibliographic Essay," War-Torn Societies Project, UN Research Institute for Social Development, Geneva, 1995.

2. Johan Galtung, "Three Approaches to Peace: Peacekeeping, Peacemaking and Peacebuilding," in *Peace, War and Defense: Essays in Peace Research* (Copenhagen: Christian Eljers, 1976), 2:297–304.

3. K. Hewitt, ed., *Interpretations of Calamity from the Viewpoint of Human Ecology* (London: Allen and Unwin, 1983).

4. For more about the "contract culture" and humanitarian relief, cf. Graham Hancock, *Lords of Poverty* (London: Macmillan, 1989).

5. Joanna Macrae, "Aid under Fire: Redefining Relief and Development Assistance in Unstable Situations," background discussion paper, Dept. of Human Affairs Seminar, ActionAid, Overseas Development Institute, Wilton Park, U.K., April 7–9, 1995.

6. Mark Duffield, "Complex Emergencies and the Crisis of Developmentalism," *Institute of Development Studies Bulletin* 25, no. 3 (U. of Sussex).

7. NORDSAMFN, *Nordic Peacekeeping Handbook,* Nordic UN Standby Forces (Helsingfors: Tryckericentralen AB, 1993), 28.

8. Cf. General Assembly, "Report of the Secretary-General on the Work of the Organization," UN Document A/49/1, Sept 2, 1994.

9. Cf. F. Cuny, *Disasters and Development* (New York: Oxford University Press, 1983).

10. R. Gorman, *Refugee Aid and Development: Theory and Practice* (Westport, CT: Greenwood Press, 1983).

11. For definitions of conflict resolution, mediation, peacekeeping, peace research, etc., cf. Graham Evans and J. Newnham, eds., *The Penguin Dictionary of International Relations* (London: Penguin Books, 1998).

12. Herbert Kelman, "The Interactive Problem-Solving Approach," in *Managing Global Chaos* (Washington, D.C.: U.S. Institute of Peace, 1996), 501–20.

13. E. Voutira and Shaun Brown, "Conflict Resolution: A Cautionary Tale," Report No. 4, Refugee Studies Program, University of Oxford, 1995.

14. Marina Ottaway and Thomas Carothers, eds., *Funding Virtue: Civil Society Aid and the Promotion of Democracy* (Washington, D.C.: Carnegie Endowment for International Peace, 2000).

15. For descriptions of various peacemaking projects of NGOs, cf. David Smock, ed., *Private Peacemaking*, Papeworks #20, U.S. Institute for Peace, 1998.

16. For a summary view of the relationship problems between NGOs and the military, cf. T. Lanzer, B. Harrell-Bond, and R. Ryscavage, "The Role of the Military in Humanitarian Emergencies," Conference Report, Refugee Studies Program, Oxford, U.K., October 29–31, 1995.

17. Adam Roberts, "Humanitarian Action in War," Adelphi Paper No. 305 (London: International Institute for Strategic Studies, 1996).

18. For example, Guus Van Der Veer, *Counseling and Therapy with Refugees and Victims of Trauma: Psychological Problems of Victims of War, Torture and Repression* (New York: John Wiley & Sons Pub [Paperback], 1998).

19. Cf. "Forgiveness in Conflict Resolution: Reality and Utility," Conference Report, Woodstock Theological Center, Washington, D.C., December 9, 1996.

20. Anne-Marie Smith, *Advances in Understanding International Peacemaking* (Washington, D.C.: U.S. Institute of Peace); John Clark, *Democratizing Development: The Role of Voluntary Organizations* (London: Earthscan Pub, 1991).

21. Larry Diamon, Juan Linz, and Seymour Lipset, *Democracy in Developing Countries*, 3 vols. (Boulder, CO: Lynee Rienner, 1989); and Guillermo O'Connell, Philippe Schmitter, and L. Whitehead, *Transitions from Authoritarian Rule: Prospects for Democracy*, 4 vols. (Baltimore: Johns Hopkins University Press, 1986).

22. Gary Dempsey with Roger Fontaine, *Fool's Errands: America's Recent Encounters with Nation Building* (Washington, D.C.: Cato Institute, 2001).

23. Paul F. Diehl, J. Reifschneider, and Paul Hensel, "United Nations Intervention and Recurring Conflict," *International Organization* 50, no. 4 (autumn, 1996).

24. Lawrence Harrington and Samuel Huntington, eds., *Culture Matters* (New York: Basic Books, 2000).

APPENDIX 1: CONVENTION ON THE ELIMINATION OF ALL FORMS OF DISCRIMINATION AGAINST WOMEN

(Abridged by omission of Arts. 26–30)

The States Parties to the present Convention,

Noting that the Charter of the United Nations reaffirms faith in fundamental human rights, in the dignity and worth of the human person and in the equal rights of men and women,

Noting that the Universal Declaration of Human Rights affirms the principle of the inadmissibility of discrimination and proclaims that all human beings are born free and equal in dignity and rights and that everyone is entitled to all the rights and freedoms set forth therein, without distinction of any kind, including distinction based on sex,

Noting that the States Parties to the International Covenants on Human Rights have the obligation to ensure the equal rights of men and women to enjoy all economic, social, cultural, civil, and political rights,

Considering the international conventions concluded under the auspices of the United Nations and the specialized agencies promoting equality of rights of men and women,

Noting also the resolutions, declarations and recommendations adopted by the United Nations and the specialized agencies promoting equality of rights of men and women,

Adopted and opened for signature, ratification, and accession by General Assembly resolution 34/180 of December 18, 1979. Entered into force: September 3, 1981, in accordance with Art. 27 (1).

Concerned, however, that despite these various instruments, extensive discrimination against women continues to exist,

Recalling that discrimination against women violates the principles of equality of rights and respect for human dignity, is an obstacle to the participation of women, on equal terms with men, in the political, social, economic, and cultural life of their countries, hampers the growth of the prosperity of society and the family and makes more difficult the full development of the potentialities of women in the service of their countries and of humanity,

Concerned that in situations of poverty women have the least access to food, health, education, training and opportunities for employment and other needs,

Convinced that the establishment of the new international economic order based on equity and justice will contribute significantly toward the promotion of equality between men and women,

Emphasizing that the eradication of apartheid, all forms of racism, racial discrimination, colonialism, neocolonialism, aggression, foreign occupation, and domination and interference in the internal affairs of States is essential to the full enjoyment of the rights of men and women,

Affirming that the strengthening of international peace and security, the relaxation of international tension, mutual cooperation among all States irrespective of their social and economic systems, general and complete disarmament, in particular nuclear disarmament under strict and effective international control, the affirmation of the principles of justice, equality and mutual benefit in relations among countries and the realization of the right of peoples under alien and colonial domination and foreign occupation to self determination and independence, as well as respect for national sovereignty and territorial integrity, will promote social progress and development and as a consequence will contribute to the attainment of full equality between men and women,

Convinced that the full and complete development of a country, the welfare of the world, and the cause of peace require the maximum participation of women on equal terms with men in all fields,

Bearing in mind the great contribution of women to the welfare of the family and to the development of society, so far not fully recognized, the social significance of maternity and the role of both parents in the family and in the upbringing of children, and aware that the role of women in procreation should not be a basis for discrimination but that the upbringing of children requires a sharing of responsibility between men and women and society as a whole,

Aware that a change in the traditional role of men as well as the role of women in society and in the family is needed to achieve full equality between men and women,

Determined to implement the principles set forth in the Declaration on the Elimination of Discrimination against Women and, for that purpose, to adopt the measures required for the elimination of such discrimination in all its forms and manifestations,

Have agreed on the following:

PART 1

Article 1

For the purposes of the present Convention, the term "discrimination against women" shall mean any distinction, exclusion or restriction made on the basis of sex which has the effect or purpose of impairing or nullifying the recognition, enjoyment, or exercise by women, irrespective of their marital status, on a basis of equality of men and women, of human rights and fundamental freedoms in the political, economic, social, cultural, civil, or any other field.

Article 2

States Parties condemn discrimination against women in all its forms, agree to pursue by all appropriate means and without delay a policy of eliminating discrimination against women and, to this end, undertake:

a) To embody the principle of the equality of men and women in their national constitutions or other appropriate legislation if not yet incorporated therein and to ensure, through law and other appropriate means, the practical realization of this principle;

b) To adopt appropriate legislative and other measures, including sanctions where appropriate, prohibiting all discrimination against women;

c) To establish legal protection of the rights of women on an equal basis with men and to ensure through competent national tribunals and other public institutions the effective protection of women against any act of discrimination;

d) To refrain from engaging in any act or practice of discrimination against women and to ensure that public authorities and institutions shall act in conformity with this obligation;

e) To take all appropriate measures to eliminate discrimination against women by any person, organization or enterprise;

f) To take all appropriate measures, including legislation, to modify or abolish existing laws, regulations, customs and practices, which constitute discrimination against women;

g) To repeal all national penal provisions which constitute discrimination against women.

Article 3

States Parties shall take in all fields, in particular in the political, social, economic, and cultural fields, all appropriate measures, including legislation, to ensure the full development and advancement of women, for the purpose of guaranteeing them the exercise and enjoyment of human rights and fundamental freedoms on a basis of equality with men.

Article 4

1. Adoption by States Parties of temporary special measures aimed at accelerating de facto equality between men and women shall not be considered discrimination as defined in the present Convention, but shall in no way entail as a consequence the maintenance of unequal or separate standards; these measures shall be discontinued when the objectives of equality of opportunity and treatment have been achieved.
2. Adoption by States Parties of special measures, including those measures contained in the present Convention, aimed at protecting maternity shall not be considered discriminatory.

Article 5

States Parties shall take all appropriate measures:

a) To modify the social and cultural patterns of conduct of men and women, with a view to achieving the elimination of prejudices and customary and all other practices which are based on the idea of the inferiority or the superiority of either of the sexes or on stereotyped roles for men and women;
b) To ensure that family education includes a proper understanding of maternity as a social function and the recognition of the common responsibility of men and women in the upbringing and development of their children, it being understood that the interest of the children is the primordial consideration in all cases.

Article 6

States Parties shall take all appropriate measures, including legislation, to suppress all forms of traffic in women and exploitation of prostitution of women.

PART 2

Article 7

States Parties shall take all appropriate measures to eliminate discrimination against women in the political and public life of the country and, in particular, shall ensure to women, on equal terms with men, the right:

a) To vote in all elections and public referenda and to be eligible for election to all publicly elected bodies;

b) To participate in the formulation of government policy and the implementation thereof and to hold public office and perform all public functions at all levels of government;

c) To participate in nongovernmental organizations and associations concerned with the public and political life of the country.

Article 8

States Parties shall take all appropriate measures to ensure to women, on equal terms with men and without any discrimination, the opportunity to represent their Governments at the international level and to participate in the work of international organizations.

Article 9

1. States Parties shall grant women equal rights with men to acquire, change, or retain their nationality. They shall ensure in particular that neither marriage to an alien nor change of nationality by the husband during marriage shall automatically change the nationality of the wife, render her stateless or force upon her the nationality of the husband.

2. States Parties shall grant women equal rights with men with respect to the nationality of their children.

PART 3

Article 10

States Parties shall take all appropriate measures to eliminate discrimination against women in order to ensure to them equal rights with men in the field of education and in particular to ensure, on a basis of equality of men and women:

a) The same conditions for career and vocational guidance, for access to studies and for the achievement of diplomas in educational establishments of all categories in rural as well as in urban areas; this equality shall be ensured in preschool, general, technical, professional, and higher technical education, as well as in all types of vocational training;

b) Access to the same curricula, the same examinations, teaching staff with qualifications of the same standard and school premises and equipment of the same quality;

c) The elimination of any stereotyped concept of the roles of men and women at all levels and in all forms of education by encouraging coeducation and other types of education which will help to achieve this aim and, in particular, by the revision of textbooks and school programs and the adaptation of teaching methods;

d) The same opportunities to benefit from scholarships and other study grants;

e) The same opportunities for access to programs of continuing education, including adult and functional literacy programs, particularly those aimed at reducing, at the earliest possible time, any gap in education existing between men and women;

f) The reduction of female student drop-out rates and the organization of programs for girls and women who have left school prematurely;

g) The same opportunities to participate actively in sports and physical education;

h) Access to specific educational information to help to ensure the health and well-being of families, including information and advice on family planning.

Article 11

1. States Parties shall take all appropriate measures to eliminate discrimination against women in the field of employment in order to ensure, on a basis of equality of men and women, the same rights, in particular:

a) The right to work as an inalienable right of all human beings;

b) The right to the same employment opportunities, including the application of the same criteria for selection in matters of employment;

c) The right to free choice of profession and employment, the right to promotion, job security, and all benefits and conditions of service and the right to receive vocational training and retraining, including apprenticeships, advanced vocational training, and recurrent training;

d) The right to equal remuneration, including benefits, and to equal treatment in respect of work of equal value, as well as equality of treatment in the evaluation of the quality of work;

e) The right to social security, particularly in cases of retirement, unemployment, sickness, invalidity, and old age and other incapacity to work, as well as the right to paid leave;

f) The right to protection of health and to safety in working conditions, including the safeguarding of the function of reproduction.

2. In order to prevent discrimination against women on the grounds of marriage or maternity and to ensure their effective right to work, States Parties shall take appropriate measures:

a) To prohibit, subject to the imposition of sanctions, dismissal on the grounds of pregnancy or of maternity leave and discrimination in dismissals on the basis of marital status;

b) To introduce maternity leave with pay or with comparable social benefits without loss of former employment, seniority or social allowances;

c) To encourage the provision of the necessary supporting social services to enable parents to combine family obligations with work responsibilities and participation in public life, in particular through promoting the establishment and development of a network of child-care facilities;

d) To provide special protection to women during pregnancy in types of work proved to be harmful to them.

3. Protective legislation relating to matters covered in this article shall be reviewed periodically in the light of scientific and tech-

nological knowledge and shall be revised, repealed, or extended as necessary.

Article 12

1. States Parties shall take all appropriate measures to eliminate discrimination against women in the field of health care in order to ensure, on a basis of equality of men and women, access to health care services, including those related to family planning.
2. Notwithstanding the provisions of paragraph 1 of this article, States Parties shall ensure to women appropriate services in connection with pregnancy, confinement, and the postnatal period, granting free services where necessary, as well as adequate nutrition during pregnancy and lactation.

Article 13

States Parties shall take all appropriate measures to eliminate discrimination against women in other areas of economic and social life in order to ensure, on a basis of equality of men and women, the same rights, in particular:
a) The right to family benefits;
b) The right to bank loans, mortgages, and other forms of financial credit;
c) The right to participate in recreational activities, sports, and all aspects of cultural life.

Article 14

1. States Parties shall take into account the particular problems faced by rural women and the significant roles which rural women play in the economic survival of their families, including their work in the non-monetized sectors of the economy, and shall take all appropriate measures to ensure the application of the provisions of the present Convention to women in rural areas.
2. States Parties shall take all appropriate measures to eliminate discrimination against women in rural areas in order to ensure,

on a basis of equality of men and women, that they participate in and benefit from rural development and, in particular, shall ensure to such women the right:

a) To participate in the elaboration and implementation of development planning at all levels;

b) To have access to adequate health-care facilities, including information, counseling, and services in family planning;

c) To benefit directly from social security programs;

d) To obtain all types of training and education, formal and non-formal, including that relating to functional literacy, as well as, *inter alia,* the benefit of all community and extension services, in order to increase their technical proficiency;

e) To organize self-help groups and cooperatives in order to obtain equal access to economic opportunities through employment or self-employment;

f) To participate in all community activities;

g) To have access to agricultural credit and loans, marketing facilities, appropriate technology and equal treatment in land and agrarian reform as well as in land resettlement schemes;

h) To enjoy adequate living conditions, particularly in relation to housing, sanitation, electricity and water supply, transport and communications.

PART 4

Article 15

1. States Parties shall accord to women equality with men before the law.

2. States Parties shall accord to women, in civil matters, a legal capacity identical to that of men and the same opportunities to exercise that capacity. In particular, they shall give women equal rights to conclude contracts and to administer property and shall treat them equally in all stages of procedure in courts and tribunals.

3. States Parties agree that all contracts and all other private instruments of any kind with a legal effect which is directed at re-

stricting the legal capacity of women shall be deemed null and void.

4. States Parties shall accord to men and women the same rights with regard to the law relating to the movement of persons and the freedom to choose their residence and domicile.

Article 16

1. States Parties shall take all appropriate measures to eliminate discrimination against women in all matters relating to marriage and family relations and in particular shall ensure, on a basis of equality of men and women:

a) The same right to enter into marriage;

b) The same right freely to choose a spouse and to enter into marriage only with their free and full consent;

c) The same rights and responsibilities during marriage and at its dissolution;

d) The same rights and responsibilities as parents, irrespective of their marital status, in matters relating to their children; in all cases the interests of the children shall be paramount;

e) The same rights to decide freely and responsibly on the number and spacing of their children and to have access to the information, education, and means to enable them to exercise these rights;

f) The same rights and responsibilities with regard to guardianship, wardship, trusteeship, and adoption of children, or similar institutions where these concepts exist in national legislation; in all cases the interests of the children shall be paramount;

g) The same personal rights as husband and wife, including the right to choose a family name, a profession and an occupation;

h) The same rights for both spouses in respect of the ownership, acquisition, management, administration, enjoyment, and disposition of property, whether free of charge or for a valuable consideration.

2. The betrothal and the marriage of a child shall have no legal effect, and all necessary action, including legislation, shall be

taken to specify a minimum age for marriage and to make the registration of marriages in an official registry compulsory.

PART 5

Article 17

1. For the purpose of considering the progress made in the implementation of the present Convention, there shall be established a Committee on the Elimination of Discrimination against Women (hereinafter referred to as the Committee) consisting, at the time of entry into force of the Convention, of eighteen and, after ratification of or accession to the Convention by the thirty-fifth State Party, of twenty-three experts of high moral standing and competence in the field covered by the Convention. The experts shall be elected by States Parties from among their nationals and shall serve in their personal capacity, consideration being given to equitable geographical distribution and to the representation of the different forms of civilization as well as the principal legal systems.

2. The members of the Committee shall be elected by secret ballot from a list of persons nominated by States Parties. Each State Party may nominate one person from among its own nationals.

3. The initial election shall be held six months after the date of the entry into force of the present Convention. At least three months before the date of each election the Secretary-General of the United Nations shall address a letter to the States Parties inviting them to submit their nominations within two months. The Secretary-General shall prepare a list in alphabetical order of all persons thus nominated, indicating the States Parties which have nominated them, and shall submit it to the States Parties.

4. Elections of the members of the Committee shall be held at a meeting of States Parties convened by the Secretary-General at United Nations Headquarters. At that meeting, for which two thirds of the States Parties shall constitute a quorum, the persons elected to the Committee shall be those nominees who obtain the largest number of votes and an absolute majority of the votes of the representatives of States Parties present and voting.

5. The members of the Committee shall be elected for a term of four years. However, the terms of nine of the members elected at the first election shall expire at the end of two years; immediately after the first election the names of these nine members shall be chosen by lot by the Chairman of the Committee.

6. The election of the five additional members of the Committee shall be held in accordance with the provisions of paragraphs 2, 3, and 4 of this article, following the thirty-fifth ratification or accession. The terms of two of the additional members elected on this occasion shall expire at the end of two years, the names of these two members having been chosen by lot by the Chairman of the Committee.

7. For the filling of casual vacancies, the State Party whose expert has ceased to function as a member of the Committee shall appoint another expert from among its nationals, subject to the approval of the Committee.

8. The members of the Committee shall, with the approval of the General Assembly, receive emoluments from United Nations resources on such terms and conditions as the Assembly may decide, having regard to the importance of the Committee's responsibilities.

9. The Secretary-General of the United Nations shall provide the necessary staff and facilities for the effective performance of the functions of the Committee under the present Convention.

Article 18

1. States Parties undertake to submit to the Secretary-General of the United Nations, for consideration by the Committee, a report on the legislative, judicial, administrative or other measures which they have adopted to give effect to the provisions of the present Convention and on the progress made in this respect:

a) Within one year after the entry into force for the State concerned;

b) Thereafter at least every four years and further whenever the Committee so requests.

2. Reports may indicate factors and difficulties affecting the degree of fulfillment of obligations under the present Convention.

Article 19

1. The Committee shall adopt its own rules of procedure.
2. The Committee shall elect its officers for a term of two years.

Article 20

1. The Committee shall normally meet for a period of not more than two weeks annually in order to consider the reports submitted in accordance with article 18 of the present Convention.
2. The meetings of the Committee shall normally be held at United Nations Headquarters or at any other convenient place as determined by the Committee.

Article 21

1. The Committee shall, through the Economic and Social Council, report annually to the General Assembly of the United Nations on its activities and may make suggestions and general recommendations based on the examination of reports and information received from the States Parties. Such suggestions and general recommendations shall be included in the report of the Committee together with comments, if any, from States Parties.
2. The Secretary-General of the United Nations shall transmit the reports of the Committee to the Commission on the Status of Women for its information.

Article 22

The specialized agencies shall be entitled to be represented at the consideration of the implementation of such provisions of the present Convention as fall within the scope of their activities. The Committee may invite the specialized agencies to submit reports on the implementation of the Convention in areas falling within the scope of their activities.

PART 6

Article 23

Nothing in the present Convention shall affect any provisions that are more conducive to the achievement of equality between men and women which may be contained:
a) In the legislation of a State Party; or
b) In any other international convention, treaty or agreement in force for that State.

Article 24

State Parties undertake to adopt all necessary measures at the national level aimed at achieving the full realization of the rights recognized in the present Convention.

Article 25

1. The present Convention shall be open for signature by all States.
2. The Secretary-General of the United Nations is designated as the depositary of the present Convention.
3. The present Convention is subject to ratification. Instruments of ratification shall be deposited with the Secretary-General of the United Nations.
4. The present Convention shall be open to accession by all States. Accession shall be effected by the deposit of an instrument of accession with the Secretary General of the United Nations.

APPENDIX 2: OPERATION AGRICOLA: THE ESSENTIALS

HAVING RETURNED from Bosnia in April 1998, I found myself preparing to go back to the Balkans in late January 1999, as the Commander of 101 Logistic Brigade,[1] to support and help implement a peace agreement that was, at the time, being negotiated at Rambouillet. The aim was to move quickly into Greece and Macedonia,[2] receive, stage, onward move, and integrate (ROSI) the United Kingdom's contribution to the NATO-led KFOR,[3] and then move on up into Kosovo itself. Events, as they so often do, were to overtake us. By mid-February, we were settled into a number of locations around Skopje, the capital of Macedonia, and had begun the process of bringing in large elements of both my own brigade and 4 Armoured Brigade. As the armored vehicles of the first battle group were being off-loaded at the port of Thessaloniki in Greece, the talks began to falter. By the end of February, over two thousand military personnel and several hundred vehicles were in theater, but with the situation deteriorating, we realized that the operation was not going to be anything like as straightforward as we had originally thought. Ships and aircraft continued to flow into theater, but by the end of March the bombing campaign had started, following the complete breakdown of the Rambouillet talks.[4]

Reports indicated that fighting inside Kosovo was escalating. By mid-March over 200,000 IDPs were reportedly on the move. Several thousand people had also crossed Kosovo's international borders into Albania and Macedonia; the refugee flows had started in earnest, and the bombing campaign served only to exacerbate matters. Numbers inevitably vary from source to source, but around twenty-five hundred Kosovars had been killed in the twelve months prior to the bombing; ten thousand more died in the three months after. Similarly, some quarter of a million Albanians had become IDPs and 200,000 refugees before the bombing; well over a half million became refugees in the month after, one million by June. These numbers, horrific as they are, need to be set in the context of the Krajina, when the Croatian Army ethnically cleansed 250,000 Serbs in three days in August 1995, and Rwanda, when 250,000 crossed into Tanzania in twenty-four hours in April 1994, another 250,000 in the next three days, and one million in July.[5]

There could be no doubt that the crisis would get worse, so we produced contingency plans; as usual, of the three options we planned for, it was the fourth that actually happened. On Thursday, April 1, I drove out to look at several sites that the Macedonian government was intending to develop as refugee camps. They were small and in poor locations, very close to the border with Kosovo. The government-led reconnaissance was badly organized and chaotic, but I was able to meet with some UN officials, in particular the head of the UNHCR mission to Kosovo, Jo Hegenauer, and a representative from the U.S. State Department, David Scheffer, an Ambassador at Large for War Crimes Issues. I outlined my thoughts on the situation. In essence, this was to construct major camps around a grass airfield and range complex, situated alongside the main road running from Pristina to Skopje, ten kilometers south of the border crossing at Blace. The location was big enough to create space to maneuver in order to deal with the refugees; it had a good river source for water and an excellent site for a logistics base. In the meantime, we agreed to help the Macedonian government construct a small camp at Bojane, some twenty kilometers away.

The following day, April 2, and Good Friday in the United Kingdom, I was contacted by the UNHCR (Jo Hegenauer). Large numbers of Kosovar Albanians had been arriving at Blace over the last few days, by road and now by train, and things were getting extremely serious; there was no shelter, food, or medical cover, and the tired and hungry people were in a bad way, indeed, some were beginning to die. Could we help? I rang my Chief of Staff (COS) and ordered him to establish our tactical headquarters (Tac HQ) at a location near the airfield and implement the initial elements of our contingency plans. The immediate task was to establish a focal point where we could work with the UNHCR, ferrying food, blankets, and medical supplies up to the border. Tac HQ was up and running within four hours. Field kitchens started to prepare chicken and rice; I ordered the release of both fresh food and operational rations, and food was being moved forward by about 2300 hours, some nine hours after Jo Hegenauer's call, on UNHCR vehicles loaded at our logistic base. The temperature was not much above freezing, and it had been raining or sleeting for thirty-six hours. Images of the thousands of people crammed into the fields around the border crossing were beginning to be shown around the world; the scenes there were disturbingly chaotic, with no evidence of any coordinated response. Pressure was mounting on the Macedonian government, and on the UNHCR, whose small team was self-evidently going to be overwhelmed. Various government officials visited Tac HQ during the following day, Saturday, April 3, most importantly, in retrospect, Julia Taft from the U.S. State Department. The United States was putting real pressure on the Macedonian government, who clearly needed convincing that the situation at Blace could not be allowed to continue. There was inevitably a great deal of uncertainty, but I was convinced that the dam at the border would break at short notice, and when it did, we had to be able to deal with the torrent of refugees that would be released. No other organization was in a position to help, and we could not stand idle; apart from the human needs it was clear to me that the Macedonian government needed KFOR's strength, and we needed them to maintain their resolve. After a night of detailed planning, I ordered construction work to start.

The brigade engineers pulled aside the crop-spraying Antonov 1 aircraft, built a bridge across the fast-flowing stream that ran alongside the airfield, opened up access tracks from our logistic base out onto the range and airfield, and began to dig deep trench latrines. Elsewhere, among a myriad of other tasks, the logistic regiment, working with the UNHCR, continued to move supplies forward to the border; the medics began to prepare their reception centers, and the first tents were set up. All of this was being done in a vacuum, as I had received no orders. Finally, and thankfully, at 0800 hours on Easter Sunday morning (in the Western rite), the Macedonian Deputy Foreign Minister, Mr. Boris Trajkovski, rang me to ask that we should, indeed, implement our plan. International pressure, particularly from the United States, had clearly worked. The tempo of work increased. Water purifying and pumping systems were set up; reception and registration areas were established. The KFOR commander visited and authorized assistance from other KFOR nations, and small, but important, attachments from the German and Italian contingents arrived to help put up tents. At 1700 hours Macedonian police informed me that the first refugees would be allowed across the border at 1900 hours. One of the sites, eventually known as Stenkovic 1, was ready to accept some, and overnight several hundred arrived; around thirty thousand were, however, estimated to be crammed into no-man's land at Blace, and the situation there continued to deteriorate.

On Monday, April 5, the dam broke. The U.K. Secretary of State for International Development, Claire Short, arrived with the United Kingdom's Ambassador and a number of other officials; a large media presence was also gathering. Authorizing DFID support, which was to prove absolutely invaluable, she asked to look around. As we were approaching the main airfield site, Stenkovic 2, a number of buses arrived crammed to bursting point with refugees. The picture of Claire Short helping them off the buses became worldwide prime-time news. Work continued, but no more refugees arrived. Then darkness fell. Suddenly buses by the dozen poured in. Arriving five at a time, with eighty to a hundred refugees per bus, they disgorged their human loads and were replaced fifteen minutes later by another five buses—

and on it went, hour after hour. As dawn broke the flow stopped, but by then around twenty thousand refugees had arrived. All through the night soldiers from the brigade put up tents, helped families into them, issued food and blankets, and provided medical support; I watched as a tiny baby died, but many other refugees, both young and old, were successfully treated by the multinational medical facility. It was a grueling night, but it was just the first of many. Day after day the brigade erected more tents and provided more water, food, and other supplies. Night after night the buses arrived. It was only later that we realized that during the day these buses were being used to ferry children in Skopje to and from school and adults to and from work; as soon as it got dark they moved to the border to ply a different trade. By April 9, there were around forty thousand refugees in the two major camps; while some were being flown out, there was little space left. Over 2,800 tents had been erected, 1,600 meters of water pipeline had been laid, tens of thousands of meals had been cooked and distributed, along with over 103,000 jars of baby food, 11,000 loaves of bread, 264,000 liters of bottled water, and 430,000 bars of chocolate; 400 deep trench latrines had been dug and thousands of refugees had been treated in our medical facilities—five had died, but twenty-four babies had been born, our proudest statistic!

In one sense the worst was over. Initially the NGO presence on the ground had been minimal. OXFAM arrived first and quickly became effective, playing a key role in the development of the water and sanitation systems. Other organizations began to arrive, but slowly. The United Nations became more effective as the week progressed. Various senior officials arrived and were briefed, the UNHCR and WFP teams were strengthened, and several key individuals emerged as real "players." For a few days the flow of refugees slowed, and the various NGOs began to get organized. On Sunday, April 11, we were able to hand over most of the medical support to MSF and the Red Cross. Although we began to plan the hand-over of all aspects of the camps, the following week was still a demanding one. The camps had to be extended as more refugees arrived, policing and security became a problem, and the temperatures began to soar. Rubbish clearance, sanitation, and the threat of disease became key issues. I knew that in Zaire, after the genocide in Rwanda, cholera had broken out; fifty thousand had died in four weeks at the height of the crisis. This, and the threat of fire, were my worst fears. Once again our military resources had to lead the way. Further influxes of refugees continued, and thunderstorms flooded the camps. The ability of the various agencies to cope remained suspect, and we were asked, by the UNHCR, to stay on for a few more days. Finally, we withdrew over the period of April 17–19, leaving behind a military liaison team.

After a gap of about eight days, during which time the brigade was immersed in the RSOI of the 2nd Battlegroup and the training program of 4 Armoured Brigade, our attention was directed back to the humanitarian aspects of the situation once again. Inside Kosovo further waves of Kosovar Albanians were being rounded up and moved to the borders. The camps in Macedonia were full, and the ones in Northern Albania, where NATO AFOR was operating, were overflowing. The Macedonian government was adamant that it would not allow additional camps to be built in their central and southern regions, and so attention focused on southern Albania. Numerous meetings were held and reconnaissance trips conducted. Finally, UNHCR and HQ KFOR agreed that we should use brigade assets to establish a series of camps in the Korce region of Albania, around forty kilometers south of Lake Ochrid. Dividing the brigade, and the HQ, over such a distance—we would now have elements of the brigade in three countries, Greece, Macedonia, and Albania—was far from ideal. My main HQ was heavily involved with military support to KFOR, particularly 4 Armoured Brigade, and our primary mission was to support the U.K. move into Kosovo; nonetheless there seemed little likelihood of any such move in the short term— indeed, we were beginning to plan forced entry options, which would inevitably take weeks to prepare and implement. The lead elements of Tac HQ thus deployed to Albania on May 8, and I joined my COS there the next day.

The problems were very different from those we had encountered in Macedonia over Easter. Although there was a time imperative, it was not as urgent as before. The UNHCR and NGO presence was considerable, and the emphasis was on developing sustainable camps, suitable for refugees to live in throughout the winter if necessary. It was, however, a demanding few weeks. Local politics was riven with corruption, and there was criminality in abundance. Superposed on this was an unclear military command structure—we were operating in AFOR's area of responsibility, with both AFOR and KFOR forces working with us— and an equally unclear link between the UNHCR in Albania and Macedonia. Our first few "situation reports" back to the PJHQ apparently read more like a John Le Carré novel than a military update—particularly when rival gangs in Korce began open warfare, and anti-corruption officials, appointed from Tirana, began to stir things up. Nonetheless, by June 6, and in very close concert with DFID, who were once again quite excellent, UNHCR, and the NGOs, four substantial camps were constructed, and other locations surveyed and planned; in all we created capacity for well over sixty thousand refugees. As it turned out, only between twelve and fifteen thousand spaces were used as, once again, events were to turn, this time for the better.

At the beginning of June, planning for the B(-) option had begun in earnest,[6] and additional elements of the brigade, still based in the United Kingdom, were deployed. At short notice, 5 Airborne Brigade and a large RAF Support Helicopter force were inloaded and configured to go north into Kosovo. Entry into Force was June 10, D-Day June 12, and by June 18, my Tac HQ had moved up into Pristina, along with literally hundreds of journalists and NGOs, of every acronym imaginable. In addition to providing military engineering, logistic, and medical support to the U.K. Forces, the brigade repaired and ran a large part of the Kosovo railway system, established a fire-fighting capability in Pristina, and a civilian criminal detention center in Lipljan; in addition, a temporary, emergency refugee camp was constructed just outside Pristina to enable several thousand Romany gypsies to be relocated. In all of these areas, we attempted, with lesser or greater success, to work with the various nonmilitary organizations and agencies, who by then were pouring into Kosovo. Individual relationships were excellent, but tensions between KFOR and the UNHCR at the operational level meant that the brigade's assets were underutilized, particularly our rail capability. By the beginning of August, the situation was settling, and we began to prepare to hand over our responsibilities. We finally withdrew and returned to the U.K. in late August.

So ended OP AGRICOLA, for me at least. Throughout the deployment I met and worked with a large number of nonmilitary organizations. Since returning I have attended two conferences, one in The Hague on NATO's involvement in humanitarian action in the Kosovo crisis, and the other at Stanford University on "Ethics and Civil Wars."[7] The following appendix will outline the insights gained from my experiences and research.

NOTES TO APPENDIX 2

1. The brigade deployed as CSSG (U.K.) but was retitled in June 1999.

2. Macedonia is more politically correctly known as the Former Yugoslav Republic of Macedonia (FYROM).

3. The initial U.K. contribution included the KFOR Headquarters and Signals Brigade and 4 Armoured Brigade, as well as 101 Logistic Brigade.

4. Bombing started on March 24, 2000.

5. See William Shawcross, *Deliver Us From Evil: Warlords and Peacekeepers in a World of Endless Conflict* (London: Bloomsbury Publishing, 2000), 344.

6. B(-) was the planning option for forced entry into Kosovo; it included around 50,000 U.K. troops.

7. The output from the Hague Conference, November 15–16, 1999, was *NATO and Humanitarian Action in the Kosovo Crisis*, Occasional

Paper no. 36, Thomas J Watson Jr. Institute for International Studies and the Humanitarian Law Consultancy, Copyright © 2000; that from Stanford University, May 26–27, 2000, the Third David Hamburg Symposium on Conflict Prevention, still has to be published.

APPENDIX 3: SURVEY OF MILITARY ATTITUDES TOWARD NGOs FOLLOWING THE KOSOVO CAMPAIGN[1]

Number shown in the left column is the sum of first choices against that response.

	1. **Causes of the Kosovar Refugee Crisis.** Do you think that NATO's air campaign:
4	*a)* Made a bad situation worse
1	*b)* Caused the whole crisis
32	*c)* Helped to prevent a greater disaster
12	*d)* Had no significant effect on the refugee crisis
	2. **Reasons for NATO's Intervention in the Refugee Crisis.** NATO diverted some of its ground troops to the provision of humanitarian assistance to refugees in Macedonia and Albania for the following reasons:
1	*a)* A genuine desire to provide emergency humanitarian assistance
8	*b)* Guilt
23	*c)* Overwhelming media pressure
23	*d)* It was a decision taken in order to keep the Macedonian and Albanian governments on side
10	*e)* Because the civilian aid agencies were not capable of providing adequate support
	f) The refugee crisis was part of Milosevic's deep battle against the West—this was NATO's response

3. Quality of the British Military Aid Effort. Once committed, the British military aid effort:

3. Quality of the British Military Aid Effort. Once committed, the British military aid effort:

a) Was well coordinated and highly effective

b) Was chaotic and poorly executed

4   *c)* Was too little too late

1   *d)* Was a token gesture

38   *e)* Was effective but hampered by poor coordination with the civilian aid agencies

4. Military Aid Capabilities. The functional areas in which the British military are *more* capable than civilian aid organizations are (rank with additional ticks as necessary):

23   *a)* A disciplined and robust workforce

13   *b)* Command and Control (coordinating military and civil aid effort)

11   *c)* Engineering (fencing, latrines, access tracks, water points, and skilled tradesmen)

5   *d)* Logistic (transport, storage, and distribution of food, people, and equipment)

4   *e)* Medical (trained personnel and equipment)

12   *f)* Security (providing a secure environment for the aid activity)

5. Command and Control. When involved in humanitarian aid operations, which are being supported by civilian aid agencies, do you believe that British troops should be:

75   *a)* Retained under British or NATO command at all times

10   *b)* Placed under command of the senior UN commander on site

0   *c)* Placed at the disposal of the most capable NGO on site

2   *d)* Kept apart from civilian aid workers as much as possible

6. Coordination of the Camps. Coordinating authority for the Brazda Refugee Camp was formally delegated to which single lead organization during the first days of occupation?

0   *a)* HQ 101 Logistics Brigade

9	*b)* OSCE
2	*c)* UNHCR
12	*d)* OXFAM
19	*e)* HQ KFOR
	f) Don't Know

7. The UN. Which phrase or phrases sum up your overall view of UN Aid workers? (Note that question 8 covers the Nongovernment Agencies.)

42	*a)* "Dedicated and effective professionals"
24	*b)* "Dedicated and caring, but not effective in a crisis"
6	*c)* "Poorly coordinated"
1	*d)* "Amateurs"
	e) "Anti-military"

8. The Nongovernment Agencies. Which phrase or phrases best sum up your overall view of the NGOs?

38	*a)* "Dedicated and effective professionals"
26	*b)* "Dedicated and caring, but not effective in a crisis"
7	*c)* "Poorly coordinated"
3	*d)* "Amateurs"
	e) "Anti-military"

9. Motivation of Civilian Aid Workers. In general terms what factors do you believe *most motivate* civilian aid workers (UN and NGO)?

44	*a)* The desire to relieve the suffering of desperate people
16	*b)* Money
6	*c)* The thrill of working in potentially dangerous places
6	*d)* Religious or spiritual conscience
2	*e)* Other factors. Explain on reverse of sheet

10. The Role of the Military. "The ultimate role of Britain's armed forces is to defeat the nation's enemies in battle." Involving British troops in humanitarian operations will:

64	*a)* Degrade fighting skills and spirit

8	*b)* Test and improve military logistic, engineering, and medical skills
3	*c)* Improve morale
	d) Upset morale

11. Operation AGRICOLA. Do you believe that British involvement in the refugee crises during Operation AGRICOLA was:

39	*a)* Right and had no adverse effect on our fighting capability?
5	*b)* Right but potentially reduced our fighting capability?
	c) Wrong, took our eye off the ball and should have been avoided?

12. Who Benefited Most from the British Military Aid Effort? Which group or organization benefited most from the British military aid effort?

8	*a)* The refugees—through actual material aid (food, water, shelter, medicine, security, etc.)
4	*b)* The civilian aid agencies—from military materiel, logistic, and manpower support
2	*c)* The British Government—through good media coverage
5	*d)* NATO—seen to beat Milosevic at his own game
	e) The British Army—excellent PR, good training and recruiting potential

Yes	**13. Preparation?** Do you think that you would have benefited from some additional pre-deployment training on humanitarian support issues? Delete Yes or No.
29	If yes, in which areas:
29	*a)* Coping with emotional stress
	b) An improved understanding of civilian aid agencies
	c) The technical support requirements of refugee support operations

14. Were You Affected? Did your experiences during the refugee crisis affect you emotionally?

8	*a)* A little bit at the time, but no long-term effects
30	*b)* More after the event than during
7	*c)* Not really at all
	d) I still experience strong emotions about that period of the operation

15. **Looking Ahead.** British troops have been required to provide emergency humanitarian support on Op HAVEN, GABRIEL, GRAPPLE, RESOLUTE, and AGRICOLA. Some believe that this is the pattern of future conflict and that the chances of British troops fighting in a high intensity conflict during the forthcoming decade are negligible. On the other hand, some believe that the world is increasingly unstable and that a major war involving British troops is almost inevitable. Which of the following do you most agree with?

14	*a)* British military doctrine and training should concentrate more on peace support operations and the provision of humanitarian aid
57	*b)* The British Forces should concentrate on the high intensity end of the conflict spectrum and continue to gear down as required by circumstances
9	*c)* Neither. State your reasons.

16. **The Acid Test.** A list of some of the civilian aid agencies involved in the Kosovar refugee crisis is given below. Indicate your view of the performance and ability of the agencies and NGOs that you came across in the camps by placing ticks (for good) and crosses (for poor) next to each. Again, if you think that any agencies were particularly good or notably poor illustrate this with two or more ticks or crosses. You will probably only have a view on a few agencies so leave the remainder blank.

Perceived performance: G = Good, P = Poor

	G	P		G	P
AAH—Action Against Hunger	10	5	NPA—Norwegian Peoples Aid	7	2
CRS—Catholic Relief Services	15	11	OSCE—Org for the Security & Coop in Europe	38	39
DFID—Dept. for International Development	15	9	OXFAM GB	25	11
DRC—German Red Cross	11	7	SCF—Save the Children	5	7
ICRC—International Committee for the Red Cross	20	9	UNHCR—UN High Commissioner for Refugees	19	36
IRC—International Rescue Committee	7	8	USAID	5	7
IOM—International Organization for Migration	3	5	World Food Program	19	5
MSF— *Médecins sans frontières*	30	12	WVI—World Vision International	2	5
MCI—Mercy Corps International	3	4	WHO—World Health Organization	7	12

NOTE TO APPENDIX 3

1. See Appendix 1 in Major R. K. Tomlinson, MBE, BSc (Hons), "Reversing the Downward Spiral: Exploring Cultural Dissonance Between the Military and NGOs on Humanitarian Operations," Royal Engineers (RE) Defense Logistics Management (MSc Dissertation, Cranfield University, Royal Military College of Science, July 2000).

THE CENTER FOR INTERNATIONAL HEALTH AND COOPERATION AND THE INSTITUTE OF INTERNATIONAL HUMANITARIAN AFFAIRS

THE CENTER FOR INTERNATIONAL HEALTH and Cooperation (CIHC) was founded by a small group who believed that health and other humanitarian endeavors sometimes provide the only common ground for initiating dialogue, understanding, and cooperation among people and nations shattered by war, civil conflicts, and ethnic violence. The Center has sponsored symposia and published books that reflect this philosophy, including: *Silent Witnesses; A Framework for Survival: Health, Human Rights, and Humanitarian Assistance in Conflicts and Disasters; A Directory of Somali Professionals; Clearing the Fields: Solutions to the Land Mine Crisis; Preventive Diplomacy: Stopping Wars Before They Start;* and *Tropical Medicine: A Clinical Text;* as well as this book and other volumes in the Fordham University Press International Humanitarian Affairs series.

The Center and its Directors have been deeply involved in trying to alleviate the wounds of war in Somalia and the former Yugoslavia. A CIHC amputee center in northern Somalia was developed as a model for a simple, rapid, inexpensive program that could be replicated in other war zones. In the former Yugoslavia, the CIHC was active in prisoner and hostage release, in legal assistance for human and political rights violations, and facilitated discussions between combatants. The Center directs the International Diploma in Humanitarian Assistance (IDHA) in partnership with Fordham University in New York, the University of Geneva in Switzerland, and the Royal College of Surgeons in Ireland. The CIHC cooperates with other centers in offering special-ized training courses for humanitarian negotiators and international human rights lawyers. The Center has offered staff support in recent years in crisis management in East Timor, Aceh, Kosovo, Palestine, Albania, and other trouble spots.

The Center has been afforded full consultative status at the United Nations. In the United States, it is a fully approved public charity.

The CIHC is closely linked with Fordham University's Institute of International Humanitarian Affairs (IIHA). The Directors of the CIHC serve as the Advisory Board of the Institute. The President of the CIHC is the University Professor and Director of the Institute, and two of the CIHC officers, Larry Hollingworth and Michel Veuthey, are adjunct professors of Fordham. The Institute offers courses in various aspects of international humanitarian affairs and sponsors symposia on cutting edge topics in this field.

DIRECTORS

Kevin M. Cahill, M.D. (President)
Lord David Owen
Boutros Boutros-Ghali
Peter Tarnoff
Jan Eliasson
Peter Hansen

Francis Deng
Joseph A. O'Hare, S.J.
Abdulrahim Abby Farah
Lady Helen Hamlyn
Eoin O'Brien, M.D.

ABOUT THE AUTHORS

Tom Arnold is Chief Executive of Concern Worldwide. He is a former Assistant Secretary with the Irish Department of Agriculture and spent ten years with the European Commission. Between 1993 and 1998, he served as Chairman of the Organization for Economic Cooperation and Development (OECD) Committee of Agriculture.

Judy A. Benjamin serves as the gender advisor to USAID in Kabul, Afghanistan. Trained as an anthropologist, her focus has been on the impact of conflict on civilian populations. As the senior technical advisor for the Women's Commission for Refugee Women and Children from 1996–2001, she investigated the gender dimensions of forced migration and the socioeconomic effects of war on women. Benjamin directed an AIDS prevention program for CARE in Nagra, Tanzania, during the Rwandan crisis. She is a frequent speaker, lecturer, and author of numerous articles concerning critical gender issues.

Fredrick M. Burkle, Jr., M.D., is Deputy Assistant Administrator at the Bureau for Global Health, U.S. Agency for International Development (USAID). He was Senior Scholar, Scientist, and Visiting Professor at the Center for International Emergency, Disaster, and Refugee Studies at the Johns Hopkins University Medical Institutions.

Kevin M. Cahill, M.D., is University Professor and Director of the Institute of International Humanitarian Affairs at Fordham University; President and Director of the Center for International Health and Cooperation; Professor and Chairman, Department of Tropical Medicine, Royal College of Surgeons in Ireland;

Clinical Professor of Medicine, New York University; Director, the Tropical Disease Center, Lenox Hill Hospital; and Chief Medical Advisor, Counterterrorism, New York Police Department.

Major General Timothy Cross has served with the British Army for over thirty years. His operational experience ranges from working as a bomb disposal officer in Northern Ireland in the 1970s to serving with the UN in Cyprus in the 1980s; the Coalition in the Gulf War in 1990–1991; and three times with NATO in the Balkans in the 1990s. He commanded the 101 Logistic Brigade in Macedonia, Albania, and Kosovo, leading the NATO response to the 1999 Easter Refugee Crisis in Northern Macedonia and assisting the UNHCR and other relief agencies in Southern Albania and Kosovo. He was appointed CBE in the subsequent operational awards and is currently Director General of the UK's Defense Supply Chain.

Francis M. Deng is a Director of the Center for International Health and Cooperation. He is also the UN Secretary General's Special Representative for Internally Displaced Persons; Ralph Bunche Professor of International Affairs at the City University of New York; and Senior Fellow, the Brookings Institution. He was Secretary of State for Foreign Affairs, The Sudan.

Ted R. Gurr is Distinguished Professor at the University of Maryland, and founding Director of the Minorities at Risk Project. He has been Olaf Palme Visiting Professor at the University of Uppsala.

Barbara Harff is Professor of Political Science at the U.S. Naval Academy and a senior consultant to the U.S. government's State Failure Task Force.

Larry Hollingworth is Humanitarian Programs Director for the Center for International Health and Cooperation. He is also Adjunct Professor in the Graduate School of Social Service of Fordham University in New York. He has served with the UN agencies in Palestine, Bosnia, Chechnya, and East Timor. Prior to that he was a British Army officer for thirty years. He is a frequent lecturer on relief and refugee topics in universities and is a commentator on humanitarian issues for the BBC.

Randolph Martin is Senior Director of Operations of the International Rescue Committee (IRC). His portfolio includes responsibility for the security of the more than seven thousand members of the IRC's national and expatriate staff members around the world. He lectures frequently on security before international donor agencies, nongovernmental organizations, and academic conferences.

Gerald R. Martone is the Director of Emergency Response at the International Rescue Committee. He has served as co-chair of the Disaster Response Committee of InterAction, the Sphere Project Management Committee, and has published numerous articles and book chapters on emergency assistance and international affairs. He is an Associate Professor at Columbia University's School of Public Health.

Richard Ryscavage, S.J., is the Country Director of the Jesuit Refugee Service/U.S.A. and the National Secretary for Jesuit Social and International Ministries. Father Ryscavage studied at the Fletcher School of Law and Diplomacy, and was the first Pedro Arrupe Tutor at Oxford University's Refugee Studies Centre in Great Britain.

Ed Tsui is the Director of the Office of the Coordinator of Humanitarian Affairs (OCHA) at the United Nations. He joined the United Nations in 1972 and has had extensive experience in the fields of social and economic development and humanitarian affairs. Since 1992 he has been closely involved in organizing and improving international response to humanitarian emergencies and disasters worldwide, having served as Chief of Staff for the Undersecretary General and Director of Policy in the Department of Humanitarian Affairs.

INDEX

abbreviations/acronyms, xi–xiii
action
  early warning for, 9
  political support for, 3
advocacy, 111, 120–21
aedes agypti, 86
Afghanistan
  armed conflict within, 4, 24
  chronic emergency in, 226
  female treatment in, 163–64
  genocide/politicide in, 27
  human rights abuse in, 137
  information management in,
    51, 80
  Internet-based Virtual OSOCC
    for, 45
  solidarity groups in, 231
  terrorism base in, 131–32, 192
African Charter on the Rights and
    Welfare of the Child, 171
African Union, 6–7, 11, 122, 128
Afrikaaners, 22
Agenda for Peace (Boutros-Ghali),
    5–6
aid
  acceptance of, 38
  corruption of, 321*n*16, 323*n*34
  impartiality of, 245
  protection through, 137
  rights-based approach toward,
    138–39
aid worker. *See* relief worker
Aideed, Mohammed, 274–75
Al-Qaeda, 131

Albania, 11, 193–94, 206, 207, 351,
    368
Algeria, 26, 27
Allende, Salvador, 25
Alliance 2015, 110
Ambassador for War Crimes, 7
American Society of International
    Law, 123
Amnesty International, 9
anemia, 184
Angola, 124, 193–94, 226
Annan, Kofi, 195, 217, 218
Annotations (Guiding Principles)
    (Brookings Institute), 123
apartheid, 22
Art of War, The (Sun), 202
Arusha Peace Agreement, 276
Assessment, 72, 73
assistance/rescue
  conflict assessment for, 3
  disaster assessment for, 55
  early warning for, 3
  humanitarian goal for, xvi
  programs for, 127
  rapid assessment for, 56, 58–59,
    62
Assistant Emergency Relief Coor-
    dinator (AERC), 42
autocracies *v.* democracies, 24
autopsies, verbal, 65–66
Azerbaijan, 4

Balkans, the, 10, 192
*Basics of International Humanitarian
    Missions*, xv

beriberi, 184
Bhutan, 4
Blair, Tony, 217
Blue Beret, 190
Bosnia Herzegovina
  British military operations in,
    193–94
  complex emergency in, 191, 216
  crimes against women in, 171
  ethnic cleansing in, 26, 279
  human rights abuse in, 137, 140,
    142
  peace efforts in, 294
  protection of NGOs in, 239
  Sarajevo in, 234
  solidarity groups in, 231
  Srebrenica as safe area in, 279
Botswana, 37
Boutros-Ghali, Boutros, 5–6
British military operations, 192–
  94, 351–59
Brookings Project on Internal Dis-
  placement, The, 123
burial practices, 100
Burma (Myanmar), 27, 226
Burundi, 4, 11, 18, 22, 27–28,
  124–25

Cambodia, 13, 86
Canadian Ministry of Foreign Affairs, 7
car jacking, 246–47
Carnegie Commission on Preventing Deadly Conflict, 7
cash grants. See funding, emergency
casualties, civilian, 192, 227
Center for International Health
  and Cooperation, the
  (CIHC), 367–68
Center for Preventive Action, 7
Centers for Disease Control and
  Prevention (CDC), 61

Central Emergency Revolving
  Fund (CERF), 48
Central Register (OCHA), 47
Chechnya, 5, 69, 192, 206, 225
child soldiers, 226
Chile, 24
China, 23, 26, 27, 30, 77
Chinese–Malay conflict, 18
chlorination, 87
civil defense, 47
civil society, 290–91
Civil-Military Information Centers
  (CMIC), 75, 321n19
Code of Best Practice in the Manage-
  ment and Support of Aid Person-
  nel (People in Aid), 110
Code of Conduct of the International
  Red Cross and Red Crescent
  Movement, 110, 136
Cold War, xv, 131
Colombia, 4, 125, 139
Commission on Human Rights,
  118, 120, 121, 127
Committee on the Elimination of
  Discrimination Against
  Women, 316n12
Common Appeal Framework, 48
Common Ground, 11
Common Humanitarian Action
  Plan, 50
communicable disease. See disease,
  infectious
Communism, 21–22
community involvement, 234–35
Compilation and Analysis of Legal
  Norms (UN), 121
computers, personal. See database,
  electronic
Concern Worldwide, 2, 80–82,
  110–12
conflict
  armed, 3–4, 319n2

Chinese–Malay, 18
containment of, 4
ethnic/religious causes of, 22
ethnopolitical causes of, 4
identification of genocidal/politicidal, 5
in Liberia, 8
prevention of, 8
resolution of, 3
society in, 3–5
Tamil–Sinhalese, 18
Tutsi/Hutu in, 11, 27–28
world's attention deficit for, 3, 5
Conflict Prevention Center, 6
Conflict Prevention Network, 6
Conflict Prevention Surveys, 9
Congo. *See* Democratic Republic of Congo
Consolidated Appeals Process (CAP), 39, 47
consultants, reviews by, 53
Convention Against Torture and Other Cruel, Inhuman or Degrading Treatment or Punishment, 160
Convention on Refugees, 121
Convention on the Elimination of All Forms of Discrimination against Women (CEDAW), 160, 170, 171
Convention on the Rights of the Child (CRC), 170, 171
Coordinator for Humanitarian Assistance (OCHA), 1, 6, 14
Council of Europe, 12, 128
Council on Foreign Relations, 7
country strategies, 70
Crisis Intervention Team (CIT), 172
crisis management
communication during, 42, 50
evaluation of, 70–72

funding for, 47–48
phases of, 16, 60, 69
warning system for, 16
crop failure, 181
crude mortality rate (CMR), 63–64
cultural relativism, 163–64
Cultural Revolution (China), 30
cultural theory, 197–98
Culture Consequences (Hofstede), 197
Culture Matters (Harrington/Huntington), 294
Cultures and Organizations: Software of the Mind (Hofstede), 197
cyclones, 55
Cyprus, 272–73

database, electronic
collection of, 61, 65, 74–75
interpretation of, 72, 77
networking by, 13
use of, 13–15, 39, 42–43, 46, 47, 49–52, 57, 60
dead, disposal of, 100
democratic process, 4, 22, 293, 319n5
Democratic Republic of Congo (DRC)
civil war in, 11, 12, 13
disaster response in, 42
Goma's disaster in, 33–35, 46–47, 51–52
Hutu refugee camp in, 140, 172
Tutsi/Hutu incursions from, 30
dengue fever, 101–102
Department for Foreign International Development (DFID), 61, 196
Department for International Development (DFID) (United Kingdom), 194

deterrence, 238–39
diarrhea. *See* disease, diarrheal
diplomacy
    Machiavelli's book on, xvi
    success of preventive, 12,
        301*n*18
disaster
    assessment of, 55
    basic needs during, 83
    definition of, 315
    population vulnerability in, 114
    prediction of, 1
    prevention of, 3
    response to, xv
    warning of ecological/humani-
        tarian, 10
Disaster Epidemiology Research
    Center, 61
discrimination, group, 4, 117–18
disease
    diarrheal, 82, 90, 100
    infectious, 68, 81–82, 90–91,
        160, 183, 185
    malnutritional, 66, 68, 181–84,
        186–87
    respiratory, 82, 106, 183, 185
    vector associated, 82, 83, 100–
        103, 183, 185–86
    water–related, 82–83
disinfection, 87
distribution system, 50
donor alerts, 47
donors, international, 8, 46, 47
drought, 55, 181

earthquakes, 53, 55
East Timor
    conflict in, 192, 194
    crisis management in, 368
    ethnic cleansing in, 216
    evaluation of aid response for,
        53

human rights in, 79, 80
    Indonesian occupation of, 281
    murder of UNHCR staff in, 225
    timeliness of aid for, 41
Eastern Democratic Republic of
    Congo, 68
Economic Community of West Af-
    rican States, 128
economic interdependency, 22, 23
Egypt, 125
El Salvador, 24, 45
emergencies
    funding for, 47–48
    reaction to, 1
emergency analysis
    component of, 5
    indicators as suitable for, 15
    uniformity in, 77
Emergency Relief Coordinator
    (ERC), 125, 127, 128
emergency, complex
    characteristics of, 75–77
    definition of, 55, 287, 314
    increase in, 192, 216
    intervention in, 79
    role of military in, 221–23
    vertical programming during,
        163
    women/children issues in,
        153–79
emergency, humanitarian
    mandate of, 135
    role of women/children in, 154
    safe house provision for, 148–49
environmental health, 67–69, 81
Epicentre, 61
epidemiological analysis, 56–57,
    59
equality, definition of, 315
Eritrea–Ethiopia conflict, 226
ethnic cleansing, 216, 279, 352
ethnicity, elite, 21–22

European Platform for Conflict Prevention and Transformation, 8–9
European Union, 6
evacuation, planning/revision for, 261–62
Evaluation Studies Unit (OCHA), 53
exclusionary ideology, 21
excreta disposal, 82–83, 89–96, 109
exit strategy, xvii, 271–72
Exodus Within Borders: An Introduction to the Crisis of Internal Displacement (Brookings), 130

Falun Gong, 30
famine, 55, 180–81, 227
fecal coliform, 89. *See also* water supply
Field Information Support (FIS), 52
field monitoring. *See* monitoring, field
filtration, 87
flash appeals, 47, 48
flocculation/sedimentation, 86–87
flooding, 55, 181
Food and Agriculture Organization (FAO), 6, 51
food emergency, 1, 6
foreign investment, 27
Foreign Ministry of the Netherlands, 7
Former Yugoslav Republic of Macedonia (FYROM), 4, 10–11, 204, 206, 210, 351, 358n2
Forsaken People: Case Studies of the Internally Displaced (Deng, Cohen), 130
Forum for African Women Educationalists (FAWE), 166

Forum on Early Warning and Early Response (FEWER), 8, 14
foster family network, 149
fuel needs, 67–68, 109
funding, emergency, 47–48

gender analysis, 118, 315
gender discrimination
    complex emergencies and, 153–79
    female role in, 81, 165
    prevention of, 141, 151
    tools for, 158–59
    violence and, 160–62
Geneva Conventions, 110, 141–42, 168
genocide, 7, 20, 21, 24, 26, 30, 278
Georgia (country), 125
Global Information and Early Warning System (GIEWS), 6
Global Water Supply and Sanitation Assessment 2000 Report (WHO, UNICEF), 82
Goma. *See* Democratic Republic of Congo
Great Lakes (Central Africa), 192
Greater Horn of Africa Initiative, 301n16
Greece, 11, 351
Guidelines on Drinking Water Quality (WHO), 89
Guidelines on the Protection of Refugee Women (UNHCR), 165, 173
Guiding Principles on Internal Displacement (UN), 121–26, 169, 173
Guinea, 155, 163, 225
Gypsies. *See* Roma, the

Haiti, 294
Handbook for Applying the Guiding

Principles (Brookings Institute), 123
Havel, Vaclav, 217
health care
  assessment for, 1, 57–58, 62, 67
  data for, 61, 63–64
  education for, 83, 103–106, 232
  environment in, 67
  HIV/AIDS and, 81–82, 160
  immunization as, 66, 185
  use of media for, 105–106
  perinatal conditions for, 82
  refugees and, 64–65
Health Information Systems
  (HIS), 59
High Commissioner on National
  Minorities (OSCE), 6
HIV/AIDS, 81–82, 160
Holbrooke, Richard, 126
Honduras, 193–94
Horn of Africa, 10
Human Development Index
  (HDI)
Human Dimension Implementa-
  tion Meeting, 129
human rights
  abuse of, 135
  concept of, 138, 217–18
  legality of, 168–71
  medicalization of, 137
  observers of, 3
  precedence of, 79
  violations of, xvi
Human Rights Internet, 9
Human Rights Watch, 9, 13
Humanitarian Charter, 138
*Humanitarian Charter and Minimum
  Standards in Disaster Response*
  (Sphere Project), 83
Humanitarian Charter, the, 110
Humanitarian Early Warning Sys-
  tem (HEWS), 6, 14

Humanitarian Information Center
  (HIC), 42
humanitarian intervention
  basic needs for, 140–41
  cultural humility in, 294
  guidelines for, 143–52, 320n11
  Machiavelli's application to, xvi
  phases of, 286–89
  protective presence of, 139–40
  safety/security during, 141–42,
    228–49, 322n26
Hutus, 4, 11, 22, 27, 30
hygiene education, 83, 103–106

ideology, exclusionary, 21–22
immunization, 66, 185
Impact of War on Women Project
  (ICRC), 172–73
India, 23, 45, 53
indicators
  for environmental health assess-
    ment, 68
  identification advances of, 57
  interpretation/evaluation of,
    15, 78
  patterns of, 69
  use of, 14
Indonesia, 129, 192, 368
information
  interpretation of, 3, 13, 14
  management of, 16, 39, 50–51
  sharing of, 51
Ingushetia, 192
Institute of International Humanitarian Affairs (IIHA), 368
Integrated Regional Information
  Network (IRIN), 50
Intelligence agencies, US, 7, 10
Inter–Agency Network, 127–28
Inter–Agency Standing Committee (IASC), 122
Inter–American Commission on

Human Rights of the Organization of American States, 122
InterAction's Security Task Force, 225, 255
interdependency of countries, 23
internal displacement
police training for, 151–52
research for, 130, 132–133
root causes for, 130–34
internally displaced people (IDP)
camp management for, 174–75
challenge for, 132–33
definition of, 311n2, 315
foster family network for, 149
gender involvement for, 151, 153–79
health issues for, 63–65, 232
information centers for, 145–46, 152
issues of national identity for, 117
laws for, 124–29
leadership committees for, 150–51
legal aid center for, 146–48
movement of, 351
NGO perception by host country and, 231
returnees' rights for, 152, 173, 288
structural protection in, 164–65
v. refugees, 115, 155–56
vulnerability of, 117
International Committee of the Red Cross (ICRC), 136, 168, 190, 191, 192, 194, 195, 319n1, 355
international community, 119, 131
International Covenant on Economic, Social, and Cultural Rights, 171
International Criminal Court, 170

International Crisis Group (ICG), 8
International Diploma in Humanitarian Assistance (IDHA), 367–68
International Drinking Water and Sanitation Decade, 89
International Federation of Red Cross and Red Crescent Societies (IFRC), 136
International Force in East Timor (INTERFET), 282
International Humanitarian Affairs Series (Fordham University Press), xvi
International Monetary Fund (IMF), 288
International Organizations of Migrants, 1
International Red Cross, 1
International Rescue Committee (IRC), 114, 171
International Tribunal, 278
Internet, 44–45, 49
Iraq, 4, 27, 193–94, 239
Islam, 21–22
Israel/Palestine, 4
Israeli Defence Force (IDF), 210

Kashmir, 5, 23
kidnapping, 247
Kissinger, Henry, 217
Kosovo
aid programs in, 206, 211
conflict in, 192, 351
crisis management in, 368
database for, 52
ethnic cleansing in, 216
human rights abuse in, 137, 217
peace efforts in, 4, 294
safety of NGOs in, 239
Kurdistan, 193–94
kwashiorkor, 182, 183–84, 186–87

land mines, 244
latrine, 90–94, 354
Laurasi Foundation, 207
Lebanon, 294
Legal Access for Women Yearning for Equal Rights (LAWYER), 166
leptospirosis, 102
Lhotshampas, 4
Liberia, 4, 8, 27, 80, 137, 155, 226
lines of operation, 204
LogFrame, 70
logical framework analyses, 70
logistics center, 46

Macedonia. See Former Yugoslav Republic of Macedonia
Machiavelli, Niccolò di Bernardo, xvi
malaria, 82, 100–101, 183, 185–86
Malawi, 37
Malaysia, 18
malnutrition
  physical effects of, 66, 68, 181–83, 186–87
  role of physician in, 186
mandate, 268–69
Manual on Field Practice in Internal Displacement (Brookings Institute), 123
marasmus, 182, 183, 186–87
Marcos, Ferdinand, 25
Marxism-Leninism, 21–22
Masses in Flight: The Global Crisis of Internal Displacement (Deng, Cohen), 130
measles, 82, 183, 185
measures of effectiveness (MOE), 70–72
Médecin du Monde, 213
Médecins sans frontières (MSF), 74, 194, 206, 207, 213, 322n24, 355

media
  coverage of, 180
  gender attitudes of, 157–158
  health education through, 105–106
  manipulation of, 208
  perception by, 323n30
  television as, 49
  timeliness of, xv
migration, forced, 12, 55
Military and Civil Defence Unit (MCDU), 46
military operations, 226, 321n19, 325n51
military personnel
  assets database for, 47
  civilian protection by, 75
  humanitarian deployment for, 219–20, 291–92
  values of, 203, 322n21
Minimum Standards in Disaster Response (Sphere Project), 58, 138
Minorities at Risk (MAR) Project, 4n5
Mission Ost, 323n27
mission statement, 269–70, 320n11
missions, country, 129–30
models
  criteria/risks of, 15–16, 302n21
  forecasting for, 12
  necessity of, in monitoring, 14, 15
  review of, 52
Moldova, 12
monitoring, field
  early warning as, 5, 13
  health focus of, 61–62
  value of, 14, 49–50
Monserrat, 193–94
Moros, 4, 24

Mortality and Morbidity Weekly Report (MMWR), 61
mosquito, *Anopheles*, 100
Mozambique, 37, 46, 52, 193–94, 221

National Displaced Women's Organization, 166
Nepal, 4
Network of Ethnological Monitoring on Early Warning of Ethnic Conflict, 8
networking, electronic, 13
NGOs in Disaster Relief, 110
non–governmental organizations (NGOs)
  acceptance of, 233–35, 248–49
  assessment/action by, 74–75, 143–45
  competition between, 213, 228, 325n40
  Concern Worldwide as, 80–82
  cultural education of, 231
  financial aspects of, 253–54
  growth of, 320n13
  interaction of military and, xvi, 214–16, 292, 321n19
  management of, 237, 250–61
  mission/mandate of, 195, 230, 231–34, 322n25
  personnel of, 324n35
  perspective of, 2, 323n30
  safety/security for, 229–63
  targeting of, 231
nonmilitary organizations
  code of conduct for, 212, 228
  commitment of, 207
  consistency/discipline in, 213, 228
  cooperation between military and, 214–16, 321n19
  cooperation/rivalries between, 207, 212–13, 228

knowledge/specialization of, 206
long-term structure in, 209
media manipulation by, 208
principles of, 205–206
response time of, 210–12
strength/weakness of, 205–16
suspicion of military by, 214
nonrefoulement, principle of, 169
North Atlantic Treaty Organization (NATO), 26
North Korea, 77, 80
nutritional assessment, 67

Office of Foreign Disaster Assistance (OFDA), 61
Office of Humanitarian Affairs (UN), 13
Office of the Coordinator for Humanitarian Assistance (OCHA), 1, 6, 33, 34, 38–48, 50–51, 123, 128
On Psychology of Military Incompetence (Dixon), 212
On-Site Operations Coordination Centers (OSOCC), 44–45
Operation AGRICOLA, 219, 220, 221, 351–59
Organisation for Security and Cooperation in Europe (OSCE), 6, 12, 122, 128
Organisation of African Unity (OAU). *See* African Union
Organization of American States (OAS), 128
Oxford Committee for Famine Relief (OXFAM), 172, 194, 195, 206, 208, 320n12, 323n29, 355

Pakistan, 27
Palestine, 4, 368

Pan American Health Organization, 73
peacekeeping forces, 76
pellagra, 184
People in Aid, 110
People-Oriented Planning (POP), 158–59
perinatal conditions, 82
personnel
mobilization of, 1
training of, 57
Peru, 45
Philippines, 4, 24, 25, 129
Pinochet, Augusto, 25
Policy and Studies Development Branch (OCHA), 53
policy, discriminatory/international, 3
policy, US foreign, 5
political elite, 24
political upheaval, 20–22
politicide, 20, 21, 24, 26, 27, 30
population displacement, 10, 55
primary health care (PHC), 66
programs
development and, 3
evaluation of, 57
for assistance, 12
Protecting Refugees (UNHCR), 136
protection intervention, 135–37, 235–37
protection. *See* security
protective accompaniment strategy, 139
protein energy malnutrition (PEM), 66
protocols
initial health assessment for, 73–74, 78
necessity of, 14
public health information, 57

rainwater, use of, 85
rapid assessment
for refugee camps, 63
indicators for, 63–72, 78
necessity of, 56, 59
rapid response teams, 40, 51
reconciliation, 292–93
Red Cross. *See* International Committee of the Red Cross
refugee camps, 108, 182
description of, 353–55
environmental impact of, 108, 182
food exploitation in, 167
foster family network for, 149
gender awareness-raising in, 153–79
health care involvement in, 59, 66, 232
information centers for, 145–46
legal aid center for, 146–48
location of, 108–109, 352
management of, 108–12, 174–75
ombudsman for, 108–109
skills training in, 167–68
structural protection in, 164–65
violence in, 173–74
Refugee Convention, 169
refugees. *See also* women/children as refugees
Convention on Refugees for, 121
definition of, 169, 315
education programs for, 141–42
flow/tracking of, 13, 55, 61, 77, 351
foster family network for, 149
gender involvement for, 151, 153–79, 209
health issues for, 63–65, 232
information centers for, 145–46, 152

laws for, 124–29, 168–71
leadership committees for, 150–51
legal aid center for, 146–48
national identity of, 117
NGO perception by, 231
ombudsman for, 149–50
responsibility for, 162
returnees' rights for, 152, 173, 288
social marketing for, 150
v. internally displaced people, 115, 155–56
vulnerability of, 117
Registered Engineers for Disaster Relief (RedR), 255
relief agencies, 1
relief worker
  as peace builder, 79
  character of, 197, 203–205, 210, 235, 252
  cultural education of, 164, 175–77, 232
  difficulties for, 211
  female, 209, 323n32
  protection of IDP rights by, 136, 139–52
  responsibilities of, 228–29
  safety/security of, 227–39
  strength/weakness of, 205–16
ReliefWeb, 6, 50
Representative of the UN Secretary–General on Internally Displaced Persons, 114, 116
Reproductive Health Consortium (RHC), 172
resident/humanitarian coordinator (R/HC), 40, 46, 49
resolution, UN adoption of, 268
respiratory infections. See disease, respiratory
response time, xv, 49

reviews, systematic, 52–53, 57
right of return, 152, 173, 288
risk, 241–49
risk factors. See models
road blocks, 248
Roma, the, (Gypsies) 12, 357
Romania, 12
Rwanda
  aid missions in, 137, 172, 213
  British military in, 193–94
  complex emergency in, 216, 287
  genocide in, 11, 18, 22, 27
  UN Assistance Mission in Rwanda (UNAMIR) for, 276

sanitation
  excreta disposal for, 82–83, 89–96
  means of, 2
  needs assessment of, 67–68
  system choice for, 90
Sarajevo. See Bosnia Herzegovina
satellite transmission, 49, 61, 77
Save the Children, 173, 195
Schaeffer, David (Ambassador for War Crimes), 7
scurvy, 184
search/rescue teams, 44, 47
security
  assessment, 1, 57, 232–49
  challenge to, 3–4
  displaced populations and, 116–18, 153–79
  financial management for, 253–54
  global NGO policy for, 250–52
  headquarters management for, 250–61
  individual's responsibility for, 263
  priority for, 57, 109
  safety v., 228

standards for, 257–61
training programs for, 255–56
women/children and, 153–54
security for staff, xvii
September 11, 2001, 131–32
Serbia. See Yugoslav federation
sewerage, 94–96
Sexual Violence against Refugees: Guidelines on Prevention and Response, 165
Shari'a law, 21–22
shelter
  qualifications for, 109
  supply problems for, 107
  emergency, 1, 2, 67–68
Sierra Leone, 4, 137, 155, 160, 163, 192–94, 216, 218, 226
Sierra Leone Association of University Women (SLAUW), 166
SLORC (Burma), 27
Slovakia, 12
slow sand filtration, 87
social engineering, 290, 294
solidarity organizations, 230–31
Somalia, 76–77, 80, 137, 182, 185, 239
  action by UN Security Council for, 273–79
  Operation "Provide Relief" for, 273
  peace efforts in, 294, 367–68
South Africa, 22, 37
Special Rapporteur on Violence Against Women, 315
Sphere Project, 58, 83, 88, 89, 90, 110, 138
Sri Lanka, 18, 192
State Failure Task Force, 19, 20–21, 23
state sovereignty, 116, 118
Status of Refugees, 169, 171
strategic framework, 70

strategies
  design time for, 3
  local context for, 80–81
  preventive, 7, 31
Sudan, 24, 129, 137, 192, 226, 227
Supplementary Human Dimension Seminar on Migration and Internal Displacement, 128–29
supplies, mobilization of, 1, 46
supplies, relief, 46
surge capacity, 40, 51
Survey of Military Attitudes Toward NGOs Following the Kosovo Campaign, 214
Swaziland, 37
Swiss Foreign Ministry, 7
Swiss Peace Foundation, 7

Tajikistan, 191
Taliban, the, 27, 131
Tamil–Sinhalese conflict, 18
Tanzania, 165, 172
technology
  advances in, 13, 44–45, 49, 50, 61, 77, 195
  computer connectivity as, 294
  identification of, 52
television, 49
terrorism, 54, 131–32, 245
threat, 241–49
Tibet, 23, 30
trade openness, 23, 24
Trust Fund for Disaster Relief, 48
tuberculosis, 106, 183, 185
Turkey, 129
Tutsis, 4, 11, 22, 27, 30

Uganda, 22, 26, 125
UN Assistance Mission in Rwanda (UNAMIR), 276

UN Declaration of Human Rights, 79
UN Development Program (UNDP), 51, 80, 288
UN Disaster and Coordination (UNDAC), 51
UN High Commissioner for Refugees (UNHCR), 1, 56, 125, 126, 136, 156, 194, 196, 206, 323n33, 324n36, 355
UN High Commissioner on Human Rights, 171
UN Humanitarian Response Depot, 46
UN International Children's Emergency Fund (UNICEF), 82
UN Joint Logistic Centers (UNJLC), 46
UN Mission in East Timor (UNAMET), 282
UN Operation in Somalia (UNOSOM), 273–74
UN Protection Force (UNPROFOR), 280–81
UN Secretary-General, 5, 8, 14
UN Security Council, 8
UN Special Rapporteur on Violence Against Women, 171
UN Transitional Administration in East Timor (UNTAET), 282–83
Unified Task Force (UNITAF), 274–75
United Kingdom (UK), 128, 351
United Nations (UN)
    action by, xvi, 8, 267–68, 326n55
    as multilateral, 196
    diplomatic/political initiatives by, 12
    response to disaster by, 1
Universal Declaration of Human Rights, 160, 168, 171

US Agency for International Development (USAID), 7, 196
US Central Intelligence Agency (CIA), 10
US Committee for Aid and Relief Everywhere (CARE), 172, 195, 206
US Department of Defense (DOD), 7
US Department of State, 7, 9

vector control, 82, 83, 100–103, 185–86
Vietnam, 294
violence, 55
    benefits of, 284–85
    definition of gender-based, 315
    population displacement as, 55
    recovery from, 285–86, 292
vulnerability, 241–44, 315

warning systems, early
    challenge for, 3, 302n22
    commitment to, 14
    concept of, 300n9
    information on, 300n10
    monitoring of indicators for, 14–15
    objectives/methods of, 9, 20, 301n16
wars of identity, 191
waste management, 83, 96–98, 100. See also excreta disposal
water supply, 1, 2, 67–68, 82–89, 98, 109, 354
West Timor, 137
women as relief workers, 209, 323n32
Women's Commission for Refugee Women and Children, 171
Women's Convention, 316n12
women/children as refugees

creation of women's committees
    for, 151
equal access to services by,
    153–55
protection of, 153, 166–67
role changes in, 153–79, 166
sexual exploitation of, 155
victimization of, 155
vulnerability of, 161–62
World Bank, 196, 288
World Food Program (WFP), 1,
    46, 194, 196, 206, 355

World Health Organization
    (WHO), 1, 58, 61, 73, 82, 83–
    84, 89
World Vision (WV), 207–208

Yugoslav federation, 9, 10–11, 26,
    69, 166, 367

Zaire. *See* Democratic Republic of
    Congo
Zimbabwe, 37, 93